WITH BRITISH SNIPERS
TO THE REICH

By

C<small>APTAIN</small> C. S<small>HORE</small>

*(Formerly officer sniping instructor at the
British Army of the Rhine Training Centre.)*

Lancer Militaria
Mt. Ida, Arkansas

WITH BRITISH SNIPERS
TO THE REICH

THE SNIPER

CONTENTS

ACKNOWLEDGEMENTS

IT IS with great pleasure that I acknowledge the help and encouragement I have received from the following to whom Sniping meant, and owes, so much: Major O. Underhill, O.B.E. (K.S.L.I.), Major the Hon. A. H. Wills (Lovat Scouts), Major R. St. C. Maxwell (Black Watch), Captain R. M. Barr (Black Watch), Captain E. H. Robinson (K.R.R.C.), CSM. A. Ross (Lovat Scouts), and CSM. J. Davidson (Seaforths).

I am exceedingly grateful to these Sniping School NCOs who were my friends, with whom I crossed the Rhine in March, 1945, worked and shot in Holland and Germany and for whose Regiment—the Lovat Scouts—I have the greatest regard: C/Sgt. A. Davidson, C/Sgt. J. A. Haggerty, Sgt. J. McKay, and Sgt. J. Morrison.

I acknowledge, too, a debt of gratitude to Major-General F. R. G. Matthews, D.S.O. formerly Commandant of the Training Centre, and Lt. Col. D. B. Lang, D.S.O; M.C. Commandant of the School of Infantry under whom I deemed it an honour to serve when attached to the British Army of the Rhine Training Centre, July–October, 1945.

And I wish to record my appreciation of my one time Unit CO—Wing Commander A. C. Neill (R.A.F. Regiment)—who for a period of two and a half years never interfered with the sometimes unorthodox instruction of his Weapon Training Officer.

AUTHOR'S FOREWORD

ON MY return to civilian life early in 1946 I decided rather naively that I would write, at a pedestrian gait, a monumental international history of Sniping. During my stay in Germany, after the end of the war in Europe, I had been toying with this idea, and had written to American sources for information about the part sniping had played in the history of American arms, and I hasten to declare that I was treated with the greatest courtesy, the National Rifle Association of America in particular being most helpful. However, early in March Mr. Samworth suggested that I write for him a book on British riflemen and sniping in World War II—and *not* at a pedestrian gait! I settled down to work at once, and although it appeared to be a terrific task I found that the thousands of words mounted steadily. And in December I wrote "Finis."

In writing this book I had a number of objects; to record the value of sniping in World War II; to pay due respect to those officers and men to whom sniping owes so much, and who strove strenuously, undismayed by rebuffs, until the greatest of all games was recognised in its true worth; to explode fallacies and myths, ignorance and misconceptions about sniping, and to do what little I could to further the cause of Sniping not only in the British, but also the American, Armies, and so on. But I desired also that the book should be of some interest to all men to whom firearms are something more than inanimate pieces of wood and metal. My own limited experiences were of low priority in my conception of the book.

In certain sections I have been critical, but, I hope, with justification and without rancour; but I do wish to record my unbounded admiration for the British Army from the highest to the lowest rank; it is only when one returns to civilian status that a full, true appreciation of Service life is obtained.

When publisher and author are thousands of miles apart one would imagine that there would be great difficulty in maintaining contact. But somehow no obstacle appears to have beset the path of Mr. Samworth and myself, and I have certainly come to regard him as an old friend, which is just as it should be between two red-hot firearms enthusiasts.

This book has been the means of starting, and cementing, another friendship—that between myself and the artist, J. Sharrock, who is known to all his friends as "Honest Joe." He is an ex-soldier and since his humorous drawings were much appreciated and eagerly sought by American soldiers in a nearby camp I have no doubt that they are, at this moment, occupying some prominent place in many American homes.

C. SHORE

Hazel Grove, Stockport,
England, July, 1948

FOREWORD / WITH BRITISH SNIPERS TO THE REICH

THE principal events and battles of World War II were, as a matter of course, thoroughly documented in the years following the capitulation of the Axis Powers. Endeavors of a lesser scale—particularly sniping, despite its contribution to the outcome of the war—received mention in passing, or not at all, however. As a result, books written by World War II snipers with actual combat experience were hardly commonplace and are still considered unique.

The most notable work, perhaps, is a first-hand account by an officer and sniper named Captain C. Shore. This book is called *With British Snipers to the Reich.* From the landings at Normandy to the crossing of the Rhine, Captain Shore presents the fascinating story of the British sniping campaign against Hitler's Wehrmacht during World War II. In addition to detailing the finer points of sniper training, tactics, rifles and telescopic sights in a combat environment, Captain Shore also provides the reader with a wealth of information pertaining to a wide variety of Allied and Axis small arms fielded during World War II.

Shore was an accomplished sniping instructor with the British Army of the Rhine, and his assessment of the value of the precision rifle fire is as note worthy today as it was forty years ago:

"I maintain that during World War II far too much emphasis was laid on superiority, or volume, of fire—fire-power or lead-spattering, have as you will—by the authorities. To many, the individual rifleman did not count at all, and it was a small wonder that the feeling spread amongst the men that the rifle was out-of-date. Everyone clamoured for a weapon which would send out masses of bullets at an alarming rate.... Only the minority cherished the rifle as it should be venerated. And if sniping schools did nothing else they did at least fill every student with a true appreciation of his rifle as a weapon of precision and of accurate firepower with practice, which gave him pre-eminence amongst fighting men. A man who could really use his rifle was more deadly than the average man with an LMG, as I have seen, and demonstrated, many times."

A classic work by any measure, *With British Snipers to the Reich* is of great importance as an account of modern warfare with the emphasis on sniping.

Peter R. Senich

BRIEF ODYSSEY

England · D Day · Normandy · Belgium · Holland
Germany · Holland · Germany · Denmark · Germany
England

I FIRST tried to get a course at a Sniping School in early 1943 when stationed in England, but without success. Because I was tremendously keen on sniping I endeavoured to obtain some sniping rifles for my unit, but here again my efforts were of no avail. This was at the time when the subject of sniping was belatedly occupying the minds of the Powers that Be since the Hun was doing some execution with his snipers in the Middle East theatre. Early in 1944 knowing that at some future, probably near future, date I should have an appointment in Europe, I endeavoured to buy a good rifle fitted with a telescope sight. I wasn't particular about the calibre, so long as I could obtain the necessary ammunition, nor the weight. But despite exhaustive enquiry and one or two hopeful, optimistic hours I had to admit defeat, and I left England in a convoy bound for the Invasion of Europe on the morning of June 5th, 1944 still without my hoped-for period at a sniping school, and devoid of the greatly desired telescopic sighted rifle. For about eighteen months previously I had done a good deal of shooting with an old P.'14 fitted with normal iron sights; it was a splendid rifle and much coveted by my CO who smiled rather grimly when he saw it stacked in one corner of the very tiny LST cabin four of us shared.

Prior to D Day there was the usual hustle, bustle and confusion resultant of the gathering together of kit and

[1]

equipment. Rifles, Stens, Brens and pistols were all examined thoroughly, some thrown out and others receiving armourers' attention. Spares were noticeable for their almost entire absence, and I well remember the unit armourer coming to me the day before we moved off to concentration area with a .38 pistol and saying that it was useless since the trigger spring was broken, and there was absolutely no chance of securing a spare. I asked him if he had a cigarette lighter, and somewhat mystified he said "Yes." He handed it to me and I saw that the flint spring could easily be cut in half and still function. So the spring was halved, one section being replaced in the lighter and the other inserted in the pistol. Everything was OK and I fired that pistol many months later, and found that it still functioned well.

I spent considerable time checking ammunition and anything suspect was jettisoned. Tracer and incendiary cartridges were difficult to obtain and it was only a matter of hours before we departed on the first stage of the long trek which was to bring us on to the Normandy beaches that I was satisfied that we had all our armament and ammunition in tip-top order. During the time in the concentration area before embarking, and we boarded our LST on the 1st, June, a thorough inspection was made to ensure that the men were carrying only ball ammunition for their their rifles, since we had been told that there would be little mercy extended to our fellows if the Hun caught them carrying tracer or incendiary. They were specifically warned too about the maltreating of ammunition by sawing off, or filing, the tip of cartridges and thus making "dumdums." Later in the campaign I heard at least one harrowing story of how woods were cleared by the use of incendiaries, and of the shrieking agony of one poor devil hit in the guts by such a bullet.

A rather amusing incident occurred in the concentration area. During the final check-up of the unit's Bren guns one of the gunners reported to his sergeant that one of his barrels had a crack in it. This barrel was duly examined by the NCO who confirmed that there was a crack present, and, in turn, he reported the matter to the CO who said that it must be changed. A day or so later there was handed to me another report to the effect that there was a further Bren barrel with a crack in it, so I decided to go along to the Armament officer and ask for a couple of new barrels. But fortunately I first asked for the barrels to be brought to my tent. Then, at first glance, I saw that which was causing so much heart throbbing to the gunners—and the sergeant. The "cracks" were the gas vents! Even now I blush to think of the figure I should have presented had I gone to the Armament officer!

We passed through the Straits of Dover at about ten o'clock in the evening of the 5th, June, and everyone expected the visitation of Jerry shells from the Calais batteries, but everything was quiet. Thinking that it might be the last opportunity for some time I donned my pyjamas before clambering into the top bunk of the tiny cabin, but took them off again on the advice of my colleagues who said that we must expect trouble with a capital T that night and it was as well to be clothed and prepared. After some hours sleep I chaffed these fellows about their fears, but was considerably shaken when they informed me that there had been a terrific bang in the early hours when one of the ships in the convoy had struck a mine, and that we were now eleven in line and not twelve. I hadn't heard a thing!

Although off the beaches in the early afternoon we could not all land owing to the scarcity of "Rhinos" and we were therefore compelled to spend the night of June 6th, on board the LST which pulled out to about a mile off shore. Just after nightfall we received the very unwelcome attentions of a couple of JU 88's, suffered 63 hits on the port side and 48 on the starboard; the ship was on fire below, she was leaking like a sieve and when we took up "Abandon ship stations" we found the floats useless and everything very badly knocked about. I had the bad luck to lose one or two of my best men, killed and wounded. I can never forget that night; the sense of oppression; the choking in the throat from the smoke generators which had been lighted on deck to "blanket" the craft from the Hun planes; the demon wailing of hundreds of ships' sirens; the headlong rush for the sparse cover; the bowel-relaxing suspense of waiting within a thin steel chamber for the inevitable attack; the sudden roar of diving planes; the scream of falling bombs; the convulsive lurch of the ship as the bombs tore the water and the sides of the craft; the tearing of steel and the moans of the wounded with the pearls of shock-sweat on their foreheads! It was the longest night of my life.

In Normandy my experiences in sniping were more of the receiving rather than the giving variety. Shortly after landing I saw an officer leave the assembly area in a Jeep, smiling broadly, driven by an harassed faced driver. A few minutes later the Jeep returned with the officer dead, a neat hole being drilled in the centre of his forehead. "Sniper" muttered the driver hoarsely. I must admit that it gave me, and the others, a shock. Apparently it was not going to be "the piece of cake" we had been led to believe at the numerous briefings to which we had listened with great interest and a growing enthusiasm. I noticed that when the men brewed the inevitable "char" they kept very close to the trucks and showed little inclination to stand upright.

It was very interesting to note the difference under fire of the men who had experienced the wiles of the Hun before and the "fledgelings" coming up against it for the first time. The majority of men with experience never took chances; they did not require telling to "dig-in" against the chance of shelling or air attack—it was never too much trouble for them. The "novices" at first looked askance at such industry, and ignored friendly advice, but after their baptism of mortar, shell or bomb fire there came a radical change of attitude. Unfortunately for many of them baptism and death were one and the same ceremony. There could be no two opinions about it—the wise man never hesitated to "dig-in" and the first job done when one moved to a new locality was to get down to it; fox-holes had priority over grub, and surely no moles were ever more industrious. The first night in Normandy there was not much digging, but more of a "scraping." When the Hun bombers came it was a case of diving into the nearest ditch or natural hole, and there was not much thinking about whether such shelters were unhealthy from the point of view of mines or booby traps.

On the second night, the battle having edged a mile or two away from us, the CO ordained that we might put up a tent, low and camouflaged, to house HQ and the signallers in the new locality. This tent was in close proximity to a ditch and since I was supposed to be, amongst many other things, the mine expert of the outfit, having undergone a very short course in such abominations way back in 1943, I had the job of looking around to see if there was anything in the nature of Hun frightfulness about. I never liked mines, in fact I disliked them intensely, and so I went about the job in no light-hearted manner. It was almost dusk, too late for sustained digging, so all the HQ chaps spread their gas capes, wrapped themselves in greatcoats and prepared to sleep in, or near, the ditch. Such is the optimism of the British soldier.

On hands and knees I crawled around and met one or two wires which on closer investigation yielded—nothing. One of the signallers came hot-foot for me to say that they had found a queer hole in their tent floor which the officer in charge there had said might be something in my line! I probed about, carefully, but found nothing. As soon as the

[5]

dusk came Jerry was over and I was in the ditch. After about quarter of an hour huddled close to the bottom of the ditch and plagued by thousands of mosquitoes whose eager diving flight could easily be imagined by the rising-crescendo whine, a sergeant crawled along to say that in his section of the ditch there were a number of wires which disappeared into the bank. I warned him not to touch the damned things, and to warn the men likewise. Later I investigated these wires which were sunk deeply into the banks, and by carefully digging around the wires unearthed a number of red metal objects, quite small, into which the wires disappeared. The CO said the best thing to do would be to get a good length of thick string, retire to a safe distance and pull! After cautiously attaching the string to the wires and metal objects I did this, and instead of a terrific roar which everyone expected, nothing happened except that the "objects" rolled down into the bottom of the ditch. These red metal tins were empty, and had apparently been placed there purely for delay purposes. I grant that our approach was cautious, but then in dealing with the wily Teuton one could not be too careful.

On the following night a couple of Army drivers with a three-ton wagon asked permission to put their truck in the bottom corner of a field which housed some of my men. It was about an hour before dusk and in consenting to their request I told them to get digging and get protection for themselves since it was a very unhealthy district, and, if they could, to bank some earth around their wagon. (In static positions all our transport was dug-in at the start of the campaign.) They said *they* would be all right sleeping in their truck. I told them not to be such damned fools. Before midnight we got a pasting and four of our chaps were hit, three of them badly. We had a wagon knocked out too with shrapnel through the engine. The Army wagon was riddled, and the two drivers who had chosen to retire in the back of it were asleep for keeps. They were in a hell of a mess, and we had the nasty pre-breakfast job of sweeping the remains together. For many, this night saw their first experience of anti-personnel bombs; these were certainly terrifying and caused many casualties. The last qualms of our men as to the "fag" of getting into the earth no matter what time of the day or night they took up a new position disappeared and ever afterwards when we moved and stopped in forward areas where there was no other form of shelter or cover everyone dug feverishly.

A FW 190 swooped in early one afternoon and "brewed" the woods close by our position. A latrine, of sorts, had been built just inside the wood and therein a corporal sat ruminating on the folly of war, and the untold, and prior to the war, unacknowledged, delights of sanitary plumbing, when a 20mm cannon shell grazed the bucket without touching him. Heedless of heavily be-trousered ankles that alarmed NCO just leaped and ran much after the manner of men engaged in a three-legged race. On the same afternoon I had a close shave from a piece of shrapnel which just scraped my nose and inflicted a short scratch on the right leg. That piece of shrapnel is before me as I write. It is a nasty looking bit of steel. I was bareheaded at the time and had it been a couple of inches different in flight I am afraid that I should not have travelled farther than the beach-head.

One night I was standing on the steps leading down to the HQ dug-out talking to the CO when a German plane came in low and dropped something about three hundred yards away; there was no noise and no thud. As the CO shouted "Duck" I saw a vivid circle of flame, crimson in the centre merging to bright orange on the circumference, and then my head, the only portion of my anatomy above ground level, received the punch of the blast, and my steel helmet, very seldom worn, was pushed from my head and the tautened chin-strap pulling back on my throat nearly choked me. I was very "shaken"!

[7]

During the early days in Normandy there was a terrific amount of nonsense printed in the newspapers about sniping. A frequent comment was that there had been a great number of snipers left behind on the initial German withdrawal from the coast and that these were causing much trouble behind the British front; again, quite a number of women, probably the French wives of the German occupational troops, possessed rifles and were sniping. One report had the story that the German snipers were using the "dastardly" wooden bullet which inflicted terrible wounds! I have before me a newspaper cutting, based on a report which appeared in a medical journal, which reads:—"Wooden bullets . . . are invisible in X-ray pictures of the wounds they make. These bullets break on solid structures such as bone, and the scattered fragments are not likely to be located by X-rays. Wooden bullets are said to be effective up to about 100 yards." This is stranger than fiction!

There was a considerable amount of this ammunition lying in machine gun positions in Normandy about two miles in from the beaches, and all I examined on the 7th, June was standard 7.9mm calibre and belted for LMG use. The year of manufacture varied from 1937 to 1943. Later I came across a considerable amount of this ammunition cartoned, and in Germany discovered many boxes labelled for LMG use and others for rifle; the only outward difference in the appearance was a serrated ring close to the the base of the cartridge case.

There were quite a number of Germans left behind in the sparse woods near the beach-head, and there was a good deal of sporadic rifle fire, but the results were certainly not comparable with what would have happened had "snipers" been left behind. An illustration of this is shown by the fact that one night I was out with a signaller who was laying field-telephone cable when we were fired on five times in a few minutes. The nearest bullet was about six feet away from us. We did not stop to argue about it, of course, and dropped to earth in much quicker time than it takes me to write this account, crawling for some yards before coming up again to renew the job. There was quite a lot of noise at the time and it was not possible to locate the rifleman responsible. Confidence grew a little with the knowledge of rotten marksmanship, but we were by no means comfortable, and I think the mental strain of working under "aimed" rifle fire is greater than that experienced under any other type of fire. And knowing something of the sniper's art makes the mental state even more trying!

In connection with this "mental strain under fire" I took part in some very interesting discussions with the men after the cessation of hostilities and the general opinion of the "nerve shattering sequence" was that mental-unease under the varying types of lethal fire came in the following order—greatest effect first:—sniping or aimed rifle fire; mortar fire; shelling; bombing; machine gun fire. In a way this was surprising, I had always felt that the men detested machine gun fire, and knowing their own very meagre gifts with a rifle I thought that they would have little respect for the Teuton riflemen, but no doubt this is just another example of the undue tributes paid to one's enemy. In connection with bombing it is a fact that air attacks are far more nerve shattering and frightening when one is afloat than when one has the good earth beneath one's feet, or stomach. On D Day the crew of our LST said the ship was the luckiest in the British Navy—had survived a direct hit at Anzio and so on—and we were comforted, but not for long! When one is on land there is nearly always some cover to be found, even if it is only a stinking Normandy drain. On board ship one feels so helpless. I certainly respect the courage of the men who go down to the sea in ships in war-time.

Being perhaps too sniper conscious I had instructed my NCOs on the last night on board ship to cover their chevrons with pieces of denim. It was noticeable that the NCOs of the beach landing parties had adopted this idea. I, and a colleague, wore roll-neck sweaters, thus hiding the tell-tale collar and tie. A few hours later I was told by my Colonel that he had ordered my NCOs to uncover their chevrons immediately, and that *his* officers must wear, and show, collars and ties. If we were to die he said we must die as officers! It was useless to remonstrate with a man who knew and realised so little, and not worth while pointing to officers passing along the road up to the line who were absolutely indistinguishable from the men.

We rounded up quite a number of the so-called snipers (the great majority of them did not merit the title "riflemen") from the woods in those early Normandy days. This matter of "beating" was treated in an almost jocular manner, as an evening jaunt, just as one would take a 12 bore here in peace-time England and walk round the shoot more as a means of obtaining a thirst to be slaked at the local public-house rather than a serious attempt to provide something for the pot. Everyone who could joined the band of "hunters," and the woods were "beaten" in a light-hearted fashion. Resistance was not great and casualties were light. Occasionally a Hun rifle spoke, but the Germans, once they saw the strength of the "posse," soon came out with their hands aloft. They were regarded as one views a poacher, without much in the nature of resentment unless they had been directly responsible for the killing, or wounding, of a comrade.

A number of these Jerries showed knowledge and appreciation of woodcraft but I am quite satisfied that extremely few of these men were "snipers." Once I heard that a "real sniper" had been taken; the report was that on his sleeve he was wearing a badge, showing crossed rifles surrounded with a wreath! I did my best to find this man, since I was not aware that such a badge existed in the German army, but was not successful and therefore dismissed it as just another story. It is perhaps interesting to record that throughout the campaign in N.W. Europe from D Day to May 8th, 1945 and afterwards in Germany from Westphalia to the Danish border I never met a German wearing the German sniper's badge, an eagle's head (which we took to be symbolic of the observation side of the sniper's art); and despite the most exhaustive enquiries, and during my time at the Training Centre I was in a sound position for making such an enquiry, I never came across anyone who had met a Hun with the sniper badge. Examination of the "pukka" German snipers killed in the field did not reveal this insignia. Naturally we thought of the possibility of the Huns tearing off such a badge, since the old adage that sniping is a dirty game is still rife in certain quarters, incredible though it might sound, and they may have feared the consequences of being discovered so adorned, but I personally examined many German prisoner's clothing, particularly those who wore the combat badge, in an endeavour to find the tell-tale "dark tone" resultant of a removed badge, without success.

The majority of men we took in Normandy wore camouflage jackets, and in some cases full suits of camouflage, complete with cowl or hood, but then the ordinary German soldier was much better equipped from the camouflage point of view than our own. Late in the campaign, factories were taken which were filled with the excellent padded camouflage jacket, with hood, with which thousands of the Wehrmacht were equipped. These jackets were very well made and, in winter, ideally warm. They were reversible, one side normal German camouflage design, brown and green in varying tones and geometric pattern, and the other, white, for use in the winter snow. Teutonic thoroughness was shown in the fact that even the metal buttons were painted with a hard white pigment on the normally worn inner-side. The British snow-suit, used a good deal by snipers in the winter of 1944–1945 and generally by troops in the Ardennes affair, bore brown buttons! To say the least of it, such an example of glaring lack of thought was exasperating!

In Normandy we heard, and read, much about snipers in church steeples, and one evening I was solemnly told by three men cowering in a ditch that a sniper was firing at them from the church spire which could be seen in the distance towering above some high trees. This spire was about 1,000 yards away, but the range according to the "sectional average" of the three men was "just about 500 yards"! I am told that the Hun's native ingenuity once gave rise to a "sniper in a church steeple" true story; to a long length of chemically treated rope suspended inside a church spire the Germans tied a number of "crackers" at irregular intervals, and then set a light to the rope which acted as a slow burning fuse. The effect of the crackers going-off at irregular intervals suggested sporadic rifle fire—to the credulous, "sniper fire"!!

Women sniper stories too were all the rage for a few days in Normandy but I never received authentic evidence of one such case. (It may be interesting to point out that in 1937 the use of firearms was introduced into the curriculum for some of the German *Madchen*. In that year the Nazis set up a Colonial school to train women as Colonial wives ready for the day when colonies went back under the Fatherland's control, and an important part of the training of a future Colonial wife was learning to shoot.)

We found a number of German sniper "hides"; these hides were often interlinked by ditch-ways etc., and in one or two cases it was apparent that one hide had been used as domestic quarters, and the other for the serious job of life. These latter always commanded excellent fields of fire and in the neighbourhood of some of them British and Canadian graves, surmounted by steel helmets which had a single hole through them, were silent, but sufficient, testimony to the efficiency of a real German sharpshooter.

For some time after D Day all the wounded were evacuated to England as soon as possible; even the slightest of wounds meant "Blighty." One afternoon I spoke to an Airborne corporal and a Commando, both slightly wounded, who were waiting to board a Red Cross Dakota bound for England. They were from the canal bank at Caen, the scene of a most gallant stand by a few against terrific odds. They told me that nearly every man "relief-prayed" at dawnlight when the first Spitfire patrol zoomed overhead It was then that they got the opportunity of loading every weapon they had, and every man possessed rifle, carbine, LMG, and pistol—and it was never very long before the necessity to re-load again occurred. The Huns threw everything they had at this canal-bank garrison, but they were strongly lodged and would not budge. They said that they did not give Jerry very much chance of sniping at them.

On the same afternoon I spoke to the most hideously wounded chap I ever saw; all that was left of him was a head and trunk. During an attack, rushing through an orchard, he had stepped on a Tellermine (the shear wire must have been almost shorn through) and both arms and both legs had been torn from his body. He was smiling quite cheerfully, and smoking a cigarette, as he lay on the stretcher waiting to be loaded into the plane. The medical orderly told me that he was really marvellous. "Does he know?" I asked. "Yes," replied the orderly. It is on such occasions when one cannot speak for a lump in the throat, when the mind is full of the horrible cost of war, and when one realises the soundness and nobility of the human heart and mind.

Many men in the invading armies felt that they were not welcome in Normandy. The people had become accustomed to the German occupation; many of the German troops had been stationed there for years and some of them had married Norman girls. In Normandy, the granary of France, there had been no lack of food, the Huns had waxed fat, treated the peasants quite decently and had been thoroughly accepted. Many of the girls who had married Germans were definitely hostile to us, but in my own experience that hostility had never a physical, or practical, manifestation.

The first prisoners taken in Normandy were a motley crew. Many were elderly men; there were quite a number of Russians, and it was rather surprising to see a number of young yellow-skinned Japs being herded together to embark on LSTs leaving for England on the morning of the 8th, June.

Throughout the campaign there was one characteristic of the Hun which never altered, and that was his love of comfort. There were many occasions when his leaning towards comfort seriously jeopardised his life, but he would have his comparative luxury. Whenever he was in the vicinity of houses, or villages, whether advancing or retiring, he chose to sleep indoors rather than rest in the open or in ditches. On numerous occasions when his British or American counterpart would have got down to rest on the outskirts of a village, holding that point by standing patrols or a small garrison, the German settled in in force, and for his brief rest occupied the most comfortable quarters he could find. And he suffered many casualties from shelling as a result. This pre-occupation with comfort was found throughout Europe, from the country just behind the beach-head in Normandy to the Rhine and beyond.

About two or three miles in from the beaches in Normandy there was left ample evidence that the Bosche was being strongly re-inforced. There were a great number of soundly planned dug-outs in course of construction, and those that were finished, and furnished in a style which bordered on luxury, were really first-class dwellings and strong enough to withstand anything other than a really heavy shell or bomb. Had the invasion been delayed much longer there is no doubt that it would have been a much graver job. The story is now told that Hitler had a last minute intuition that the invasion would take place in and around the Cherbourg area, and the signs of feverish activity which were to be found in all sectors behind the beaches revealed that the intuition was being acted upon.

To many of us in Normandy during the terrific storm which stopped all landings a few days after the initial assault it was a constant puzzle, and a great relief, that the Germans did not launch an all-out counter-offensive during those few fateful days when the great storm lashed the coast and the Channel. Had he then attacked in his greatest strength I believe that we could not have held him. I had only to look at my Colonel's face in the early morning when I made my dawn report to know that the position was hellishly serious. Later I was told that for once the German meteorologists were wrong in their forecast; they had ventured the opinion that the storm would last for three or four days longer than it actually did, and that was one reason for the delay in the attack. I am quite ready to believe this story since, without doubt, much importance was laid on the theories of the German weather men. After all, during the Blitzkreig of 1940 their forecasts upon which the lightning attacks were based, had proved to be absolutely correct.

I know that the Allied airforces did a magnificent job of work during those fateful storm days in harrying German convoys and communications (and the German High Command had ordered convoys, including armour, to move by day rather than by night—had they moved during the hours of darkness the number reaching the rendezvous point would have been far greater than it actually was as a result of day movement) but their undoubted power alone could not have been responsible for the—to the Huns—disastrous delay in the counter-attack.

It was a great relief on the morning of D plus 14 to dash back to a vantage point on the Crepon road on a motor-cycle and watch for a few minutes the mass of men and materiel being hurriedly unloaded in the artificial harbour. Had the Huns launched an all-out attack during the height of the storm it could not have been another Dunkirk; it would have been impossible to get away after a German break-through, and such a catastrophe would have resulted in stalemate for many months, if not years, and, by such time, the Germans would have undoubtedly brought into being many of the ghastly and deathly things which we found in the almost complete stage on the mad dash through from Holland deep into the Reich.

One of the greatest sights of the whole war was the 1,000 Lancaster bomber raid on the city of Caen on the evening of July 6th. And never before, or after, did I see so much flak in the sky. As the marker planes went in it seemed impossible that any aircraft could go through that sky barrage and live. It was interesting to see the flak dying gradually as wave after wave of the heavies sailed in to drop their loads. I think it was on that night that everyone who saw the spectacle knew that the war was won no matter how long it would be before Jerry quit. Any nation, or nations, capable of putting so many heavy aircraft into the sky at the one time simply could not lose a war. And for thousands of Jerries who survived that holocaust the writing must have been very plainly on the wall.

We moved up into the Cristot area just after the fierce battle which had taken place there. Matters were still damned unhealthy. The stench, or stenches, were terrible; the nauseating smell of violent death pervaded the whole place. The batteries in our rear pounded away nearly all day and night, and the air was in perpetual torment with the sighing of shells winging their way towards the Hun. There were some Jerries at Juvigny with 88s and mortars, and after leaving us in comparative peace for the first couple of days they opened up on the third night and then for eighteen consecutive nights they let us know that they had not been liquidated. One night a terrifically large piece of shrapnel shattered the rough shelter covering seven of my men and shrieking through, missed the whole cowering bunch! We cussed our gunners a little on these nights too since they kept up their infernal racket practically throughout the hours of darkness, and the flash of their guns brought Jerry planes round like moths to a candle. On their run-in to the guns in our rear they usually sprayed our area for fun.

It should be said though that the German planes attacked in their greatest strength just after dusk, not that they ever attacked in strength as we, the British and Americans, knew air power. And their primary targets were always the beaches and the bay.

When at Cristot we nightly expected German patrols and took the necessary precautions, but there was never a clash. We were not a big unit, and we appeared to be entirely alone and divorced from everything, and everyone else. Every night, just in front of us on a ridge, there appeared what seemed to be hundreds of Bren carriers with Vickers guns, etc. They charged up to the top of the ridge discharged thousands of rounds of ammunition and then ran down again. We got some marvellous views of the old Typhoons dive-rocketing the German armour-harbours. Those chaps certainly did a magnificent job of work throughout the campaign. The Caen area was never healthy.

This part of the country had a number of small woods, or copses, and there I found one or two dead German riflemen. Their scattered, and in some cases, camouflaged positions showed that they were not just ordinary infantrymen, and there was ample evidence that they had done some execution. But all that remained of their rifles revealed that none had been equipped with telescopic sights.

One of my colleagues complained that for a couple of

days his sleeping place, a lean-to close to a ditch, had become unbearable as the result of a terrible stench. For quite a time the weather had been very hot, and he was not really anxious to change his abode since it was shady, and anyway everywhere stank in that area. After a day or so of exceptional heat we got about thirty hours of torrential rain which effectively stopped all movement on both sides and we settled down to a short period of peace such as one expects from reports of Chinese wars which apparently stop when the rains come. Due to the rain there was a slight subsidence of the floor of my colleague's lean-to and he awakened in the morning to find a German hand sticking out of the ground about three or four inches from his nose. The body had been buried only a very few inches below the surface. My colleague found another place!

It was in this area that one afternoon I did about a hundred yards in something under "evens." I had been talking to a number of chaps who were resting behind the line and spending a pleasant hour testing captured German weapons, including Schmeissers and Lugers, and was just going back to HQ when I saw a plane shoot out from the wood about 600 yards distant. It was a FW 190. Within a split second a couple of hundred men disappeared into the earth. There was absolutely nothing for me to fall in so I ran faster than I have ever run before, or since, spurred on by the rattle of the FW's machine guns. Reaching the tiny orchard which masked our HQ I cleared a terrifically high hedge and fell on top of the cook who was grovelling in his garbage pit. An exotic lady's boudoir could not have smelled so sweet! The FW secured only one hit—one chap having taken a bullet through the right shoulder. The wounded man was smiling happily. He had little pain and was talking excitedly about "Blighty"! And he was in the centre of a slightly envious crowd!

In Normandy, and throughout the campaign, there was

a good deal heard about German snipers in trees. I am quite sure that the majority of *riflemen* will share my doubts as to the efficiency and effectiveness of tree-shooting. There certainly were Germans in trees, but I am of the opinion that they were acting as observers rather than snipers. There are comparatively few men who can shoot with sniper-accuracy in the off-hand position, let alone the far more difficult position which arises from almost any stance in a tree. The Germans used slings for these "Tarzans" and, of course, such a contrivance captured the attention and fired the imagination of war artists and correspondents, with the result that a most graphic, if not entirely factual, portrayal resulted. The most notable tree merchant I saw—smelled would be a more fitting word since there was little left of him but smell—swung lazily in his sling in a large tree near Cristot in July. He reminded me of highwaymen's remains swinging from the gibbet in the "good old days." A burst of machine gun fire and the hot sun was responsible for this excrescence. When speaking of this monkey-business it is only fair to mention that, according to German small arms manuals, training in tree shooting was practised.

After eighteen very colourful days and noisy nights, the only comforts of which were twice undressing for a bath in a bucket and sleeping at odd times in greatcoat and blanket in, and on, Mother Earth, we were pulled back about fifteen miles mainly to rest. For the first two nights the silence was uncanny, and no one could sleep. Here I took the opportunity of looking around for a suitable place to re-zero and test the rifles of the Squadron, and found a rough, a very rough, 30 yards range in the headquarters of a replacement unit. The butts were just a dug-out plot with a rock background which provided many alarming ricochets, and here men just going up the line gave their rifles a last testing. These people had no targets, but fired at tins, etc.; I wanted something a little more elaborate, so I had one or two small frames made and got the orderly room people to make a stencil of the "Rommel's Runners" target which was in the copy of the National Rifle Association Journal which I had brought across with me. Although the "printing" was not good the targets were certainly better than corned beef tins. When we started to fire there were a number of officers sitting about in the sunshine, within fifteen yards of the butt. When I told them that I proposed to start firing they said "All right, old man, carry on; we shall be all right here." But they did not stop long. As I have said before— there were many alarming ricochets!

Even at this early stage this particular replacement unit had quite a good museum of captured German weapons and equipment and I spent an interesting hour studying the specimens. But I found that the officer in charge of the "museum," although having some knowledge of the stuff on view, had not that unbounded enthusiasm of the true weapon devotee; he did not really "know"! This kind of superficial knowledge I found prevalent throughout the Services both in England and overseas. I could quote many examples, but here are two to illustrate my points:—R.A.F. armament officers in England had never heard of the Mk. VIIIz ammunition; many Army officers to whom I showed some rounds of the round-nosed British Mk. VI cartridges said "Oh, dum-dum bullets"! Even officers of years of experience were woefully lacking in their knowledge of firearms and ammunition, and I often thought that had these men occupied a corresponding position in a civilian business house they would not have been employed long had they shown such a lack of interest in the equipment of their job.

❁   ❁   ❁   ❁

Normandy Night

There are three men in the signals trench; a signaller on the RT set, a corporal with the field telephone and an officer. They are seated, cramped and uncomfortable, on empty biscuit tins. Above them forming a roof are the trunks of shell-spattered trees loosely covered with earth, proof, they all devoutly hope, against shrapnel and machine-gun bullets. Overall is a low, perfectly camouflaged tent, through the odd bullet holes in which a star occasionally blinks obscenely. The harsh discordant chatter of the wireless set is nerve-wracking. The thoughts of all three men are similar. They are thinking of their wives and their homes; the homes they now realise were never fully appreciated in the halcyon days of peaceful civilian life. The officer, one time poet and author, prays silently with head sunk into the upturned collar of his greatcoat; although late June it is cold and damp in the trench. His prayer is semi-pagan in its simplicity—"Guard my beloved wife. Grant me the guts and courage necessary to be an example to my men. Grant us a speedy victory, and that the sanity of peace may return to a mad world. I ask these things in the name of Christ, the Perfect Man."

The corporal is garrulous and drones away interminably about nothing if given the opportunity or encouragement. The radio-operator, a dark, saturnine Welshman, with something of the quiet brooding mystery of the Welsh mountains about him, is almost sullen, and he reads his small home-town newspaper, received that afternoon, with unblinking eyes in the yellow light of a battered hurricane lamp. The officer reaches for the rifle which stands in one corner of the trench, and polishes the already gleaming butt with his handkerchief. It is a P 14 and a much loved weapon.

Suddenly out of the south comes the ominous drone-note of approaching hostile aircraft. Above the cacophony of the RT set ack ack guns of all calibres spring to guttural life. It is easy to differentiate between the short snake-spitting hiss of the Bofors guns, the deep tone crack of the 3.7s, the harsh cough of the 20mms and the monkey chatter of the LMGs. Above all rides the ear-splitting roar of the heavy field gun which now opens fire some distance to the rear. As the big calibre guns shake the earth and the tent tosses as though shaken by a mischievous wind, the officer shudders. He takes his cigarette case from his left breast pocket and hands it to the signallers. As he strikes a match and passes it to his two companions his fingers are perfectly steady; that pleases him.

The earth vibrates to the impact of HE bombs dropped a short distance away. Closer comes the sharp crack of bursting anti-personnel bombs with the resulting shower of hissing shrapnel seeking lodgement in shrinking flesh. All sound is magnified by the acoustic properties of the tent. The men crouched in the trench force themselves to talk, but no attention is paid to that which is said. They feel that they are trapped, and they want to scream and to clamber out of the trench and run headlong into the night.

Outside there is quiet again. The telephone orderly closes his eyes, and the wireless operator reads the most popular Sunday newspaper, many days old. The officer lights a pipe and bites hardly on the stem, re-arranges his blanket beneath him on the biscuit tin, endeavouring to loosen cramped limbs and ease aching buttocks and thighs. He polishes the rifle butt again, and thinks of his dogs and his guns and of long, glorious days in the field and on the range. And he thinks of War. If there had ever been within him any romanticism regarding war it had been killed during those first few violent days when the stench of death filled the mouth and choked the throat, and indelibly printed on his mind was a picture of a death-dilated cow lying obscenely with legs and udders stiffly, starkly pointing to the sky—the Mecca of a million flies. His eyes close and his head droops lower and lower. Suddenly he is vitally alert again as the mad symphony of the night war rises to crescendo. The corporal shivers. "Here they are again, sir," he mutters. "How long to dawn?" The officer glances at his watch. "Two hours." During the brief air attack the men's nerves and muscles are taut, but there is no fear on their faces. But a month of strain is becoming apparent; there is a slight trace of grey about the temples of the officer, and below the eyes of all three there is a delicate, web tracery of exhaustion.

Except for the crackling chatter of the radio set all is quiet. Occasionally the staccato report of a rifle shot and the angry "drrrp, drrrp" of a Spandau comes out of the night. Frequently the three men are covered by showers of dirt as some industrious mole, a lovely little creature of shining black velvet, undisturbed by the manifold noises of war, burrows assiduously and forces his tunnel out into the gaping chasm of the trench, the brown, damp walls of which are changed to smooth elephant grey in places by the impress of great-coated backs. A beetle in shining ebony armour moves quickly along the arm of the officer. With a woman's tenderness he allows it to run on to a piece of paper and then places it on the parapet of the trench. It does not seem strange to him that he who will, and must, kill Man, will not crush out the life of a lowly beetle.

Cramped and with legs and feet tingling with pins and needles the officer slowly climbs out of the trench, crawls through the darkness of the low tent and passes out into the cool night. He breathes deeply. Behind him the dark sky is slashed with the crimson, yellow-shot, flash glow of heavy artillery. He and the corporal who has joined him, exchange a few words with the two-man patrol who slide up like grey wraiths. A large fire reddens the south horizon. To the north-west, over the beaches, the tracer of naval pom-poms climbs lazily and eccentrically into the blue velvet of the sky weaving fantastic patterns. Vivid blotches of orange and red, like ink stains on a blotting pad, mark the bursting of heavier calibre shells. The scene and the atmosphere remind the officer of the grotesquerie of the ballet. Only the blue-silver gleam of the few stars is constant.

Across the dull muted note of our own batteries comes a harsher, more piercing wail. "Shells—Jerries" shouts the officer, and he and the corporal dive into the tent and fall into the trench. They lie with thumping hearts and brains on fire. The ground shakes and earth pours down through the crevices in the trunks covering the trench. Sweat rises on the foreheads of the three men. The officer shakes his head, and struggles for his cigarette case—always the cigarette—the consolation of thousands of men throughout two great wars!

And so the night drags on, seeming interminable. And then comes the dawn. The officer goes out into the open. In the east the sky is crystal grey and green, and shafts of mauve, scarlet and gold herald the slow approach of the sun. The dawn wind is swishing the corn a hundred yards away. The officer thinks of slim pale-backed women in long, rustling evening gowns.

The corporal joins the officer. Together they look skyward with gladdened eyes. There is relief in their hearts. The subaltern feels that he wants to laugh and sing. As he goes to his ditch leaving an uneven-trail through the dew-drenched grass, he knows that for a couple of hours he can sleep secure in the knowledge that no Hun will haunt the

[24]

blue Normandy sky whilst Spitfire, Thunderbolt and Lightning gambol in the sun. He shakes the mud from his blanket, and scrapes the dried earth from where it has sealed the crevices in the buttons of his greatcoat. He finds pleasure in dallying over such trivialities.

He lies down in the bottom of the ditch, places his rifle beside him, and happily draws a blanket over his weary body. Above in the sky the Allied planes ride like triumphant hawks, hurtling in the burning blue and gold of the morning.

The subaltern sighs. He is oblivious to the many discomforts of his bed. He sleeps.

Another long Normandy night has slipped into vivid, agile memory!

❖ ❖ ❖ ❖

Belgium

After one or two relatively unimportant German riflemen incidents across the Seine I ran into a little desultory German sniping in Belgium, not far distant from Brussels, the city which gave us our most tumultuous, spontaneous and sincere welcome. Many Germans took to the surrounding woods on the occupation of the capital city and for a night or so were a nuisance, but the Belgian Maquis attended to most of them in no uncertain fashion. They believed in bringing back concrete evidence of their kills. I was offered a real souvenir of a German sniper for ten cigarettes—a left ear in a match-box!

The majority of the members of the Maquis were a blood-thirsty crowd who would stop at nothing; they had many interesting tales to tell, but we found their demands for cigarettes too exhausting. One of their officers pressed upon me a perfect example of the German Mauser carbine, the Kar 98K with which I later did quite a lot of shooting. The Maquis had gathered together an enormous quantity of German weapons, rifles, machine carbines and pistols, and I have no doubt that some of them amassed a small fortune from souvenir hunters. I actually saw a Luger sold to an American for the equivalent of £27.10 or over $100! This I found amusing since the same pistol had been offered to me the previous day for the equivalent of twenty dollars; an offer which was turned down in the same scornful manner as my counter-offer of four dollars!

I could never understand why men should be so foolish as to pay such extortionate prices for German weapons. Many men who had no real interest in firearms clamoured for Lugers and Walthers, and I am quite sure that even if the British police authorities had not launched their campaign of calling-in all such weapons 99% of them would never have seen the light of day again; once they had been shown to admiring relations they would have been thrown into a neglected drawer and forgotten. It quite frequently happened that a chap who really *was* interested in firearms and had considerable experience with them before the war could not obtain anything interesting, or by use of his common sense would not pay the fantastic prices demanded. I have often thought it most peculiar that the majority of Service men think the weapons of the enemy are better than those with which they themselves are armed. But perhaps the Germans thought the same! I know they were certainly interested in the British Enfield .38 pistol, and even brought out a pamphlet about it.

We went into the Dutch salient, the narrow strip bordering the road from Eindhoven to Nijmegan a few days before the end of September 1944. The reception we got in Eindhoven was cold and austere, somewhat to be compared to that received in Normandy. The first troops in Eindhoven had been welcomed vociferously and with great enthusiasm; national costumes had been worn and the national orange flag flown everywhere. But on that first night there was quite a big German air raid on the town and that had certainly dampened the ardour and enthusiasm of the Dutch. We English are very prone to the idea that the Teutonic mind has no sense of humour, but I think we sometimes err; when the Hun raided Eindhoven on the first night of its liberation the marker planes dropped *orange* flares over the town!

Due to Jerries' penchant for cutting the Eindhoven-Nijmegan road at that time we were ready for anything as we moved northwards up the salient. Notices along the road warned all traffic to "Keep moving" and we needed no urging. There were, however, few incidents. I was riding a motor-cycle and on the instructions of the C.O. a colleague and myself were riding near to the centre of the convoy. About ten miles north of Eindhoven we were joined by a Don R and a sergeant, both astride motor-cycles and they jogged along beside us for some time. It was only later that I learned from the Don R that they had run into some machine gun fire and rifle fire at the end of the convoy, and had thought it was high time they took up another position! We were fired on a couple of times before running into our objective, but sustained no casualties.

Our goal was one of the biggest airfields in Holland; it was one of the largest I have ever seen, and one which Jerry had vacated very hurriedly, intact, when the first British recce cars had swept in to the place. But the recce unit being weak in strength had had to withdraw, so in came the Hun again and very effectively blew the place to hell before retiring for good. And the Hun knew something about demolition! It was a barren and desolate place and I spent the first two nights curled up on the ground between ammunition boxes. About this time I got a really severe cold which stayed with me for three weeks. And there is only one thing, or perhaps I should say, two things, worse than a cold when on active service—tooth-ache and dysentery! One certainly feels hellishly miserable. Our first night in occupation was a signal for the Bosche to come across and drop his invitation card, but no damage was done other than swallowing a little Dutch mud and manure as a result of diving for cover. There was a lot of small arms fire about, and the next morning it seemed that the line was just in the front garden, or shall I say circular garden since the noise of minor battle was all around us. A few miles before reaching this spot we had passed a sign which stated that such and such a Division's Battle School was situated in the direction of the arrow! That was one of the most amazing things of the campaign to me—the quickness by which Battle Schools sprang up just behind the advancing armies and the fluid front line. On the next day when I visited some of my chaps and watched a marvellous display of German mortar fire not many hundreds of yards away I was amused to find that some of the men thought it was part of some training going on at a Battle School!

On the way through the corridor we passed many American airborne troops. Some of them were nonchalantly carrying out patrols in the woods bordering the road. I shall never forget seeing one Eaglet who carried three pistols slung in his belt, and his Winchester carbine over his shoulder, the muzzle of which was covered by a certain rubber article which is never mentioned in drawing-rooms and which was serving a most useful purpose in preventing the rain, which was falling rather heavily at the time, from entering the barrel.

There were many isolated pockets of Huns in the salient, and these were a damned nuisance for some days. Here again though quite a number of shots came our way from the woods it did not merit the title of sniping, since no one was hit.

As an illustration of how long some of these pockets remained it is enough to say that on October 13th, I went down to Eindhoven and about five miles from the town I was ambling along in a Jeep behind an ambulance, and there was another Jeep in front of the Red Cross van. Suddenly there was the deuce of a row and everything stopped —myself about two inches from the ambulance. My batman who was in the passenger's seat shouted "Mortaring" and we dived for the convenient ditch in the approved not-hitting-the-ground-from-the-Jeep style. One mortar bomb had dropped immediately in front of the leading Jeep, left a tiny crater in the road, but had not touched either the vehicle or the occupants. The latter, along with the ambulance crew, were our immediate companions in the ditch. A few more bombs came over, landing unpleasantly close, and then after a couple of minutes' silence we all boarded our respective vehicles and went like the wind Eindhoven-wards. I afterwards learned that an isolated Hun mortar plastered this particular section of the road at the same time each morning, and had the range to a T. I understand that a few mornings later a tank was detailed to wipe out the pocket, and that was the end of those Jerries.

A day or two after arriving at the airfield we received a message that some British planes had been fired at by a 20mm gun from a wood about a couple of miles from the airfield. The CO and myself went out to have a look at the area specified; it would have been a battalion task to search only a tenth of that wooded area!

We were in one of the hardest-hit, and poorest, parts of Holland, only a few miles from the German border and there is no doubt that close proximity to the border in-fluenced and coloured the outlook of the people in our area. These Dutch in the main, were sullen and uncommunica-tive, and obviously suffering from lack of nourishing food. The children in particular were glaring examples of mal-nutrition, and many of them, only about seven years of age, had the faces of ancient crones.

The appearance of some of the Dutch Free Forces, or Maquis, was not prepossessing, and when they turned out in force they resembled nothing more than the old Key-stone comedy cops, since many of them effected a peculiar green English-constable-type steel helmet, the efficiency of which I would have taken great delight in testing. They had very little idea of even guerilla warfare, and when in their company, as I was on occasion, I always gave their riflemen a wide berth. To more than one of them with whom I came into contact *any* type of ammunition fitted the German Mauser. One morning I went to great pains to tell a Dutch Maquis that he was seeking trouble with a capital T in endeavouring to fire British and American rifle ammunition in a Mauser, or 9mm cartridges in other calibre pistols, but I have no doubt that no notice was taken of any such warnings. I have no information available as to the casualties caused by such abysmal ignorance of firearms knowledge, but I am confident that there were many. This ignorance of firearms and ammunition was pretty prevalent throughout these guerilla forces, except where Allied officers had been parachuted in to the irregulars, and had given them a good deal of instruction. They had not the slightest knowledge of any safety rules, and when one worked with them there was always much more danger of being shot in the posterior than being laid low by any lurking enemy. I do think there is too much emphasis laid on safety by military authorities, but the Maquis people went to the other extreme!

A considerable quantity of arms, and ammunition, had been dropped to the Free Forces throughout Europe, but many of these were ruined and of no use when the time came to use them, because an entire lack of firearms consciousness had resulted in their being stored in places where they were subject to deleterious weather conditions. A quantity dropped in one area in Holland in which I worked had been collected and buried in the ground about three feet deep. The weapons had been buried without being oiled or wrapped in some form of protection material. When one considers that in that area the ground was about six inches under water during the winter months, and even in summer it was possible to find water at a shallow depth the condition of the weapons when lifted had to be seen to be believed. I was present at one such exhumation. The parcel of weapons had consisted of Enfield .38 pistols and Sten carbines. I have never seen weapons in such a terrible state. Being considered something of a magician in the art of cleaning and repairing firearms I was asked if I could do anything with the pistols. Well, I did my best, and spent hours and hours on them during the long winter, noisy nights when sterner things had not to be done, and used all manner of patent cleansing agents and some personal recipes, but in the majority of cases it was hopeless. I managed to get a couple of the Enfields in fair shape, and I believe they were used quite successfully later. But it made the heart of a gun-lover bleed to see such desecration. The Sten guns were absolutely ruined. This weapon was never a thing of beauty and good finish. After some months buried in water-soil every firearms-fan will realise something of the state of these carbines. But as I have pointed out previously this lack of firearms knowledge or consciousness was by no means confined to such people as the Maquis. Officers and men of the British Forces often showed a woeful lack of firearms knowledge.

The Dutch Maquis like the French and Belgian were armed with all manner of weapons, rifles, machine carbines and pistols. I think that practically every make of weapon in the world could have been found in an exhaustive search of the Maquis's armouries.

One of the Dutch irregulars had an American carbine with which he would not part even for cigarettes. It was red with rust and the butt was badly cracked. I am quite willing to wager that if he ever fired that carbine his name is now duly inscribed on the Dutch Maquis Roll of Honour! This carbine must have been subjected to really rough usage, since the Winchester I used, and of which I have written elsewhere, had been found in the Wilhelmina Canal just north of Eindhoven, and must have been there some time. I spent some hours cleaning it, and at the end of that period the barrel was brilliant, and the whole weapon as good as new, a fact which speaks well for the manufacturers and the materials they used.

For some time in Holland my platoon carried out a nightly protective patrol in rather nasty wooded country, but there was not much excitement other than occasional and sometimes dangerous clashes with Dutch police patrols!

After some shelling early one Sunday morning I was sent out with my platoon to look for an OP which the Powers that Were decided must be in the area between us and the thinly held front line. It took some considerable time to find even one section holding an extremely fluid and elastic line, and when I finally found a subaltern and asked him to mark the line on my map, as laid down by higher authority, he told me that he couldn't possibly do that since he really had no knowledge of it, and that I should have to go down to HQ—and the HQ, of course, was many miles astern! In the particularly flat terrain in our area there was really only one possible OP and that was in a village church. But there was certainly no signs of the upper regions of this church being used for years except by rather unclean birds! This was a typical example of the wild goose chases in which I found myself forced to indulge from time to time.

❋   ❋   ❋   ❋

A 1944 Version of Ten Little Nigger Boys

It was a miserably wet Dutch Sunday morning in early October 1944 and for our sins we were in and around a German airfield not far from the German border. The airfield was devastated as only German sappers can blow anything. To the east, south and west the surrounding country was typically Dutch—dyke-boundaried flat fields; to the north it was heavily wooded. The people around the area were in bad shape, particularly the children with their spindly legs and large skeleton-like heads; all of them were afraid that the Hun would be coming back, just as he had told them he would.

We were just getting used to the idea that the salient had been widened a little and that there was much less chance of our being surrounded again. It was really miserable, and to fill my own personal cup of woe to overflowing I had one hell of a streaming cold, and felt like creeping between my damp blankets on the floor of a draughty and "bomb-shifted" hut we had cleaned up for our signallers, and passing out completely! At 10.30 hours a message came from HQ that the CO wanted to see me. I clothed myself in ancient gas clothing to keep out the rain, donned a crash helmet, perspired very freely when kicking up my motor-cycle and then skated down the greasy dirt lanes to the farm which had been taken over by Squadron headquarters.

The CO was bubbling over with good humour, at complete variance to my own state of mind. A Dutch Maquis scout, complete with rusty Sten gun, had come in and reported that (a) there were ten Germans in the adjacent wood and (b) that the leader of the local Maquis band had kept the Germans under surveillance and wanted some assistance to round them up. Apparently the scout had called in at one of the platoon's HQ farther down the railway line which passed between our area and the woods, and there the officer in charge, "K," had collected ten men and gone hot-foot in the direction given by the Dutchman, no doubt thinking of the decoration which would come to him if he were successful in bringing in ten Huns! The CO wasn't satisfied about the situation at all, and cursed "K" roundly for going off like that when it was my job to do such things, my platoon being kept specially for such purposes. He told me to get a truck and a couple of sections and go back with the Dutch scout who had now begun to scorch rather vilely having stood before the CO's fire for some time. Out into the pouring rain I went and routed out my sergeant, and in a few moments two sections appeared struggling with equipment and LMGs and cursing not softly! We climbed into the truck and were off. The Dutchman was placed on the back of my Don R's motor-cycle and led the way.

After about twenty minutes tortuous snaking of forest tracks, my map was a lousy one and after about five minutes journeying I was completely lost, we arrived at the spot where the local leader of the Maquis was standing with his trusty henchmen. They were a motley crew, and with the possible exception of the scout only the leader could speak a little English—and it was a little! The band was armed with German Mausers, Stens and pistols, various, in successive stages of rust and disintegration. After some minutes of deaf and dumb and tiring gesticulation I gathered that "K" had gone into a section of the wood about one hundred yards away, and that there had been some firing. As best I could I asked the leader how many Germans there were in the wood. He said "Nine." The numbers were decreasing.

I was rather surprised that "K" had committed his men to the wood since it was really extensive, and it would have been a comparatively simple matter for one or two Jerries to have wiped out the whole lot. To comb that stretch of wood was really a Battalion task. I did not want to commit my two sections unduly so I sent off a couple of men to endeavour to contact "K." I don't think they relished the prospect but they went speedily enough. Immediately afterwards another Dutchman appeared to report that he had seen the Germans in the far end of the wood a few minutes before. "How many?" I asked. The answer was the spreading of eight fingers, then as if to correct his mistake he pulled one finger down again. Ah, seven!

I waited ten minutes during which time the Dutchmen showed terrible signs of impatience which was brought to a head when yet another of their kith and kin appeared to report by the now established sign language that the Huns —six of them—had left the wood and headed for some farm buildings to the east. The men I had sent out to contact "K" came back at this juncture, looking pretty white about the gills, to report that they had seen nothing of "K" or his men but they had been fired at twice, once on the outskirts of the wood, and once inside, and they had not been able to locate the firer.

I decided that I would make for the farmhouses which the last Dutchman had reported as being the objective of the Germans and moved forward with the Dutchmen immediately behind me, and my two sections led by their NCOs on either side of the track. I left a couple of men behind to await a possible call, or news, from "K." At a bend in the track we encountered another Dutchman, really they were as plentiful as daisies in the Spring, and he had seen five Huns heading for the farmhouse which could be seen in the distance. We carried on, self keeping a most anxious eye on the rifles and carbines carried by the Maquis—they were all pointing in my direction. We almost fell over another very wet Dutchie who reported seeing the Germans— all four of them! This was rapidly becoming a farce, and I felt sorely tempted to throw my hand in and return to the Old Man and tell him that the Dutchmen had imagined the whole thing. But I carried on, wet and snivelling and wondering why I had deserved such a life.

Suddenly as we dashed over a break in the hedge hidden track we ran into some hefty machine gun fire. Well, I thought that I was quick in throwing myself into the convenient ditch but I fell on two Dutchmen! I found myself almost hung by the nose on one of their Mausers and hastily pushed it away. A second or two later as I peered round I saw that two of the Dutchmen's rifles were buried, muzzle first, in about six inches of mud; and thereupon decided to give these merchants a particularly wide berth once we were out of the ditch. The machine gun having given up the ghost, fortunately none of my crowd were hit, we pushed on again. The Bren crew which my corporal had pushed up on the bank in order to return the fire had seen nothing; I left them there with orders to do their stuff if the firing re-opened. Like the devil at a pantomime another Dutchman bobbed up when we had gone a further hundred yards, and, yes, the Germans were in the farmhouse—the three of them!

Very cautiously we approached the farmhouse, and beckoning the sergeant I gave him his orders. Along with one of the Dutchmen I crawled along to the hedge bordering the farm, and then was startled to hear a shout from the leader of the Maquis who was some yards behind me. He was pointing to the open country. About six hundred yards away I saw the figures of *two* Germans running like the devil over a ploughed field. Realising that there was very little we could do about it I calmly settled myself down on the damp grass, took a bead on the second Hun using my No. 4 rifle, and squeezed the trigger and hoped for the best. It seemed an unconsciously long time before the Hun went down—and then there was ONE. But not for long since the hit Hun got to his feet and before another shot could be fired he disappeared limping behind some outhouses in the wake of his colleague.

We moved up to those buildings at greater speed and with more energy than had been shown previously that morning, but after another hour's search in the pouring rain by which time the Maquis had disappeared one by one I called the hunt off. I was quite pleased with the shot, but realised that it was outrageously lucky! I picked up my very wet and miserable men who had been left to await news from "K" and endeavoured to return to HQ. That was easier said than done, and it took a long time to get out of that wood.

When I finally arrived back it was to find that "K" and his men had been in some time; they had seen a couple of Germans and had fired at them but missed. The Huns had thrown away their rifles, and these "K" had picked up. One of his Bren gunners having seen movement in a hedge-covered track about four hundred yards away had opened up, but he was not quite sure whether they were Huns or not! My speech about that part of the report cannot be printed. We were the "movement"!!

❋   ❋   ❋   ❋

At Sniping School

It was early in October 1944 when driving down to Eindhoven that I saw the usual indicative arrows on which the magic words "Sniping School" were emblazoned. Desires which perforce had been dormant for some time sprang instantly to life and from that day onwards I so pestered my Colonel that finally he said "For Heaven's sake write for an officer vacancy on an instructor's course and I'll sign the letter." That letter was typed—instantly and personally. But to get the vacancy was not very easy, and it was not until March 1945 that I left my unit, I must confess, very gladly, and went down to the School.

I shall never forget my time at this war-time Sniping School. It is the golden period of my service life. There I found a comradeship, a keen spirit and enthusiasm for which I had looked in vain in my own Regiment, and there a man was a sniper before anything else. In a sniping school there is to be found an atmosphere which is absolutely characteristic, and is not found at any other school of military instruction. And so a great enthusiasm is engendered.

The dominant instruction was in shooting, stalking and observation. The informality was pleasing, but, of course, there was discipline—it is an essential awareness of the sniper that there is great need for discipline—self-discipline, the hardest form of control. The whole atmosphere of the place was meat and drink to the ardent rifleman. I was the eldest officer on the course, and although the only one who had been on the Continent since D Day the other much younger subalterns, platoon commanders all, had each seen more infantry action. But the camaraderie was magnificent.

At the school, binoculars became part of oneself—in many cases for the first time. We enjoyed long stalks under the hot sun, for the weather was phenomenally good for that time of the year. We could not have enough shooting, and the fiery eloquence of the Chief Instructor rendered his lectures on sniping and shooting generally by far the finest I have ever heard. Throughout the course there was a fever of expectancy since we all knew that the crossing of the Rhine was imminent. We saw the open-doored Dakotas going back from the initial assault of the Rhine, and very soon afterwards we ourselves were across the river on a tour of the forward areas—the last few days of each instructor's course was taken up by the most excellent idea of "practise what you preach" and arrangements were made for the instructors and students to go up into the line and "do the job." But we had little fun and games; the Hun was running too fast. The armour had broken through and everyone knew that it was the beginning of the end. We recrossed the Rhine thinking there might still be something doing on the Dutch front, but here again "the hunt was too much up." But I am still proud of the fact that I crossed the Rhine for the first time in the company of these men before the end of March 1945!

My fellow students were a mixed bunch, but with one exception they were a sterling crowd. I roomed or "attic-ed" in a Dutch house with "Mc" a young subaltern in a famous Welsh Regiment. He was about 21 and recently married, and superficially full of the joy of life, but behind the forced gaiety there lurked the tragedy of war-horror on a brain too young to stand up to it. "Mc" often spent his evenings in writing letters and knowing that he had not been married very long I naturally thought that each and every letter was to his wife. But I was wrong. Those letters, eleven in all, were to the next of kin of the eleven chaps in his platoon who had been killed in the hellish fighting in the Reichswald Forest. On the last night at the school after some drink he broke down and cried like a child. It was left to a young Polish officer, "George" (who had lost all his family and everything he possessed in Poland in 1939 and had nothing to live for but kill Huns) and myself to see "Mc" to bed and endeavour to comfort him. After he had calmed down a bit "George" left us. I shall never forget that night lying in bed in that rat-infested attic listening to the chest-shattering sobs of the sleeping boy. They were much more terrifying than the roar of the doodle-bugs monotonously passing overhead. It was on such occasions when one realised the true hellishness of war. In action it is not so bad; there is no time for reflection or reflective thought, and the horrid sights are fleeting motion pictures rather than "stills" in hard print. It is during the long night watches in the lonely outposts when one's ears and nerves are strained to screaming point and when one is forced to *think* that the full horror is manifest. Waiting is always the hardest task.

"Mc" had an intriguing little batman, "Marco," whom he shared with me during my stay at the school. "Marco" had an Italian surname, and when he was captured in the first battle of s'Hertogenbosch this name had been the cause of his being wounded in as "dirty" a manner as any man throughout the whole campaign.

After being captured he was taken before an SS lieutenant for interrogation. The SS officer speaking in English charged "Marco" with being an Italian. In vain the batman protested that he was English, that his father had been an Italian but had married an English woman after living in London for many years and had been naturalised. The SS man would have none of it, and persisted in his accusation that the batman was an Italian in English uniform. (The

Italians, of course, were not popular with the average German.) Finally he told "Marco" to "Get out" in such a ferocious tone that the little fellow turned and started to run from the room. Just as he reached the door there was a shattering explosion and he was conscious of a terrible burning in his shoulder. As he spun round and crumpled to the floor he saw the revolver in the SS officer's hand. When he recovered consciousness he was amazed to find himself in bed in the hospital in s'Hertogenbosch, being carefully attended by a couple of German medical orderlies and a German doctor who in fluent English set "Marco" completely at ease by saying that he "understood" the case perfectly and that he, "Marco," must not judge all Germans by the unfortunate "accident" that had befallen him. During the time he was in the hospital "Marco" had nothing but praise for the work of the doctor and the medical orderlies; they shared their few cigarettes with him, and he secured whatever good food there was available. Just before the second attack on the town the medical orderlies came to him, told him that it would not be very long before he was with friends again and left him as comfortable as possible. When "Mc" reached the hospital, his platoon being the forward unit in the sector attack, he was amazed and relieved to see the grinning face of his batman swarthy and dark against the whiteness of the pillows. To the Huns generally "Marco" bore no ill-will, but had he ever met that SS lieutenant again the result would have been most interesting to the Borgia family!

Shortly after leaving the Sniping School "Mc's" platoon ran into serious trouble; they were lying close to the corner of a street preparatory to going-in to an attack when an 88 shell fell directly amongst them. The only "whole" survivors were "Mc" and "Marco" and they were both taken prisoner. For some weeks they were posted as missing and my letters to "Mc" were returned to me marked to that effect. It was with great joy that I received a letter from him in August 1945 to say that he was safe at home after being in the hospital; his nerves were in a bad shape and he had been down-graded medically, but was confident that peace and quietness would pull him round.

One of "Mc's" favourite weapons was the .5 Browning. During the fighting in the Reichswald he had found a knocked out armoured vehicle in which a .5 Browning was intact. Two of his handy men collared it, improvised a ground mounting and placed it in a strategic position since it was expected that Jerry would counter-attack at first light. He did, and when "Mc" spoke of the execution that Browning did his bespectacled face shone with an almost divine radiance! The .5 Browning was a very popular weapon with many British officers—not without justification.

Another character amongst the students was "Joe" a young Canadian subaltern who, despite many months of serious scrapping still, on occasion, thought war a delightful game. He entered into the sport of sniping with a boundless enthusiasm, and a new interest entered into the hitherto sacred trinity of Wine, Women and Song! I was amazed to find that he had never tasted Martell's Three Star Brandy until he sampled the bottle I had with me one evening; but having once smacked his lips appreciatively he was not content until I turned down an empty bottle. There were times when "Joe" was serious, no one can see War at first hand and remain absolutely untouched, but his sombre moods did not last long against his inherent, bubbling boyish humour.

"Louis," the French-Canadian lieutenant, was miserable of face and mien, but this belied his native lightheartedness. He was slow on the uptake, but was officer in charge of his Battalion Scout platoon with scores of night patrols, many of them "sticky," to his credit. He was not a good shot, but he was very keen and tried as hard as anyone. When he was not doing so well on the range he looked as if he were going to burst into tears, but then settled down in an earnest attempt to do better. Twenty-eight years of age he was nearly an ancient when compared with the remainder of the officer students except myself!

Peter, a young Irishman, belonged to a famous Regiment. He was 19 and a platoon commander of quite extensive experience. He was the worst shot on the course, a fact which he first attributed in some measure to the sniper rifle he had brought with him, which was a fair example of many of the rifles which made their appearance at the school, and which were incapable of hitting a twelve-inch bull at 50 yards, and in some cases would not have contacted a four foot square target at that range. The CI and the NCO instructors were very patient with Peter for he was a likeable boy, but his difficulty was flinching and he never conquered the habit.

"Pig"—so nick-named—was corduroy-trousered, flying-jacketed—of the officer type the mordant cartoonist likes to guy. He was the only subaltern on the course who was actively disliked by his fellows. He knew everything and had been everywhere, and on the first night at the school went along to everyone—except me, since seeing my Regimental flash he thought that I was definitely an outsider—asking when they came into Normandy. When he discovered that no one had been in on D Day, D plus 1 or D plus 2, he assumed the mantle of great experience and started to "shoot a line." I allowed him to talk until the look of malevolence was on every listener's face and then I asked him what he thought of my two rifles, the old P' 14 which I brought across on D Day and the No. 4 I picked up out of the sea on D plus 1! I plead that *my* "line-shoot" was pardonable. The others told me so anyhow. "Pig's" face was worth the proverbial "guinea a box"! "Pig" played up to the instructors, with no avail as regards the Lovat Scout NCOs whose quiet integrity was proof against anything in the nature of soft-soap. During range practices he always fired six shots instead of five! Naturally we did not say anything about that, but such a trick is the best indication of the man's calibre. He secured a very good pass on the course, but he cannot have deluded anyone—least of all, himself!

The two young Polish officers were good fellows and with a natural ability to "see" and shoot they brought a deadly hatred of the Bosche which in years of waiting had become a cold, calculating ferocity which boded ill for anything German. Unfortunately one of them was killed two days after he left the school.

"The Kid" was 5'3" and of slight build. He was not long from OCTU, and with a school cap perched on his fair hair he would have passed for a schoolboy of fourteen years of age. He had been out from England for the mere matter of three weeks and had already become notorious in his unit for volunteering for night patrols, not from inexperience of what was a most detested job, but rather from a desire to indulge in something which smacked of nocturnal, schoolboyish pranks. It was good to see the manner in which his batman, a man old enough to be his father, mothered the boy.

"Dennis" the young Marine was an exceptionally nice fellow, addicted to smoking heavy, curled pipes. He was quiet and restrained, and his whole manner radiated a confidence which must have comforted his men. A good shot, he was a splendid companion whether in peaceable or war pursuit. His batman was a typical old English butler type— a gentleman's gentleman, whose placid looks belied him since he had a splendid service record, and was more than game for any mischief that might come along.

The officer students had a farewell dinner on the last night of the course at the officers' club of a Dutch town which still had a periodic visitation from Jerry's artillery. It was an hilarious evening, with much champagne. There were many speeches, and one of my most treasured possessions is the menu signed by every member of the party, representing all types of Regiment. It was a fitting conclusion to a marvellous period. When I left the School next day the handshakes were all firm and strong, and I, with no trace of shame, confess to a lump in the throat. I know that some of these very fine chaps did not live very long after leaving the school. My memories of them, and of the school in which we worked, shot and played together, are golden.

At the school I was trained by NCOs of the Lovat Scouts. These men in their distinctive bonnets bearing the large silver badge with the stag's head and simple inscription "Je suis prest" ("I am ready") and their almost uncanny prowess in observation, stalking and shooting, earned my greatest admiration. They were quiet and restrained, not so eloquent maybe as the average Army instructor, but easily forceful. In their eyes lurked the quiet shadows of hillside forests; they were not loquacious, but in later months when we hunted together in German forests, the contents of my flask and the leaping flames of our camp-fires unloosened tongues and I was content to sit drowsily before the fire and listen to stories of Highland stalks, of great kills, and of their regard for the chief of the Fraser clan, Lord Lovat, Commando Brigadier, who was badly wounded in the early Normandy campaign. They were filled with a deep, passionate love of their Regiment. Their bonnet was sacred and they proudly wore it when in forward areas. Certainly no Red Devil of the Airborne Forces had more regard for his red beret than the Scouts for their unique bonnet. And because they knew of my respect and admiration for their Regiment they accepted me as one of themselves and said that nothing would please them more than that I should wear the coveted bonnet.

For some months in Germany I lived, trained, stalked and shot with these magnificent men of the Lovat Scouts. I hope to do all these things again when I visit them in their Inverness-shire homes.

I met Major Underhill for the first time on the cold afternoon in October when I went along to the Sniping School to make enquiries as to the possibility of my getting a course at the school. He was standing on the firing point, clad in a Denison smock, his ruddy face with its keen eyes and sharp slant of nose, radiating enthusiasm. He welcomed me warmly. I explained that which I wanted, laying emphasis on my rather peculiar position, but he said that he didn't give a damn what unit I belonged to so long as I was keen on sniping, that he would be delighted to have me at the school and that if I applied to Divisional Headquarters he felt sure that they would grant the necessary vacancy on the next instructor's course. The matter took some time but as I have previously stated I eventually arrived. Overshadowing everything else at the school was the forceful, even dynamic, personality of the Commandant, or the "old man" or "Uncle" as Major Underhill was affectionately known to every member of the staff from the Lovat Scout NCOs to the cook. Here was a man definitely knowing his subject from A to Z, and stoutly maintaining that the only place to teach sniping in wartime was in the field, in the forward areas, as close as possible to the line. He was not boastful, but supremely active and keen, working with unflagging zeal and energy. He was certainly the finest and most fiery lecturer on sniping and shooting I have ever had the good fortune to hear. He had a great hatred for the Bosche—"the grey 'illegitimates' "! He was a master coach, instilling confidence in the man he was coaching on the firing point, and to see him shoot was a joy to the eye; handling perfect, his position such that he became part and parcel of the ground. Respected and admired he was really liked by everyone with whom he came into contact. I can see him yet, as I shall always see him in my mind's eye, his slightly rotund but straight figure stamping along the quiet Dutch village street, waving his stick cheerily in salutation of the vociferous greetings always given to him by the

Dutch kiddies to whom he was affectionately known as "Poppa." I consider myself richer by having made his acquaintance.

When writing of the sniping school it would be an injustice not to mention the fatigue-men, many of whom had been front-line troops, down-graded medically as the result of wounds. They too, were filled with enthusiasm for their job, and sniping, and in their number there were one or two really excellent shots.

Despite a rather nasty hand wound (three of the five stitches were pulled during the shooting practices) I did not shoot too badly at the school and managed to reach the "V.G." classification. As a result of the pulled stitches the hand became infected and in spite of penicillin etc., the wound did not heal until June 1945.

We travelled up to, and over, the Rhine in March in trucks loaned to the school by the famous Highland Division to which we were to be attached. The trucks were crowded and everyone was complaining of cramp and stiffness before we had travelled a dozen miles. When we stopped for a very brief period to attend to the dictates of nature, within a minute of the men dropping out of the wagons there was the devil of an outcry from a military policeman who dashed out of a near-by cottage shrieking that some so-and-so had pinched his chickens—two of them. He reported the theft to me and suggested that perhaps some of the men from my wagon had been responsible. I said "Impossible." After seeing everyone on board I scrambled into the wagon myself, and just as we started off again the same MP ran up to say that all six of his chickens had now disappeared. After looking round the wagon I told him, rather sharply, that none of my chaps had taken them, and that I took a damned poor view of his accusation. It was impossible for him to stop the convoy and ask the CO for a search (I would have liked to have seen the CO's face had such a request been made!!) since once one got into the stream of traffic on the way to the Rhine at that stage in the War there was no drawing out of it. After the wagon had moved a few yards I was amazed to hear cheerful cacklings proceeding from the dim forward end of the truck. I am sure that a good meal was had by all—more tasty and succulent perhaps because the raw material for the feast had been provided by the "red-caps" for whom most soldiers have very little love, although the majority gave the military police full credit for doing a most splendid job of work, and a sticky one many times, from the beaches of Normandy to Berlin. No doubt those MPs had themselves won those fowl from some other unfortunate beings!

Approaching the Rhine the smell of death was nauseating. Hundreds of dead cattle with legs and udders stark to the sky were lying bloated and stinking. Herds of them had been pushed forward in front of troops and those that had not found mines had died much more miserably.

Anyone east of the Rhine before the end of March certainly saw that Jerry had taken a pasting. I spent the last night of that month sleeping (?) on the wooden floor of a much battered house between that which was left of Rees and Bocholt, cheek by jowl with a lance-corporal of the Royal Scots, a Lovat Scout sergeant and a lieutenant in a French-Canadian Regiment. It was a noisy night with a symphony of shell-fire, bombing and the occasional chatter of a Spandau. During the shelling, masses of plaster dropped from the remaining half of the roof, and I should not have been unduly surprised had the whole lot collapsed, but there are times when one, after months of campaigning, cheerfully accepts any form of shelter no matter how great the shortcomings. And there were rats too, but these were not of the same venturesome species such as I encountered in my Dutch civilian billet where on many nights in my attic bedroom I was awakened by large rats scampering gaily across my face. A queer noise which added to the disturbed quality of this night was a mysterious clinking sound; this was explained in the very early morning when the Lovat sergeant went out to return a few minutes later with a mess tin of fresh warm milk, straight from the cows which were tethered to the outer side of the wall.

It was in this area that a large number of the Volksturm fought their first and last battle for the Fatherland. The ditches and roads were littered with corpses, and one was that of a white bearded old patriarch who appeared ancient enough to have been a veteran of the Franco-Prussian war of 1870. Close by there lay the shattered remains of an old musket. It was in this area too that I heard of an old bell-mouthed blunderbuss being picked up. There is no doubt that the British Home Guard was a magnificently equipped force compared to its German counterpart. Not that I should have liked to have been in close proximity to that blunderbuss when it was fired!

The Lovat sergeant and myself had a good look round the ruined house in the early morning, and having made our way upstairs by the simple expedient of climbing a fallen beam we discovered a sporting rifle, which bore no maker's name, but was a close cousin of the normal Mauser in appearance. It had been badly knocked about and was useless in itself, but another member of the party finding a similar weapon in the same district it was thought possible that one complete rifle could be made from the whole parts of both, so they were both whisked back to the school. I found some ammunition to fit these rifles, thick squat cased 8.3 mm lead-tipped cartridges. Some months later I had the pleasure of firing the "composite" rifle and found it quite a useful weapon. In the same house we discovered a much shattered .22 rifle, and many boxes of .22 ammunition of an unfamiliar type; this I later discovered to be of Russian origin.

The villagers in this area were in a pitiable state. All the women were crying bitterly, and the only males left were very young boys and very old men. But the most harrowing sight to me was an Alsatian dog; it was bomb-happy and running about tirelessly and hysterically with tongue hanging out of a gaping mouth.

Soon after leaving the BLA Sniping School application was made to the appropriate authorities for my return as a sniping instructor. Nothing would have given me greater joy, but the application was refused on account of "operational" grounds. A further application, backed at my end by my Group Regimental Officer, after the cessation of hostilities was more successful, and I joined the School on attachment in July. By that time it had moved into Germany and formed part of the BLA Training Centre, later to become known as the British Army of the Rhine Training Centre.

I do not need to refer to my diary to obtain the date when I last experienced the uncomfortable thrill of a near-miss from a German rifleman's bullet, observe I again do not write "sniper." The date is indelibly stamped on the brain since it was so near to the end of hostilities in Europe— May 5th, 1945. With my platoon I had taken over a rather important German experimental factory, at the same time accepting the responsibility of keeping alive the Director of the place, an invaluable German scientist, whom the authorities thought might be liquidated since he had refused to obey the order to blow the factory to save it from falling into Allied hands. In the grounds of the factory there was a hutted German service hospital—effective camouflage—which was in process of evacuation. My Colonel, platoon sergeant and myself were speaking, or trying to speak, with a voluble and excited Frenchman who had been pressed to work at the factory when we heard the crack and thump of a rifle shot. This was, of course, nothing unusual for there had been quite a bit of small arms fire in the area that morning. A second shot which caused consternation and death in a pen of sheep directly behind us resulted in the partial disappearance of the Colonel and the Frenchman. A third shot which passed between the faces of the sergeant and myself—we were standing almost touching each other—gave us something to think about—once we had hit the ground to which I was borne by a rugger tackle from the 170 lbs. sergeant. On the ground we both perspired very freely. After a few seconds we crawled away to some bushes. I sent the sergeant to bring up my platoon sniper, a young fellow who was an adept at fieldcraft and a good shot (once during an exercise in England he reached, unobserved, a manure heap close to the "enemy" headquarters, burrowed into that stinking heap and for his skill and fortitude "killed" many of the "enemy big-wigs") and when he arrived, pleased and keen, the two of us made a stalk in the general direction of the "thump." We found a Mauser, the carbine model Kar 98K, about a quarter of a mile from the spot upon which we had been standing, but no Hun. I sent a section out to go through the surrounding woods but knew that the quest was hopeless. It was a very close shave!

Shortly after crossing the Rhine for the second time I was given the job, with about twenty men, of going along to a salt mine in which the report stated there were some 200 SS troops! Fortunately for me a much bigger formation got there first!

When we took over the airfield which was the Cranwell of the German Air Force it was not all healthy. Like many German airfields it was surrounded by woods and from time to time rifle and machine gun fire swept over the airfield from the large number of Huns who had taken refuge in the close terrain. For a night or two it was the custom to withdraw the ack ack guns from their positions on the airfield just before dusk, and the gunners were mighty glad to pull into the comparative shelter of the ruined hangars and blitzed buildings.

For some miles before reaching the airfield one had to

run the gauntlet of woods many of which bore the pleasing signs of the passage of flame throwers, and one afternoon a Hun sniping from cover some two or three hundred yards from the road had a couple of extremely quick shots at my CO in his Jeep. Both shots missed but they were far too close to the CO's head for his peace of mind, and knowing the speed at which he invariably drove his Jeep I am inclined to think that the German was certainly in the marksman class to get so close to his target.

It was in this area that an amusing incident occurred in which I was the central, and rather ludicrous, figure. Fortunately there were no witnesses otherwise I should have felt a damned fool. I was bowling along a road at about 35 miles per hour in a Jeep when I heard a sharp crack and instantly a neat round hole from which many cracks radiated appeared in the windscreen. My heart leapt, and pulling up as quickly as possible I manoeuvred the Jeep into cover at the side of the road and, complete with rifle which I always carried with me at that time I jumped out. I spent a tense quarter-of-an-hour looking around and hoping that there would be another shot (well away from me, of course!) and then returned to the Jeep. Just as I was about to clamber into the driving seat again I noticed a sinuous length of steel wire lying on the ground, close to the front offside wheel. Closer investigation revealed my "rifle" shot—the wheel had picked up the steel wire, which had wrapped round it a number of times before the free end had whipped up and shattered the windscreen so effectively. To say I cursed is needless; I cursed more when I had to spend nearly half-an-hour unwinding the wire from the wheel and the axle!

We had with us for some time an officer who shot a terrific line to his people back at home, and his early letters about D Day were published in his local small town newspaper. He was quite convinced that in every German munition factory there was some type of lethality which was being made specially for him. Whenever he went out, and that was seldom since he preferred to have plenty of people about him, he always had a narrow escape from either death or mutilation. There cannot have been another man in the whole of the Allied Forces who was sniped at so much from the beaches of Normandy to the Reich, and although he had even felt the burning of passing bullets he came through unscathed. There were times when we wished that at least one bullet had not missed! About the best of his fairy stories was that he had been sniped at in a little Belgian village he passed through when moving up into the Dutch salient in September 1944. The bullet had actually grazed his nose as he was jogging along on his motor-cycle at about 30 mph; he imagined that it had left a red streak! Some innocent fly or bee had a good deal for which to answer! Every doodle-bug which passed over our area on its way to Antwerp and other places he imagined was his potential slayer; each bomb dropped from Jerry's jet kites up at 30,000 feet had been deliberately aimed at him; and every shell which fell close or near had his name written across it! His nerve having become as flexible as a gut cast it was a darned good thing when he landed a job at Headquarters and departed for much quieter pastures. Curiously enough, he was the most fortunate chap in the unit at finding enemy weapons, and having, on D plus 1 become the rather nervous owner of a P 38 in marvellous condition, he stuck to it throughout despite being offered big sums for it on numerous occasions. I shot with this pistol a number of times, and after seeing that I suffered no hurt he consented to have a few shots too!

We had another very queer customer, "X," posted to us some weeks before the end of the war in Europe. When I first met him in the Squadron Mess on the first night I returned from my course at the Sniping School he reminded me of a sore-eyed monkey possessed of a countenance which expressed surprise and perpetual incredulity. He said that he was a rifleman and a firearms fanatic, and knew a good deal about weapons, ammunition and the like. I experienced a sense of elation at the prospect of having a kindred spirit who was as fanatical as myself. But after about five minutes conversation I was bitterly disappointed; he knew little and that little was distorted! One thing I will say for him though and that is he could beat my head off at pistol shooting—providing he wore his spectacles. Without his glasses he was as blind as a bat and one could approach within three paces of him before recognition dawned.

His handgun was a long barrelled S. & W. .38 and he could certainly use it. I never saw him use a rifle; although he said many times he would accompany me when I went out to range-shoot he just never made it. As a sporting shot on the one or two occasions I was out with him he was hopeless. When he was out alone he always had good bags but left the kills for the starving Germans! Such compassion touched me deeply! The only thing I ever actually saw him bring in was one small duckling; the carcass was a mass of shattered feathers and pellets. He had a great penchant for losing himself; only once was he given the job of leading a convoy on a trek through Germany and he was adrift for many hours, finally arriving at the destination about eight hours after the unit had got into position; fortunately the convoy had not followed him! Shortly after the end of the war he used to go out alone for a day's "hunting" as he called it; he never seemed to realise that to knock about heavily wooded areas which still contained many Wehrmacht and SS troops was courting trouble. And curiously enough he never found it!

On every possible occasion he would take a trip to arms dumps and return loaded with firearms of every description, yet it was rare that he brought back anything of value. One night he rang me up on the field telephone and asked if I would go down to his quarters to see some really good stuff he had picked up. Thinking that at last he had actually got something my motor-cycle ate up the five miles to his HQ. There I found him surrounded with a motley array of rusty shotguns, parts of pistols and revolvers, swords and scabbards. The junk was placed in three stacks; the first was for the CO because as "X" said "He gave me permission to go to the dump," the second was for himself and the third was for anyone else. I had a look at the first collection and other than a couple of nice looking swords there was nothing worth having; his personal dump was mainly scrap iron. He said that except for a rather good Smith and Wesson .38 which had been adapted to .22 there was not a wholly sound pistol in any of the dumps. He pulled this S. & W. out of a drawer and handed it to me. It was a curio. The cylinder had been sawed in half, and that which remained had been most crudely and geometrically adapted to take .22 cartridges. The barrel had not been touched however, and therefore when the pistol was fired the .22 bullets leaped merrily across space from the sawn-off cylinder and disappeared into the cavern of the .38 bore! It may sound Ripley-esque but believe it or not "X" had not noticed these things and later when he spent considerable time shooting with this hybrid he bemoaned its lack of accuracy!

In the third pile of junk my eye instantly caught sight of a very fine example of a German dress sword without scabbard. I asked him why he had not kept that in his pile, to which he replied that since it hadn't a scabbard it was of no use to him. I pulled his swords from their scabbards and was amused to find them rusty. The scabbard-less sword, a perfect example of its kind, hangs on the wall in front of me as I write. In the throw-out pile I also found the parts, complete, of a neat little "Owa" pistol of 6.35mm calibre. "X" was very annoyed at having overlooked this since he had definitely wanted a pocket pistol. There were a number of shotguns, all except one of which were virtually useless. That one was quite a good example of the shotgun-cumrifle, the rifle barrel being slung underneath the web. I was greatly amused when "X" described the rifle barrel as being the "cleaning rod housing"; he regretted that he had not been able to find the cleaning rod in the arms dump! When I pointed out to him that the "cleaning rod housing" as he so picturesquely put it was, in effect, a rifle barrel, he told me that that was probably what a number of boxes of long cased ammunition were for—and which, of course, he had not bothered to bring back with him.

I used that combination gun a good deal later and since it was extremely difficult to find that particular type of ammunition I often cursed the memory of "X." When I was visiting his quarters one morning he asked me to have a look at his beloved long barreled S. & W. .38 which for some unaccountable reason had become red with rust. It was in a hell of a state. The whole pistol was covered with a particularly malignant looking rust. Knowing that I had along with me all the cleaning tackle dear to a rifleman's heart he asked if I would take it back to my platoon HQ and see what I could do with it. I agreed, and spent the best part of an afternoon cleaning it, at the end of which some of its pristine glory had been restored. I sent it back to him by Don R. A couple of days later he brought it into me again. He told me that he had oiled it on the previous day and now it was as rusty as ever. What was the matter with it? I asked him what oil he had been using, and he said that he didn't know really, but it was some German oil which one of his men had given to him; he had the oil container with him, and produced it forthwith. The German oil container was the bottle of bleach or some such oil which was contained in the small orange coloured box which housed Jerry's compact anti-gas kit!! I don't know the formula of that oil but it certainly could produce rust! I often wondered whether the fellow who handed "X" the "gun oil" did it as a joke, or whether it was done in good faith. Perhaps only his rifle could have brought verification!

"X" also practised the firing of doubtful-fitting cartridges in his pistols, without incident or hurt. He certainly bore a charmed life—not only from firearms! When we were in Denmark, at the conclusion of a rather riotous party he dashed down to the beach, stripped naked and ran along to some high rocks, and made a beautiful dive, head first, into about two inches of water. Any normal man would have broken his neck but "X" didn't. The last time I heard of him was in the island of Sylt when I was running a sniper instructor course there; one night he achieved distinction by driving a Jeep into the Mess wall and displacing a number of bricks; a few moments before that incident he had taken a bend rather sharply and thrown out the sergeant who was seated alongside him, much to the detriment of the NCO's wrist, which was broken. On the following night he found himself locked in the apartment of a lady, and airily dismissing her plea that he should wait until her husband came and unlocked the door he decided that it was far more simple to climb out through a window, after all the flat was on the ground floor. He opened the window, climbed on to the sill and fell twenty-four feet down into the basement—without breaking a bone, but bruising himself from head to foot, and sobering himself at the same time!

In May 1945 "X" spread the news about my great interest in weapons so much that I became inundated with shotguns and rifles to repair, renovate and clean, and I was finally forced to enlist the aid of my Platoon sergeant, and we turned one of the rooms in our truly palatial headquarters into a gun-room and there spent every minute of our leisure time.

After a short spell in Denmark where amongst other things I formed part of a Guard of Honour for the Queen of Denmark I flew home on leave and then back to Schleswig-Holstein. Twenty-four hours later I was on my way, on attachment, to the Sniping School at the BLA, now BAOR,

Training Centre, travelling down to Westphalia in a 15 cwt. truck. There I was received most warmly and made to feel at home instantly. Since there was an order in force at that time that all motor vehicles must have more than one man aboard I had taken down with me a couple of drivers from the Squadron, and having reached the School in good order and condition I told them that in view of the length of the return run coupled to their tiring journey down there was no need for them to return on the following day, but that they could make a start on the second day. I remember telling them this standing at the gable end of one of the school buildings. They had just expressed their thanks when we were all spattered with concrete chippings as a few bullets hit the wall end just above us. They thereupon decided that they would return the following day! Actually they didn't, but I am quite sure that they were of the opinion that I was going to have one hell of a time!

The shooting turned out to be the result of over-exuberant Russians in the camp quite close to the School. There were many hundreds of Russians in this camp and every evening it appeared as though they selected "sides" much as we do football teams and "played" a pitched battle in which rifles, machine guns, grenades and Verey pistols all played a part. In the earliest days of the Sniping School in that area it was customary for bullets to hiss and whistle around the school buildings, and one's person, at any time of the day or night. I never discovered how many casualties the Russians inflicted on each other but I am quite sure that not all of them lived to tell graphic tales of such "pacific" warfare to their families in Russia, if indeed, a large number ever reached home.

The close proximity of a large German ammunition dump was an irresistible magnet to the Russians and one evening a number of them decided to experiment by placing a case of large calibre shells on a roaring bonfire. The result was certainly colourful and noisy, and there were quite a number of casualties amongst the participants. The fire being thrown in all directions by the explosions caused a great conflagration, and spread rapidly to underground shell chambers. For some hours the serenity of the countryside was shattered and torn by a series of heavy explosions, and flames, forty feet high, leaped above the tall trees. It was like old times to hear the shrieking whistle of shrapnel tearing the air as the shells exploded.

The Germans in the district were terrified of the Russians, many of whom had apparently elected to work voluntarily for Jerry. Once the war was over some of these Russians had gone berserk and there were very few families which had not suffered in some way. The British Tommy was hailed as a saviour and it was rather queer when one was returning to the school after an evening stroll to be greeted with a cheerful "Good night" by every German one passed. It was illuminating to note that at this time there were very few German frauleins abroad in the streets of the villages. Some weeks later when the Russians were removed the young German girls appeared from their period of hibernation.

When the Russians wanted to do any shooting there was never any question of safety rules and red flags so well beloved of the British Army which has the safety bug fastened on to it so tightly by an unknowledgeable and inconsistent public. (Even during the war this "safety" question reared its head on every conceivable occasion, and many commanding officers when their units were engaged on field firing exercises had ever-present visions of "bowler-hats" because someone might be killed, or frightened out of his wits, by a straying bullet—if the corpse or near-corpse should be a civilian it was a far more serious crime. Now we are "peaceful" again the position is much worse. A thousand people can be killed on the roads of Britain without more than passing comment, but if Mrs. Jones who lives close to a rifle range has one tile of her bungalow roof broken by a stray bullet, then all hell's a poppin'! To me this is nothing but cant, ignorance and hypocrisy.) The firers just lay down and loosed off at any target, preferably a heap of stones since they caused alarming ricochets and weird wailing noises. Seeing such shooting always reminded me of the story of the two Afridis who were arguing about the accuracy of their respective rifles. To settle the argument, and the wager, both fired at an old woman working in a nearby field. Although the result was disastrous to the old lady, the argument was not settled satisfactorily and the wager withdrawn.

The Russians kept a guard of sorts at the camp. These guards were armed with the Mousin rifle, and took great delight in using them whenever a chance presented itself. If, for example, they saw a bird settle in a tree, or a rabbit cross a path anywhere near them, up would go the rifle and the sharp crack was only rarely co-incident with the falling of the bird or the rolling over of the rabbit. Guard duty was always a good opportunity for some indiscriminate firing. When the guard thought that his tour of duty was over he merely placed his rifle on his shoulder and fired three or four rounds into the air; at least, they were mainly fired into the air, but the guard was not particular as to where the shots arrived eventually. A remark frequently heard in the area at that particular time was "it's a damned sight worse than being in the line." Once or twice I took the opportunity of looking at the rifles used by the guards; in nine cases out of ten I wouldn't have risked firing a single shot through their rifles. I never actually heard of a rifle barrel blowing, but I am convinced that it must have happened. Throughout service in Europe I saw innumerable cases of the mis-use and total lack of care of firearms, but the prize for the worst maintenance would have to be divided between the Russians in the school area and a certain party of Dutch Resistance "troops" with whom I hunted Germans one very wet morning.

When the school buildings guard was taken over by the Belgian forces stationed in a small nearby town we expected a little excitement—and got it. The guard room wall was soon suitably adorned by the futurist carving of rifle bullets, and one morning there was a spot of almost hysterical confusion, the whole guard dashing furiously about with the exception of the man who was the central figure of the commotion, and really the most concerned, since whilst seated in the guardroom playing with a German pistol he had shot himself in the leg!

Other urgent demands precluding the training of snipers I found myself working with the Lovat Scouts on general platoon weapon training. It was certainly good to be back at the school and I was very happy. In addition to practical work I lectured on such subjects as the History of the British Service rifle, Small Arms Ammunition and Comparison of British and Foreign Weapons, etc. The sniping side of the game was never lost sight of for a second by the enthusiastic instructors and leisure time was spent, when not hunting, in preparation for the future. I had many hunting trips and these were greatly enjoyed. The Lovat NCOs and myself went out in the early evening, and stalked and shot until nightfall, and then we would go back to a glade on the outskirts of the forest, build a huge fire, brew tea, have a sandwich and then smoke and yarn before the flames before curling up in a blanket and sleeping until an hour before dawn; tea again and then hunt until about 07.30 when we rejoined the truck and scooted back to the School arriving in time to have a wash and shave before the first parade. Not only were these outings recreative but they were instructive since it was a salient idea that actual hunting was one of the nearest approaches to sniping, and it was the intention to include a period of hunting in the syllabus of future sniper training.

I returned to my unit, very regretfully, some months later, and spent the last few weeks of my service in training sniper instructors for my Regiment at Schleswig and Sylt, the latter being a sniper trainer's paradise. Being given an entirely free-hand in the type of instruction to be carried out I put into practice a number of strongly and sincerely held theories on sniper training, a full description of which is given elsewhere.

*　　*　　*　　*

Combat men are often asked "What was the war really like? What does it feel like to shoot a man? Were you scared?" and so on. My experiences were by no means so hard and trying as thousands of others, but for what they are worth I can set down my reactions to war in N.W. Europe. Blitz experience in England helped a good deal since countless men before they experienced the torments of war in Europe, and elsewhere, had become only too conversant with sudden death and hideous injuries.

For many men "war" was just like an exercise, and when one actually came under fire of any description and men were hit and dropped alongside one experienced a queer sense of surprise as though the other side were not playing fair. And it was strange to think that the fellows on the other side whom you could see and hear—and sometimes smell, there's no doubt one could smell Germans at times (I had some previous experience having lived in a London boarding house with four Germans some years before the war)—would kill you if they had the opportunity. One was scared but more afraid of showing fear than frightened. I do not think the majority were terrified of death, but rather that they would not see their homes and loved ones again. And I think thousands, seeing their comrades maimed and killed, consoled themselves by thinking—wishfully—"that just can't happen to me."

The average American and Englishman is averse to killing and many, having been forced to kill, suffer from remorse. But it is a fact that a sniper will kill with less conscience-pricking than a man in close combat. Personal feelings of remorse or questioning of motives will slow down a man's critical killing instinct and the sniper who allows himself to fall into such a train of thought will not last long. It is imperative to look upon the killing of an enemy as swatting a fly, an unthinking, automatic action. Two things only should really interest the sniper—getting the job done and getting away unscathed. To become accustomed to "sniper killing" is not so difficult or hard as close quarter killing. A man dies more slowly than the average person thinks; he often grins foolishly when he's hit, the whites of his eyes roll upwards, death sweat gleams on his forehead and he sags to the ground with a retching gurgle in the throat—and it is difficult to hear that gurgle without emotion. The sniper is usually spared all this unless he's quick enough to get his binoculars on his victim, or the "sniped" is at such close range that the telescope sight will give him all the motion pictures he needs.

Sniping is not the vague, haphazard shooting of the unknown in a sort of detached combat. It is the personal individual killing of a man in cold blood, and is an art which must be studied, practised and perfected. I often heard it said that a sniper should be a man filled with a deadly hatred of the Hun, or enemy. But I found that the men who had seething hatred in their hearts for all things German, such as those who had lost their wives and children and homes in the blitzed cities, were not the type to make good rifle killers. The type I wanted was the man of cold precision, the peace-time hunter who had no hatred for his quarry but just a great interest in the stalk and the kill!

When one was in position for a shot there came an "inner freezing"; the breathing was not quite normal; the hearing sense was magnified and there came too that sense of excitement which all hunters know and which results in an unconscious nerve-hardening, and once the Hun was in the sight and the pointer steady at the killing spot there was no qualm of conscience about hitting him or taking life. The true hunter is never a butcher; he does not desire to kill for killing's sake, but there is something elemental in the stalk and the slaying which swamps every other feeling and makes the heart and brain exultant, and filled with action-elation.

It always seemed an unconsciously long time from the impersonal squeeze of the trigger to the shot going home and the Hun sagging slowly to the ground. Then followed two emotions. First, the heart leapt; and then one was very quiet inside.

There is much to be said for the Russian maxim that "One must not kill an animal unless it is necessary 'but to kill a man is different.' "

There are still many unenlightened people who think that sniping is "dirty," "horrible," "unfair." I maintain that it is the highest, cleanest game in war. It is personal and individualistic; a game of great skill and courage, of patience and of forbearance. And if one loses to a skilful opponent one should never be conscious of it. Death-night to the sniper's quarry should always be of a tropical, sudden intensity.

Compared with many my Odyssey was not hectic. But I had seen and experienced much. Nor was my return to England without incident. Between Hamburg and the Dutch frontier the train on which I travelled crashed into a stationary locomotive and there were many killed and injured. And as the ship left the harbour at Ostende at seven o'clock in the morning the BBC news was prefaced by a "Gale warning to shipping" in the Channel! But I enjoyed the trip standing on the top deck and being lashed with hard-driven spray. And my thoughts went back to that June day in 1944 when I left England on the Greatest of all Military Adventures—and I remembered those men of mine who will never return.

❊   ❊   ❊   ❊

The Story of a 29427

It was a No. 4 Mk.1. Rifle and it was first issued to Pte. X, a recruit of a famous Infantry Regiment. Pte. X was a small man and therefore A 29427 possessed a short butt of dark stained wood. It took some considerable time to instill into the dim consciousness of Pte. X that his rifle was his best friend, but eventually an enthusiastic platoon commander and an equally keen, and more forceful, sergeant made him realise that in his rifle he had something which might one day ensure that he returned to his home in the squalid street of a North of England town.

A 29427 unlike some of its contemporaries was an excellent weapon, and in the hands of a marksman it would have been capable of a very high performance. But Pte. X was not a good shot, although he tried and that is something. After a long time he mastered the intricate, to him, mathematics of the flip sight, and just before he took part in the Great European Adventure he was capable of an eight inch group with five shots at one hundred yards.

Pte. X was a D Day man and as the craft in which he sailed closed into the Normandy beaches it met trouble and so did Pte. X. And there he disappears from our account with our fervent hope that he survived. He certainly lost his rifle, and with its muzzle proudly sticking up out of the sand at low tide it was found by an officer in the early afternoon of D plus 1. The officer saw in this rifle something of an omen, and plugging it from the sand he passed it along to the Company armourer when he went back to his unit with instructions that all the sand and salt water be removed and then the rifle passed back to him.

During the next few weeks there were many sticky moments in the life of that officer but occasionally he found solace in the thorough cleaning of A 29427; a rifleman of pre-war vintage, he had with him all the cleaning kit so dear to the heart of the man who loves firearms. The first time he used the rifle was on an improvised 30 yards range and he was extremely pleased with it. It carried something more than the normal kick, but it was deadly accurate and there was a good "feel" about it. It saw a little successful action later, and was carried across the breadth of France, Belgium and then into the Holland salient in September 1944. There the officer managed to shoot frequently on an old German 100 metres range and he found that A 29427 was capable of putting five shots into a two inch circle. Being an enthusiast the officer sent home to England for a supply of T.S. Mk.1 Hun Head targets and at any odd moment he set up these targets and tried his skill. A red letter day in the history of this No. 4 rifle was when it dropped a Hun at a range in the neighbourhood of six hundred yards —a lucky shot maybe but one which could not have been possible to the officer with any other rifle. It accompanied the officer to sniping school, and over the Rhine in March 1945. After the war it accounted for deer when rations were meagre, and it was used a good deal for target practice. And then it returned to England along with a German hunting 'scope and when the long awaited composite rifle and telescope sight is finished the officer thinks that he will be possessed of a combination which might win for him a "real" sniper competition should such an event ever appear in the programme at the Mecca of English riflemen.

A 29427 of the highly polished bore has seen and experienced much, and the dark, gleaming butt bears several scars, relics of shrapnel splinters. It is a well-loved weapon.

B.L.A. SNIPING SCHOOL

1944 ... 1945

ALL SNIPING

Adventures of the Sniping Section of a Scottish Battalion
Stories from a Rifle Regiment • German Sniping
Russian Sniping . . . and the Great Myth • Sniping in
Italy • Japanese Sniping • Australian Snipers • Pro-
tective Clothing • History Repeats Itself • Ideal Sniper
Rifle • Sniping Shot vs. Bisley Tiger • Sniping
Opinions • Future of Sniping

ADVENTURES OF THE SNIPING SECTION OF A SCOTTISH BATTALION

ON PRACTICALLY all occasions when the Battalion
took over a section of the line the task allotted to the
sniper section was the domination of No Man's Land.
This shows that someone with a true appreciation of the
sniper's worth was in command. It was the sniper section's
job to despatch promptly any German who was unwise
enough to show his nose above ground during the hours of
daylight, and by constantly plugging away at every target

offered this particular snipers' section claimed, with every justification, that on several occasions they forced the enemy to live constantly underground, and to have consequently undermined the morale of the Hun to such an extent that the subsequent attack was rendered much easier than it would have been otherwise. In short the snipers were used as they ought to be used, and fulfilled their task to the utmost.

Shortly after D Day this Battalion had a section of the line east of the River Orne near the village of Ranville. The country was typical Normandy terrain, being covered with small orchards, bushes and hedgerows, and therefore by no means ideal sniping ground since it was very difficult to get a decent field of fire in excess of one hundred yards. The forward platoon of "X" Company, who were the left forward Company, were troubled every night just before dusk by a Spandau which was pushed forward to within a couple of hundred yards of the British line. Things were hot and uncomfortable for an hour or more, and then Jerry would retire circumspectly back to his own line.

After this unpopular performance had run for three consecutive nights the snipers were asked if they could do anything about it, and they certainly thought that they could. Three snipers, including a corporal in charge, set out on a selected line of approach and finally reached a position close to a cart-track. It was by no means an ideal position, being blind on one side owing to thick bushes, but in lieu of something better the snipers decided to stick it out and await developments. They had not long to wait. Suddenly, less than fifteen yards away, the bushes were parted silently and three Germans appeared, complete with Spandau. With speed and silence they set up the gun on the cart-track. Since it was impossible to see the British line from this position it was clearly evident that the gun was sent out as nuisance value only. The Huns were much too close for the snipers' liking, but the 36 grenade which each carried in his pocket felt very reassuring. (Two 36 grenades were laid down as part of a sniper's equipment at the BLA Sniping School, and this aroused some controversy since many students held the opinion that if a sniper went out on an operational tour equipped with all the things laid down by the school authorities he would be festooned like an "adjectival" Christmas tree! But in the particular instance now being quoted the grenades were certainly worth their weight in gold; these snipers had been told that in view of the type of country in which they were working grenades should be carried for emergency use, and they had very wisely carried out the suggestion.) The corporal, hardly daring to breathe, cautiously slid his hand into his pocket and his fingers closed eagerly over the 36. Still using extreme caution he withdrew the pin, and waited until all the three Huns were in a huddle crouched over the gun, and then coolly, and with excellent aim, he threw the grenade. The results were as good as the throw. Waiting long enough to make sure that all three of the Jerries were dead, the snipers grabbed identifications, very effectively dealt with the Spandau and then beat a hasty and cautious retreat. As this was their first kill, not perhaps in the orthodox manner but conclusive evidence of the soundness of their all-round training, they arrived back at our lines feeling very elated. There was no more trouble from "Spandau Pete," as the nuisance had become to be known in that particular sector.

Shortly before the attack on Caen this same Battalion held an area of the line locally known as the "Triangle." The enemy were in a strong position in a wooded area about three hundred yards distant from the British line. The Battalion snipers found some excellent positions out in No Man's Land, and by dint of careful fieldcraft they were able to reach these positions in daylight. The practise, in this area, was for a pair of snipers to man each position from first light until mid-day; at mid-day they were relieved by another team of two snipers who remained in position until dusk. It was arduous and tiring work, but definitely a sniper's real job and it was tackled in the finest spirit. On this particular sector the slightest movement in our lines invariably resulted in a fairly severe mortar "stonking" and since it was clearly evident that our positions could not be seen from the ground level, it was realised that the Hun must have an observer up aloft—in a tree. But patient and diligent observation by the snipers with telescope and binoculars failed to locate the observer for some time. One of the sniping posts was inside a wrecked German armoured car, and on the third day the mid-day relief had just been effected and the two snipers going off-duty were crawling back to our lines when a low whistle and whispered injunction halted them and caused them to re-crawl the ten yards or so they had covered back to the post. One of the relieving snipers bringing fresh eyes to the job had spotted the German observer; he was high in a tree, excellently camouflaged, but he had made the most elementary mistake of lighting a cigarette—no doubt it was a case of "familiar contempt." A whispered conversation between the four snipers followed as to the range to the German observer; they could not agree. Two of them said they estimated the range to be between 250 to 300 yards; the others said it was nearer 350 yards. The matter was settled in rather a novel manner. Three of the snipers set their sights at 250, 300 and 350 whilst the fourth sniper took the binoculars and kept them riveted on the prospective target. When quite satisfied that he was in the area of the observer he coolly gave the three men a fire order; the three rifles "spoke as one" and the Bosche came somersaulting to the ground.

When the Battalion relieved another unit near Best in Holland they were informed that the enemy in front was extremely active and had even penetrated our lines in broad daylight and burnt down a house in which some of our troops were resting. When the Battalion took over it was determined that such practices should cease forthwith, and the sniping section was allotted their customary task of completely dominating No Man's Land. It was expected that such domination would only be achieved after a stiff struggle but complete success was obtained fairly easily. Just after daybreak on the first morning an unarmed German was seen to sneak into an abandoned chicken-run. A careful watch was maintained and when he re-appeared carrying the eggs he hoped to have for breakfast he paid the full penalty—very quickly. A little later another Jerry who was acting as observer for mortars was spotted on the top of a roof and he too was speedily liquidated.

After three days in this area during which six certain kills were recorded, and the Huns were tamed to a great extent, they had very clearly decided that it was far healthier to remain underground during the hours of daylight, it was ordained that Jerry should receive a little of his own medicine, or, at least, the medicine which he had administered to the Battalion's predecessors. Two of the snipers penetrated the enemy lines before daylight and moved very carefully along the bottom of a deep, dry ditch. Occasionally coming up on top for cautious observation they moved forward slowly, and must have been at least half a mile inside the enemy's F.D.L.'s when they heard guttural voices very close at hand—too close for comfort. Freezing like hares they remained immobile for some time but since the voices neither receded nor came nearer they finally decided to have a look-see prior to turning round and beating it the way they had come. Carefully the snipers peered over the top of the ditch and were a little shaken when they saw pointing towards them, and only about ten yards away, the evil looking muzzle of a Spandau. Fortunately the owners, or lessees of the gun, were not manning the weapon, but lying talking—probably discussing the now problematical future of the Third Reich—

in a slit trench close by. The snipers had a good look around and seeing no evidence of further slit trenches, or habitation, they decided that if the fates were as kind as they should be to all snipers and scouts, they would very effectively deal with this post and get clear away. Moving very cautiously out of the ditch they crawled forward, gathered themselves up and simultaneously leaped, with fierce, but not loud, cries on top of the Germans in the slit trench. They had expected to find two men only, but there were three. The Huns were completely surprised and bewildered, and immediately deciding that discretion was the better part of valour they raised their hands well above their heads.

The snipers decided to waste no time in getting back to our lines with the prisoners, but before they could prod the Huns out of the trench a section of five Germans appeared about fifty yards away and approached at a quick run. Quick as lightning one of the snipers grabbed the Spandau, turned it in the direction of the oncoming Germans and opened fire. One long burst accounted for three of the enemy before the gun jammed. Throwing it over, the sniper seized his rifle, threw it to his shoulder and with his companion following the same action, took a bead on one of the remaining Germans, and fired. These two remaining Huns were only about twenty yards away by that time and were both firing from the hip; as both the snipers' rifles "spoke" the two Bosche toppled over and lay still. This small action had taken far less time than it takes to recount, and the three Jerries who had surrendered, although completely ignored by the snipers, just stood there nonplussed. Quite satisfied with the job the two snipers, plus the three prisoners and the Spandau, left the scene hurriedly and reached our lines safely. Naturally there was much elation over this episode, and there can be little doubt that the Hun must have wondered greatly at the miniature battle going on in his rear.

[74]

The Battalion were holding one bank of the Nederweet Canal in Holland with the Germans on the opposite bank. The distance between the combatants was only about twenty-five yards and it was possible for the snipers to hear the Germans speaking quite distinctly. There was a very high bank on each side of the canal and although the Battalion snipers waited patiently for hours on end Jerry was very careful, and remained in the safety of his own towering bank. But one afternoon the snipers' patience was amply rewarded, since for some reason or other the Germans decided to have a celebration, and proceeded to get really drunk. The first Hun to be accounted for had a bottle of wine to his lips and was in the act of taking a long draught. Perhaps that is as good a way to die as any! The shot caused a little consternation in Jerry's camp, but not much. The interpreter from the Battalion Intelligence section was alongside the sniper who had "bumped-off" the imbibing one, and he was delighted to translate the resultant conversation for the edification of the snipers. Immediately after the shot had been fired and the German with the bottle killed, a wine-thickened voice bellowed, "Who in the name of Venus fired that shot?" A reply in a similar voice was, "I don't know, but who's the silly —— who's been shot anyway?"

That afternoon drinking party was very costly for the Hun for before nightfall the snipers had killed five. It was really too easy. One wonders what the German platoon commander thought about it all next morning when he awakened with probably a damned bad head and found that his platoon had indeed been sadly depleted in strength.

Stories from a Rifle Regiment

This incident and the one which follows concern a sergeant who "won" a German sniping rifle (standard pattern rifle with large 'scope sight) in France. Although he knew nothing about the rifle, and was of questionable calibre as a rifleman, he was fascinated by it and would not part with it despite the greatest of pressures exerted upon him. He stuck to it like a leech!

The time of the incident was January 1945, and the company was sitting in a static position just east of the Maas and only a few hundred yards from the German border. The village, Neustadt, small and isolated, stood on the Sittard-Roermond railway about four miles north of Sittard. The village was being held as a company position, forward of the main line, with a troop of tanks and various odds and ends. The enemy were holding the line of a "beek" small drainage canal, in the angle of which the village stood, being flanked by it on the North and East at a distance of about 500 and 300 yards respectively.

It is the east side which concerns us in this story. One platoon was astride the railway to the north, but here there were woods between us and the enemy and these had been heavily mined both by Jerry and the former occupants of the British position. Any movement in this area was not only difficult but too dangerous for comfort. The whole place was a very eerie spot, with Jerry very much alive on two sides and nothing on the other two sides between the holders of the position and their nearest neighbours, two miles to the South-West. The platoon to which the intrigued sergeant belonged was on the western end of the village itself and had a more or less unimpeded view of the drainage canal's banks about 250–300 yards away. The enemy was known to be there because apart from considerable reciprocal activity the smoke of his brewfires was seen coming continually from behind the bank, and occasionally actual movement to and from the hamlet of Millen, about three hundred yards from the other side of the canal which he was occupying was visible.

Our policy here was one of strict "non-firing" in order to keep the Hun guessing and make him nervy, which certainly proved to be the case in the end. But the sight of a German gunner OP officer, easily recognisable at the range, calmly surveying our village through his binoculars proved too much for the sergeant one morning. He was observing from the loft of a house in his platoon area and saw this Hun officer sitting there in full view and smirk-suggestive in his arrogance; the sergeant became so incensed that ignoring all rules and regulations he took his German sniper rifle, which so far as anyone knew he had never zeroed or fired before, and very calmly shot the officer slap through the head! There was no counter battery so the assumption was that the desired result had been obtained!

This incident certainly made Jerry keep his head down in this area, too much so for the sniping enthusiasts on the British side of the canal, so resort was made to cunning. The gunners and mortar people put down a brisk "stonk" on the other side of the canal and then laid smoke along it carefully leaving a gap in the smoke opposite the platoon position in the hope that Jerry thinking something was on might be tempted to show himself in the gap and so give the snipers a chance to do their stuff. This stunt was tried on three separate occasions but the wily Hun never rose to the bait, or used periscopes to his smug satisfaction of being more astute than the cunning Englanders! In that area there was never another sniping chance.

The next story with the same sergeant as the central figure occurred during the operation immediately following the period of static warfare referred to in the previous anecdote, when the Division, along with others, was given the task of clearing the remaining enemy from the pocket between the rivers Maas and Roer south of where the two join at Roermond. An advance of about seven miles had been made from the line formerly held, when a hold-up occurred at a little straggling village called St. Joost, just east of the main Sittard-Roermond road up which the advance had been made, and which it was intended to leave at that point in order to move east towards the Roer River.

The village commanded a wide stretch of the very flat countryside and it was essential that it should be taken. It was, however, very strongly held by some of those extremely redoubtable gentlemen, German paratroops, supported by tanks and SP guns. One company, which was put in first, had an extremely rough time, and even with strong tank support and the additional help of several Crocodile flame-throwers only succeeded at length in gaining a foothold in a few houses, at the extreme south of the village. The German paratroops were some of the bravest men our fellows had ever seen, or heard of, for time and time again having been forced out of a position by the flame-throwers—not a pleasant business—they would come back before our men had established themselves.

Finally it was decided that one platoon of the company should be sent up to occupy the houses the others had won, leaving them to push on. The chosen platoon was the one now being commanded by the "German-sniper-rifle-fetish" sergeant. A visit by the company commander later in the day found the platoon in three of those typical Dutch houses with no hedges around them and completely open to view from ground-level up; the platoon was in great spirits but movement outside was distinctly tricky on anything but the home side. The sergeant was greatly excited because someone had been having cracks at his boys from another house about 400 yards away which was plainly visible, and he was convinced that he had singled out the window from which the shots were coming. Accordingly he produced his beloved Jerry rifle and settled down behind a chair in one of the windows to have a go at the first opportunity. Just as one of the officers was about to warn him that he might be silhouetted—as indeed he was—a shot came through the window, passed through the chair and missed the sergeant's head by a matter of a couple of inches. At that range it was a really good shot; a much shaken sergeant agreed. That shot marked the end of

[78]

direct sniping activity there, for the common-sense, as opposed to the sporting, way prevailed. A tank was called up, and the Jerry's house was very effectively sprayed by means of a couple of belts of Besa and the odd 75mm shell. Not sporting—not sniping—but effective, and War! There was no more trouble from that house. Maybe that German sniper if he were as good as we thought had vanished before the tank proffered its visiting cards.

Whilst the Canadian Army was engaged in clearing the Walcheren area and pushing up to the mouth of the Maas near the sea the Division, with others, was given the job of pushing across from s'Hertogenbosch, then on the western edge of the Arnhem corridor, to meet the Canadians as they came northwards. (This was in October 1944.) The limit of the unit's advance was the canal which runs north to the Maas and south to Antwerp and which lies immediately on the west of the town of Oosterhout, about thirty miles west of s'Hertogenbosch. They entered the town, after a slight unpleasantness outside, more or less unopposed one evening, and settled down quite happily for the night. The next morning they were cleaning themselves up and generally taking things easy when one of the Tank Regimental Squadron Leaders approached a platoon headquarters and asked the officer in charge if he could borrow a sniper rifle, or better still a sniper complete! The platoon commander said that he had no sniper rifle to loan, but the Squadron Leader could have a sniper plus rifle—"what about it?" The Tank Squadron Leader explained that some of his tank crews were performing for them the very unusual task of sitting beneath the thirty feet high banks of the canal just outside the town with one member of the crew out of the tank and poking his head over the bank "keeping watch." The tank men were quite enjoying this novel form of amusement but were worried because they had seen quite a lot of the enemy and not being able to bring their tank armament to bear because of the canal banks and not having anything more lethal in the shape of small arms than their revolvers and Stens they could not do anything about sending some of these Jerries "home." The platoon commander said that the other could by all means borrow his sniper provided he could go along as well and have a look at the lay of the land. Off they all went.

The sniper, the one and only in that platoon at the time, was a young lad just out from England, who had done a sniping course but to date had no opportunity of putting into practice that which had been "preached unto him"; and the platoon commander was anxious to give him as gentle a breaking-in as possible. When the party arrived at the canal bank at the most likely hunting spot they found a tank well tucked in beneath the bank with three members of its crew happily brewing up and the fourth perched on top of the bank in some bushes having the whale of a time looking for Huns. The platoon commander and the sniper had a good look around and found that Jerry, as was often his custom in these spots, had made small tunnels through the bank with fire positions quite well camouflaged on both ends of the tunnel. They decided to observe from one of these until they knew exactly how the land lay, and then do any necessary sniping.

They found that they could get excellent views of the other bank and the country about a hundred yards or so beyond though not, of course of the area immediately behind the other side of the bank which like our own tank position was well hidden. The platoon commander stayed with the sniper for about twenty minutes but saw nothing. He did not like the idea of going back to his headquarters, but since he had received orders to move his platoon to another section of the town by mid-day he left after warning the sniper not to fire from the present position, good though it was, but to find somewhere less likely to be known to the enemy who must, after all, have been occupying it twenty-four hours before. He also reminded him of moving periodically or when he'd had a shot, and so on, and fervently hoped that he would open his score and that it would not be a single!

The sniper returned to his platoon three hours later on the Tank Leader's Scout car his face alight with a grin which spread from ear to ear. He claimed one killed and one wounded. His story was:—shortly after the platoon commander had left him and he had established himself in the bank itself a Jerry bobbed his head up from a similar position to the one which he had just left, had a quick look round and then ducked down again. The sniper had watched and waited and within a few minutes the same thing happened again. Very wisely the sniper left the Hun unmolested in the hope that he would eventually gain confidence and present a rather less fleeting target. However after the performance had been repeated several times without any time variation he decided to have a go next time, and settled down with his eye to the 'scope. Up came the Hun's head again and the sniper fired. The Hun jerked up, fell forward against the parapet and then very slowly slid backwards out of sight. This was fairly convincing evidence of a kill in view of the target presented and hit—head and neck. Shortly afterwards the sniper had a shot at a German moving amongst some houses about 300 yards away, but although confident of a hit from the manner in which the Hun fell he could claim nothing more than a hit. At this juncture the sniper decided that it was time to move, and it was a fortunate decision, since Jerry started to mortar that area. The sniper reported that the light mortar "stonk" was very disconcerting, especially to the tank crew who were the nearest to the frightfulness. After this Jerry kept his head well down and although the sniper hung on for some time he did not get in another shot.

❋   ❋   ❋   ❋

This incident occurred in Holland in December 1944 when the particular unit concerned was static. They were occupying a village through which runs the Sittard-Roermond railway. The railway ran north into the German lines at this point and my colleague's platoon was astride the railway with Jerry's FDLs about 250 to 300 yards away, also astride the railway.

The British position was by no means a healthy spot in daylight since it was very exposed from "up the line" and the woods on either side were heavily mined. Therefore, in daytime, they normally pulled back leaving a couple of men with a field telephone to "observe and report."

One morning when my colleague was visiting the men on duty he was astonished to see a party of about a dozen Germans working on their line near a station some 300 yards or so inside their own FDLs and upwards of 600–700 yards from his own position. He could not really define what the Huns were doing but surmised that they were laying mines. It was certainly not a good target for the sniper rifle which the British trio had with them for various reasons—range, type of target, and a salient fact, their position was the only possible spot from which a shot could have been obtained and it was certainly not advisable to give that position away unnecessarily (thus was followed the wise maxim "Never fire from your own unit positions!").

The solution was simple. My friend got on the 'phone to the Gunners, explained that which was transpiring and where, and lo and behold, the first salvo, a battery one—from the "dear old R.H.A." which arrived in a matter of seconds landed slap bang in the right place!

❋ ❋ ❋ ❋

The Battalion was holding the line in front of a small Dutch village near Schyndel, and the sniping section had done some very useful work and the prowling element of the enemy was very subdued. Some four hundred yards in front of the line there was a house which had suffered severely from shell-fire as the gaping holes in the roof and walls testified. Very regularly a Hun observer was seen in this house but since he dodged very quickly from hole to hole he never gave the snipers a sporting chance. By virtue of his agility he became known to the section as "Bomb Happy" and each night his activities were a topic for discussion. Something had to be done about him, and it was decided that rather than risk a quick snap shot at that range with not a great chance of contacting use should be made of the haystack—the stack had an umbrella-shaped "roof" about two feet above the actual hay—which was situated about one hundred yards from "Bomb Happy's" house. As the ground between our line and the haystack was absolutely flat and totally devoid of cover a plan had to be devised to cover the retreat of the snipers should they be lucky enough to get a shot from the stack and then find themselves under Spandau fire from some unlocated German position. Having decided that the best method of covering such a retreat was by smoke, the section enlisted the aid of one of the forward sections of the rifle company and armed them with four two-inch mortars and a goodly supply of smoke bombs and a signal for their use!

On a really black night four of the snipers left the British line and crept stealthily towards the haystack, all attired in their excellent camouflage smocks, rubber shoes and cap comforters. The sniper leading the way carried a Sten gun at the ready just in case the selected post should have a German tenant; he was followed by the two snipers who were to do the job with "Bomb Happy," nursing their sniping rifles, and the rear was brought up by the fourth member of the party armed with a ladder! The haystack was reached silently and without incident, and to their relief it was unoccupied. As soon as the two snipers had cautiously climbed the ladder and had nestled down on top

[83]

of the hay the ladder was withdrawn and the "ground" members returned to our line. It had been left to the snipers' discretion when they would withdraw after giving the signal for the laying of the smoke.

It was hours after dawn before the first shot rang out from the stack, but the forward section looked in vain for the smoke signal. An hour passed and then there came again the ringing crack of a rifle shot, followed by the pre-arranged signal. As soon as the perfectly laid smoke screen was dense enough two triumphant snipers slid down from the haystack and scuttled back to our lines. "Bomb Happy" and his relief would never dodge again, and the snipers said that had it not been for the thought of sausages and bacon sizzling in the improvised frying pan for a late breakfast they would willingly have stopped in their very comfortable position all day.

During the same period, but on a different Company's front, or as the snipers called it "beat," the section had an observation post on the roof of a derelict barn. Day after day they saw a German observer who was using a high tree as his OP. This tree was some eight hundred yards away from the sniper post and the intervening country was barren and so devoid of cover that it was decided it was impossible to get anywhere near enough to make sure of a kill. This Hun was a very cocky individual, swinging up into the tree, having a good look round with his binocu-lars, and then swinging to earth again for a rest and a smoke. Naturally it was not long before he became known to the snipers as "Tarzan" and his monkey-tricks were looked upon with a mixture of amusement and chagrin.

Having decided that they really couldn't do very much about it the section leader asked the Forward Observation officer of the artillery who was with their Battalion Head-quarters if he could help to liquidate "Tarzan." The officer said that he would be delighted to try, and a field tele-phone was laid from the snipers' post back to the battery.

The artillery officer went up to the post next morning had a good look at "Tarzan" doing his acrobatics in the tree and then became very engrossed in his map, plotting the target. Finishing that task he rang up the battery, gave them "the dope" and ordered one round to be fired. And that one round scored a hit on the tree! When the snipers looked again there was no sign of "Tarzan." After witnessing such shooting the snipers were forced to admit, laconically "Not bad for the first attempt"; but really they were very impressed, and from that time onwards the artillery officer was treated with great respect. After all to snipe with a 25 pounder is great work! Later when the Battalion moved forward "Tarzan's" helmet, bearing a great shrapnel gash, was picked up. And in it was part of his head!

❈   ❈   ❈   ❈

That a knowledge of wild life was invaluable to the sniper is shown in the following:—a sniper was lying up on the fringe of a wood in the early dusk one evening. He was damned uncomfortable for a thousand and one insects were having a tribal dance about him, and occasionally sitting-out down his neck. From a shallow stretch of water about 250 yards away in front of him came the harsh chorus of bullfrogs. A man of some experience the sniper was calm, cool and alert despite the insects and the noise. Suddenly the frog song stopped. To the sniper that meant only one thing—there was movement near the water. He cautiously raised his binoculars, a type which were ideal for dusk work, and that which he saw caused him to lay down the glasses and quickly but unhurriedly take up his rifle. And so he waited until the crawling forms were delineated in the 'scope.

❈   ❈   ❈   ❈

In the early morning a sniper had seen two Huns creeping cautiously down a hedge about six hundred yards away. In view of the range and his own position which was not ideal for such a shot he waited patiently. From their line of advance he knew that he would lose sight of them about 450 yards away and that they might not re-appear for some time. There was a good deal of cover before him, and for a moment he was undecided whether to stay put or to move forward to meet them. He decided to remain but to keep an all round watch since on his left flank there was a small copse from which a narrow path ran parallel to him and then branched away immediately in front. About ten minutes later a small rabbit came very hastily down the path from the copse, and keeping to the path dashed off in front of the sniper. Suddenly the rabbit appeared to brake, paused and then jumped into the brushwood at the side of the track. Knowledgeable in his art the sniper under-stood—the Huns had separated, one of them was in the the copse and the other was creeping down the path. And so it proved. When the Germans met on the path a moment or so later the war, for them, came to an end.

❊　　❊　　❊　　❊

Long Range Sniping in World War II

In the closing stages of the Norwegian campaign there was some really effective long range sniping by the Nor-wegian mountain hunters, who were brilliant shots. When the Panzers overran their villages these men cleared out to the high vantage points overlooking the villages, and made the streets untenable by the Huns during the hours of the long Northern daylight. From, in some cases quite high up, the mountain side these white-robed and cowled snipers kept the villages under constant watch and many Nazis fell kicking with a bullet from out of the snow-blue. There was much of this kind of "passive resistance" on the part of the Norwegian riflemen.

❊　　❊　　❊　　❊

Comparatively speaking there is not a great deal to be said about German *sniping* and *snipers*. Stories of *real* sniper shooting by the Hun are rare when contrasted with the use of snipers by the British in the period 1944–1945.

There is abundant proof available that the German "snipers" were by no means so numerous as the various battle and newspaper reports would have had us believe. This "wholesale German sniper tale" was debunked many times and I can recall seeing a report which stated that in almost every bulletin received from Italy and the N.W. Europe theatre emphasis was laid on the activities of "German snipers" and the casualties they inflicted. But closer investigation revealed that these so-called snipers were, for the most part, not specialists at all but stout-hearted, well-trained riflemen who infested areas and shot with the ordinary German service rifle from concealed positions, often carefully built or constructed. Mention was also made of many snipers in trees and it was recorded that "the impression that they were not selected snipers was confirmed later when it was found that they were using ordinary rifles without telescopic sights." These riflemen "were brave men and prepared to fight to the last as individuals—they were responsible for many British casualties." Their effective range was anything up to 300 yards, and they had the most unpleasant trick of firing single shots intermittently into Headquarters; a habit which needless to say was termed annoying. There are times when under-statement is a salient feature of official jargon.

Another mis-statement which appeared from time to time was that the German snipers were using the Schmeisser machine-pistol! One report which dealt with this matter stated that a number of "snipers" so armed would place themselves three or four miles outside towns and villages along the roads leading to these communities. They would then cut in on the leading elements of the company or battalion in order to hold it back, and after running out of ammunition they would jump out into the road and give themselves up. In such actions the Germans were usually well-camouflaged, and frequently had their weapons camouflaged too, by painting or adornment with leaves. At best such actions could only result in delay, but they were of nuisance value. But they were certainly not *snipers'* actions!!

But, of course, the Hun had a number of real snipers and used them to the full; the testimony lies in many lonely graves.

Much was learned by our Commando troops in the raid on Dieppe. A costly lesson in one sector was that the Germans had expert riflemen at certain defensive posts. Whilst it was not disclosed whether or not these men were using telescopic sights, the fact remains that they were expert marksmen and inflicted many casualties on the attacking troops by skilful and selective fire. In referring to the Dieppe raid I am reminded of the story of the Canadian rifleman in Wallace Reyburn's "Rehearsal for Invasion"—"I talked to a half-caste Indian named Huppe. He's spent most of his life in the backwoods of Canada as a hunter and trapper and he's become an outstanding rifle-shot. Just before I arrived on the scene he'd picked off ten Germans in the space of half an hour or so."

I know of one occasion when a Scottish Battalion met some real German snipers, and, according to the Battalion sniping warrant officer it was the only time they came across *true German sniping shooting*. It was outside a small village, Francofonte in Sicily. The Battalion bumped rather suddenly into a German Parachute Regiment which was holding high ground, and their snipers made some really remarkable shooting at ranges of 600 yards. They stuck to their positions and kept up their brilliant shooting even when subjected to heavy shell-fire. They were, of course, well dug-in in previously prepared positions. When they were eventually driven out by the advancing troops, the majority of these snipers got away by the use of most excellent fieldcraft. It is the considered opinion of many sniping experts on our side that the average Jerry felt much more comfortable lying behind a Spandau than he did behind a rifle, and according to the authority who gave me the details of the above incident it was only on rare occasions that German snipers were used to do their proper job as snipers—in the full sense of that word.

That there were some Germans in N.W. Europe who merited the title of sniper is shown by the following stories. The first was told to me by one of the victims who, though seriously wounded, eventually recovered after some months in hospital. He certainly bore no malice, in fact, being something of a rifleman himself he was actually filled with admiration for the Hun who did his job, and shot, so well!

This fellow and his section commander were having quite a good time potting at a number of Huns who from time to time dashed across from some farm buildings to a barn, the range being about 400 yards. The two Britishers were behind a low hedge which they deemed gave them cover from view, and they were quite convinced that although the hedge was thin and sparse towards the base they were safe. The nearest farm house on the other side of the Albert Canal was some 350 yards distant and from their earlier observation was thought to be untenanted by Jerry. They continued their pleasing game of Hun-potting for some time, and had the satisfaction of seeing one or two fall and drag themselves along the ground to cover.

The recorder of the incident was standing, and his corporal kneeling. Suddenly there came a throat rattling cry from the corporal and his companion, looking down, saw that he had been hit, the bullet having entered the head just below the rear brim of his steel helmet. He knelt beside the NCO and was hastily fumbling for his field dressing when he felt a stunning blow at the back of his neck and head and knew nothing more until he recovered consciousness an hour later in an emergency dressing station. Later he learned that the corporal had been killed, and that the bullet which had laid he, himself, low caught him in precisely the same spot as that which hit the corporal but the angle at which his head must have been due to leaning over the NCO had resulted in the bullet ploughing up the back of his head, and emerging through his steel helmet. In the corporal's case the bullet had gone straight into the head and hit the brain.

The German sniper, who caused further casualties in that area, had certainly been some sharpshooter. The range was every inch of 350 yards, and his two shots in the space of very few seconds had been dead on the same spot; these two factors, coupled to the fact that the targets, even though the hedge was thin in texture at its base, must have been difficult to pick up, show that the Hun could call himself a sniper.

One of the last, and one of the best, sniping shots of the war in Europe was German too!

Round about the 26th April 1945 the 7th Armoured Division reached the line of the Hamburg-Bremen autobahn about ten miles south of Hamburg at the little village of Dibbersen. It was getting late in the day and orders were for the leading armoured Regiment to "firm base" the village and thus dominate the autobahn which here runs in a valley overlooked by the village and only about half a mile north of it. There was a clover-leaf crossing at this point where the old north-south Hamburg-Soltau road crosses the autobahn and though the bridge itself had been blown the approach roads and remainder of this crossing were intact. In view of this it was decided that there should be something pushed down as close as possible to the autobahn itself, not only to give warning of any impending counter-attack but to prevent any enemy moving up or down under cover of darkness. Therefore a troop of tanks, and a motor-platoon under the command of a very great friend of mine, were sent down to the old main road and almost to the blown bridge to the point where the auto-bahn approach road joined it and from where a good view of the autobahn itself, only 200 yards away, could be ob-tained. The position was taken up at last light and "M's" men dug-in around the tanks as usual, having left their own half-tracks some fifty yards nearer the village under cover of the cutting into which the road ran between the village and this point. As soon as it was quite dark a party went down on to the autobahn itself and laid a couple of strings of anti-tank mines across the two approach roads so that any vehicle trying to get on to, or off, the autobahn on either side, as they would be forced to in order to circum-vent the bridge which was now lying across the main tracks, would have something to think about! After this the men settled down for the night. No one expected much trouble since the Hun had been running hard all day, and it was considered unlikely that he would make any serious stand before the southern outskirts of Hamburg itself were reached. There had been quite a lot of accurate fire on the village from an 88 about a mile north of the autobahn dur-ing the evening and this continued spasmodically although it was comparatively nothing to worry about, and apart from this the night was quiet. There was one other inci-dent and that was the arrival, heralded from afar, of one hilariously drunk PW who wandered happily up to the position about midnight. He was only a boy and in his naturally talkative state quickly provided enough informa-tion to get our own guns on to the aforementioned 88 with sufficient accuracy as to effectively discourage it for the rest of the night.

In the early morning a thick mist swirled up and at dawn it was impossible to see the autobahn from the position. However a party went down and removed the mines without any trouble and by about 6 A.M. the visibility was sufficiently good for "M" to carry out the normal procedure of pulling his men back into the village from what was then a rather exposed position, and leaving the tanks quite happy to look after themselves. "M" told the sergeant to take the men back in the half-tracks to the village and set about the pleasing task of preparing breakfast, and expressed his intention of having a walk up the road, and then following the men on foot in a few minutes. "M" stayed talking to the tank troop-leader for some time; the tank officer was sitting in the turret of his tank with just his head visible, and "M" sat beside him on the turret, seeing what they could in the improving visibility.

About ten minutes passed and then "M" left; when he had covered about three hundred yards he met the tank squadron leader coming down the road from the village in his Scout car. He stopped and told "M" that he had just had a radio message to say that the troop leader had been badly wounded. Astonished "M" went back to the tanks and found that the troop leader had been hit full in the face with a rifle bullet. The bullet glancing off the cheek-bone had gone down through the lower jaw and out at the side of the neck inflicting a terrible wound. The officer was made as comfortable as possible, morphine administered and after the MO had quickly made his appearance the troop leader was removed. Although it was a touch and go business he eventually recovered.

There was only one shot and it was a clear-cut case of selectivity of target—the most important man. "M" thanked his lucky stars that he had not stayed for a couple of minutes longer asprawl the tank for he had presented a much bigger target than the troop leader. Everything was done to locate the sniper without success. Unfortunately a widespread search was not allowed since the tanks of another Regiment were due to pass through to continue the advance. As some form of consolation the troops were allowed to "brass-up" the suspected area with everything they had; even if the sniper were still there, which was extremely doubtful, he certainly would not have stayed long after the start of the "stonk." Taken all round this was a very fine shot—one of the best I heard of throughout the campaign. The visibility was poor, the target was small and "M" is quite certain that the sniper could not have been closer than 300 yards. As he said to me "To put it in training terms it was the equivalent of scoring a "central" on a Hun Head target at 300 yards or more in very poor light and with the first shot from a—presumably—unwarmed rifle. Damned good! I would have liked to have met that sniper, for more reasons than one!"

Later the same day "M" was himself sniped at from the hills surrounding the village. He was riding a bicycle at the time and since the sniper's "aiming off" was slightly at fault he was not touched. But he certainly did not give the sniper any chance of correcting that "lead" and pedalled furiously for home!

Another sniping incident, again on the British receiving side, occurred in Normandy a day or two after we landed, and is worth recording. Two of our officers had taken motor-cycles and visited part of our unit which was some distance away. They were returning to HQ along a typical, narrow Normandy dirt road; it was almost dusk and anyone would have said that anything in the nature of long shooting was impossible. They were riding in single file, some twenty yards separating them. As they approached a narrow cross-roads there was about thirty yards of the road which was open, the high hedge bordering each side of the road upon which they were travelling terminating very abruptly. As the leading officer slowed for the cross-road a bullet hissed nastily in front of his chin; he accelerated immediately and shot across the junction without any thought of what traffic might have been on the other road. The second officer, also slowing, heard and felt the path of the bullet which scraped his neck. He accelerated quickly too! They came into HQ in a serious frame of mind. I went out to the spot myself at first light and found that the nearest possible point from which the shots could have been fired was about 250 yards distant from the cross-roads. Those two shots at that range in bad light at moving targets could have been fired only by a man who knew his job. At that time there were still a number of German riflemen hanging around inside the British line, which was of course never very deeply penetrative of the bridgehead. That there was a miss forward and rearward signifies that the rifleman had nearly corrected the amount of aim-off. Had the first officer not decreased speed sharply he would certainly have brought up with that first bullet.

The German snipers missed a glorious opportunity of executing great damage on the many airfields which sprang up like mushrooms throughout N.W. Europe. In many cases these airfields were bordered by thick wooded country and it was always a source of amazement to me that Jerry did not leave behind a number of snipers in these areas to harass the construction groups and later take toll of the airfield personnel who came in to take over. I am sure that a good resolute sniper, well versed in his craft, would have added many scalps to his totem without running too serious a risk himself in these areas. Later in the campaign this lack of embracing absolutely wonderful sniping opportunities suggested that the Huns were short of first-class riflemen. The occasional well-aimed shot tearing its lethal way over an airfield to be, or a completed airfield, would in many cases have been regarded by us as just a stray shot fired by one of our own troops. When we overran German airfields the opportunity presented was even more golden since here again many were bordered by woods in which a German sniper might have escaped detection for a very long time. And using a British rifle and ammunition he would have been even more free from detection since had his victims been examined closely and the bullets recovered the fact that English ammunition had been used would have been sufficient to establish the apparent fact that it was an "accident."

Yes—undoubtedly a man of courage and initiative, skilled in woodcraft and camouflage, movement and stalking, equipped with a good rifle and TS, a master shot and brimful of confidence in his ability would have taken a heavy toll of important personnel. He would recognise that the war was virtually over but *he* could *enjoy* himself! Taking into consideration the fanatical zeal which pervaded the ranks of many German units I should have thought that action such as that outlined above would have appealed to many Huns. I am confident that had the circumstances been reversed and the Americans and British been in the German position, such wholesale sniping and execution would have taken place. In connection with these wood-bordered airfields it is noteworthy that men who were sniper-conscious—not a bad thing provided it was not carried to excess—certainly treated the situation with more circumspection than those who knew nothing of the game.

✼   ✼   ✼   ✼

RUSSIAN SNIPING . . . AND THE GREAT MYTH!

Many fantastic stories have come out of the Slav mists which envelop the U.S.S.R. but none more grotesque than the extraordinary fables of Russian snipers and sniping.

I do not think there was any subject about which there was so much balderdash printed and published during the whole course of World War II than Russian sniping. If we are to believe every report we read about the terrific casualties inflicted on the Germans by the Russian *snipers* it was amazing that there were so many Germans left to face the Americans and British in N.W. Europe! I do not think I am guilty of any exaggeration when I write that hardly a week passed in the British press that one did not read of " '——

sky' the Russian sniper has accounted for so many hundreds of Germans"! It became so bad, indeed, that if mention was made of sniping to the ordinary man-in-the-street he thought that one was using a Russian word. Figures of over 100 Germans per Russian sniper were common. "One bullet per man" was a widespread slogan and somewhere I read that one Russian had killed 127 Germans in 128 shots, another 187 Germans in 189 shots and so on. (Both these performances are, however, poor shooting when compared with the individual cited in "The Red Army" a book published by Messrs. Hutchinson who accounted for 304 Huns for the expenditure of 304 rounds!)

After the War I questioned many Germans who had fought on the Russian front and asked them about sniping. I was told that there was actually little sniping on the Eastern Front as the Americans and British—and Germans —know it. These Germans had no axe to grind at all; they were not currying favour, nor seeking to decry the Russians. Their answers were spontaneous and carried the ring of truth.

In the English press there were published, from time to time, photographs of Russian snipers with their weapons, and I seem to remember reading that weapon butts were heavily scarred by notch-tallies of their victims. If we are to believe some of the scores there could not have been much butt remaining! I have one of these photographs before me. It is a very poor reproduction, but seems to portray a Russian "sniper" peering without caution through some bushes, clad in steel helmet, and accompanied by a TS carbine and a fixed bayonet. The photographed one is detailed as having killed 181 Germans to date—summer, 1942!

One V. Galichenko claimed that by the beginning of February 1942 he had personally accounted for 153 Nazis, and that two of his trainees had killed 100 and 81 Germans respectively. He stated that in his unit there were 250 snipers and "I consider that every Red Army man can, and should, become a sniper." I know that rifle shooting was very popular in Russia before the war, but when one comes across such startling figures and statements one just wonders why the Russians ever bothered to use machine guns and the like. The statement that every man could become a *sniper* is ridiculous. Any sniper instructor knows that not one average man in a hundred will make a sniper. It is not merely a question of shooting.

I have met some Russians who had been Red Army men, and saw them shoot in the summer of 1945. If their shooting prowess be taken as a criterion I think that the printed Russian figures of sniper casualties should be divided by a hundred and the result taken as being something like the number of Germans accounted for by Russian *snipers*.

There is no doubt that many Russian reports of sniper activity covered sub-machine gun actions—close quarter work. All riflemen will wholeheartedly agree that sniping is not lead-spewing!

The *real* sharpshooters of the Russian Army were much respected. But these were not the tommy-gun artisans so beloved of the war correspondents and the Russian information bureaus, but hunters from the Urals and Siberia, the prototypes of the Australian kangaroo hunters and the Scottish deer stalkers, capable of killing at ranges up to 800 yards. Specialists without doubt and not of the "cone-of-fire" fraternity. No doubt one thing which forced the importance of real sniping into the Russian mind was the rather uncomfortable experience suffered at the hands of the Finnish snipers who were equipped with excellent rifles and telescopic sights during the brief Russo-Finnish war. Many of these Finnish snipers were eider duck hunters and as such were accustomed to shooting their quarry at short and long ranges in such a manner as not to spoil the plumage. An acquaintance of mine who travelled a lot in Finland some years ago spoke with great enthusiasm about the uncanny marksmanship of these hunters, and undoubtedly they took very heavy toll of the Russians when they put their skill to the sternest of tests—War. In addition to being wonderful shots they were adept, by virtue of their calling, in field-craft and camouflage. The combination resulted in many severe headaches, from which there was no aspirin relief, amongst the Russians.

In keeping with the cloak which appears to shroud all things Russian it was difficult to discover anything officially tangible about Russian sniping, snipers and sniper training. The wholesale butchery which hit the headlines so much during the war was quite legitimately treated as a farcical myth by anyone who had a real conception of the snipers' art. From the meagre information I was able to secure it would appear that the general plan for the use of "snipers" was something as follows:—

In defence snipers would operate on well studied terrain from previously prepared positions. In an offensive role, in the initial stages of a battle the sniper's place was with the combat troops on the start line, or in front. If it were decided that the snipers should be in front they were sent up accompanied by sappers, the latter accounting for any obstacles in the path, and reached a position where they could lie up as close to the enemy as possible. Once having reached such a position and made it tenable, the sapper returned and the sniper stayed. Just before the infantry moved off the artillery would lay down a barrage on the hostile defence, and then started the sniper's rush hour. It was thought, and it is a good point, that the sniper's fire would be unnoticed in the general din and confusion. Snipers could remain in such positions for some time, and there is no doubt that once the barrage stopped they might get quite a number of targets since that is the time when the enemy become very active and liable to give their positions away by undue movement as they prepare for the attack which they know to be inevitable after a barrage. It was laid down that the sniper, by firing at embrasures, would deprive the enemy of any possibility of observing and conducting fire. Runners were special targets, and so also were artillery observers. The Russian sniper was made aware of the German's habit of digging himself deeply into the ground once he had taken over a position and using special observation apparatus such as periscopes, and the Russian was told that such apparatus was a priority target and that accurate fire must be brought upon it. After the initial break-through snipers were to be located behind the attacking infantrymen, preferably to a flank, so that they could adequately deal with any machine gun fire, etc., which may have been by-passed or unnoticed by the advancing troops.

The Russian snipers were frequently equipped with special protective metal shields. "Covered by such a shield the sniper could calmly observe the field of battle and pick out and destroy important targets, or indicate with tracer bullets targets for tanks and artillery." Ability to observe keenly, quick finding and evaluation of targets were points which were stressed as being of great importance to the combat work of snipers. It was emphasised that when the target was out of the reach of the sniper he could indicate it to artillery by the use of tracer bullets, ensuring that he moved himself quickly to another position immediately after using tracer so as not to be discovered. During the retirement of the enemy the sniper was supposed to move forward and, together with groups of tommy gunners, infiltrate farther to the routes of the possible or probable retreat of the enemy so that from ambush he could kill officers, crews of fire elements covering the retreat, drivers of prime movers, motor vehicles and tractors—and horses.

Summing up from the information one is able to obtain about Russian sniping and sniper training it would appear that it is not sniping as we know it, but suggests rather close quarter fighting and maybe sharpshooting in its lowest form. When mention is made of targets being out of range of the sniper, and he indicating such targets to the artillery by use of tracer, one thinks of artillery firing over open sights at short ranges at mass targets, with a battle-field reminiscent of Waterloo. Again, *accurate* indication of a target, *out of the reach of a sniper*, using small arms tracer is, I suggest, a most difficult task!

It has been impossible to gain information as to the equipment of the Russian sniper—whether or not he used telescopes and other aids to the job which were part of the tout ensemble of the British sniper.

When in Denmark I saw and handled a Russian sniping rifle owned by one of the Danish Resistance Movement. The rifle was a Moisin—M 1891/1930—fitted with a large tele-scope sight, mounted on the receiver. There were no iron sights. The 'scope mounting and the TS itself followed the standard Russian pattern; on the mount were the elevation and deflection adjustments whilst the power of the 'scope (although not detailed on the sight a brief examination showed that the power was about x 4) apparently made eyepiece adjustments for range necessary.

In every way the rifle was smaller than the Moisin M 1891 with which I later became familiar, and could be compared with the trim sporting rifles the Germans used occasionally in World War II (and a good deal in World War I) for sniping. Barrel length was about 26 inches; the small of the butt had been finely reduced—a really work-manlike job—and the furniture throughout had been modi-fied and was certainly good to look upon. The weight of the complete rifle was a shade over eight pounds, and alto-gether it appeared to be something in the nature of an ap-proach to the ideal sniper rifle. The cartridge used was the standard 7.62mm—rimmed; pointed bullet.

On questioning the Dane who had the rifle he told me that it had been taken from one of the German occupational troops who had served on the Russian front and who had been very loathe to part with it. The method of transfer was not discussed! I should imagine that that German was of the true rifleman breed and was responsible for the modifications on the weapon for it showed signs of recent work. The Dane had fired it and found it to be exceptionally accurate; in fact it was so good that he would not sell it to me for the countless cigarettes I offered—and at the price which cigarettes were selling at that time in Denmark he would have had no further interest in work!! When I saw the evidenced neglect in the form of rust in the bore—the Dane had not bothered to clean the rifle after firing—I was doubly anxious to do a deal, but the owner was obdurate. I was permitted, however, to handle the rifle and fire it. It handled beautifully, and was dead-on. My efforts to purchase were renewed, but there was nothing doing!

Some time later I shot with a number of the old M 1891 Moisins and found them damned heavy and clumsy, but one or two of them were accurate, at short ranges particularly. The one I used most was about four feet long and the forestock ran almost to the muzzle; a long cleaning rod was sunk (and stuck) into the forestock. The barrel length was 32 inches (I don't think it had been cleaned for years until I took it over) and the sights were barleycorn front and V rear, the rear sight being adjustable from 400–2700 *paces*, evidence of the age of the rifle. I give the dimensions of this particular rifle, since it followed the standard pattern very closely; the majority of these old Moisins were each and everyone dissimilar, due to a variety of causes, the apparent experimenting of amateur and clumsy gunsmiths, fair and unfair wear and tear, and just disintegration due to senile decay.

Just before the end of hostilities one of my men took a small carbine from a displaced Rooskie who was running amok and causing a good deal of trouble. This carbine was slightly smaller than the Winchester, and fired a 6.5mm cartridge. The ammunition "borrowed" at the same time as the carbine was rather bloody looking—lead-pointed, and there were also one or two hollow-nosed cartridges. I did not get much opportunity to carefully examine this weapon since we were rather busy at the time, but I couldn't resist the opportunity of having a crack with it and through the medium of a spam tin target found that it seemed to be fairly accurate up to 150 yards. It certainly was good to use. After firing I handed it back to its owner and told him that I would like to use it later. But during the next hurried trek to pastures new the carbine was lost, to my great regret.

The Russian Simonov automatic rifle was first produced in 1936 but the later war version was brought into being in 1940 and known as the "Tokarev." The barrel was 24½" long, the cartridge used being the standard 7.62mm and the action was gas-operated after the manner of the Garand. Many hundreds of these rifles were fitted with telescopic sights, and their wide use in this form does not indicate that an unusual standard of accuracy for a weapon of this type had been obtained; it merely confirms the repeated opinion that the Russian idea of sniping and sniping ranges (except for the true Russian sniper, the hunter from the Urals, I have mentioned previously) was not consistent with the American and British conception. And it is difficult to conceive why a telescope sight should be thought necessary for the short ranges at which the Russian automatic rifleman did his so-called sniping.

The Germans were to a great extent fully equipped for a campaign in any part of the world, but they had hoped to beat the Russians before the nigh-Arctic winter set in and were therefore caught a little on the hop in the winter of 1941/2. But in many things they were quick to learn from the Russians, and kept their weapons lubricated with oil of a specially thin Arctic type, and small arms which gummed up were first wiped entirely dry, then lubricated with kerosene and fired prior to normal lubrication. In one respect they were far-seeing; during the winter they used red tracer

BRITISH SNIPER EQUIPMENT

Showing telescope, binoculars, compass, watch, head and face camouflage veil, camouflage (Denison) smock and the No. 4 telescopic sighted Sniper rifle.

BRITISH SNIPER

Note pockets in smock, telescope slung across back and use of veil. Rifle sling kept slack. Smock fastened at bottom by strap which passes under crotch, preventing smock from riding up at back.

cartridges for ground to ground work and these were very effective against a snow background; the Russians at that time had only white tracer for any weapons other than ack ack.

SNIPING IN ITALY

Although snipers were used fairly extensively in the campaign in Italy the organisation of the sniping section varied considerably in different Battalions. In some units the sniping section was placed in the Support Company and received its orders from the Battalion commander via the Support Company commander. Frequently a sergeant was in command of the sniping section, and he was responsible for the detailing of the snipers to their various tasks and he supervised the whole running of the section both in and out of battle; he usually had the assistance of two junior NCOs. (It was the general idea in both World Wars that the Battalion Intelligence officer should run the sniping section, but in the majority of cases this did not work out in practice. Many sniping authorities strongly held the opinion that the sniping section should have come under the strict supervision of an officer, and there is no doubt that a sniping officer, knowledgeable, keen and enthusiastic, in direct command of the sniping section could have increased one hundredfold the effectiveness and use of snipers throughout the British Army.) The men operated in pairs, and the choice of their mates was left to them; in this way the right men got together. There could be nothing worse than a sniper team which consisted of a pair of men who were mutually antagonistic and hated each other's guts.

In Italy where one unit laid down the qualities for a sniper as:—*Courage;* a good shot; reasonable intelligence; an independent spirit and outlook; patience and a good knowledge of fieldcraft, camouflage and movement: good snipers were by no means easy to find. When men with the fundamental qualifications were found they were given some training, and a specimen syllabus of such unit sniper training was something like this:—

Shooting. Constant practices at targets made as interesting as possible up to ranges of 400 yards. Each man was, as near as possible, given a rifle which "fitted" him.

Fieldcraft. Mainly individual stalks, one sniper against another. In this way full realisation that his life depended on his proficiency dawned on every man.

Camouflage. Whilst some instruction was given, and camouflaged denim suits issued, the camouflage of weapon and person was left to the individual; by this it was held that a man would be instilled with a self confidence which would not be gained if a certain type and design of dress was forced upon him. (In Italy it was of course much warmer than in N.W. Europe where snipers were happy to wear their Denison smocks in both winter and summer.)

Occasionally the snipers went out on a tour looking like shabby old poachers, carrying only their sniper rifles and no equipment. One report stated that "they used their eyes rather than telescopes." This "observation" may have passed muster in certain types of terrain, but it must always be remembered that the sniper team should be the "eyes" of the Battalion and higher formations, and there is a terrific amount which the telescope will pick up, define and determine which no naked eye could possibly see. One of the leading British sniping authorities, Major Wills of the Lovat Scouts, has said that nothing impressed him more during his experiences in N.W. Europe and in an Italian tour than the terrific advantage which the telescope afforded to the British sniper, an instrument which the enemy did not use, or did not possess.

Some instruction was given in the selection of fire positions, and emphasis laid on the fact that the atmosphere in the early morning tended to make muzzle smoke hang about and that muzzle blast tends to result in dust flying, or disturbance. (It is interesting to recall that during the course at Sylt a demonstration of sand disturbance by muzzle blast was staged, and after three rounds had been fired it was possible to pick up the contour like swirls of sand in front of the muzzle with the telescope at appreciable distances.) Emphasis was also laid on "the Jay walker dies" and the example quoted of the sergeant who was killed when he did not remove the pipeclay from his chevrons immediately he got into the line.

The general maxim to the sniper was that he should attain the standard of the highly skilled and cunning poacher.

In operation role the snipers were sent out to the various Companies before dawn and came back at dusk; they did not usually stay with their duty company but were pulled back so that they were ensured as good a night's sleep as possible. Frequently the Company to which the snipers were sent provided a section to give them covering fire when they went into No Man's Land in order to ensure that they were not surprised. The same snipers were invariably sent to the same company since it was apparent that each got used to the ways of the other, and, in addition, the system fostered a competitive spirit which was all to the good of the game. The snipers' task was invariably the same—to dominate No Man's Land and the enemy's forward defended localities when possible by killing Huns and making sure that the enemy's movements were restricted as much as possible.

The following are three short instances of such snipers' activities:—One unit had advanced to the Senio River and was holding a sector in which improvement of positions was made during the hours of darkness. The forward platoon of the unit was in and around a cluster of smallish houses about 200 yards from the bank of the river. From the roof of one of these houses there was a good clear view of the top of the bank held by the Hun. Snipers watching this bank observed that the Germans changed their sentries every even hour with monotonous regularity. At first the

Hun was cautious and our snipers withstood the temptation to shoot hoping that targets would become more favourable when the Jerries had lost some of their caution. Later in the day the hoped-for happened, and at 1200 hours six of the enemy could be seen from the waist upwards. There were four of our snipers on duty and having their set plan of execution ready they each selected a Hun and fired. Three out of the four Huns aimed at fell, and shortly afterwards their bodies were carefully dragged from the top of the bank by their comrades concealed below. At the 1400 hours relief the sentries were again very cautious and the snipers did not get in a single shot. But at 1600 hours two more Huns were sent to their particular Valhalla. It was a long and tedious day for the snipers with only two "volleys." But it was a good day's work, five Germans having been accounted for without loss to our men.

A unit was in position on the Lamone River. A patrol had crossed the river on the previous night and having run into a German position a short, sharp fight had occurred. The patrol got back with but one man missing. In the morning at first light the missing man was seen lying wounded on the German side of the river. As he could not swim it appeared as though he would have to be left there all day, but a very bright scheme was born, and executed. All the Battalion sniper section was ordered to cover and dominate about 200 yards of the river immediately opposite to where the wounded man lay, and then followed a most intense sniping match which lasted for six hours and resulted in the Germans being unable to show their heads even for a split second without running the risk of an immediate, and maybe, painless, death. At 1500 hours a two-man patrol crossed the river in a boat, collected the wounded man and brought him back to our side and to safety, and it speaks volumes for the efficiency of the "mass sniper scheme" when one can record that not a single shot was fired at the rescuers on the outward or the return journey.

Our snipers claimed five Germans killed without loss to themselves. Three days later when the Battalion crossed the river four named and dated graves were found close to the river bank, and the date in all cases was that of the day of this small yet vitally interesting action.

The Lamone River figures in another sniping incident. The British and the Bosche each had control of their respective banks. There was a considerable amount of rifle shooting backwards and forwards across the river, some of it sniping and some not! Our snipers kept a very careful watch and one day enjoyed themselves hugely for a few seconds. On this day the Bosche playfully placed some steel helmets on sticks and proceeded to walk along the river bank sticking up the steel helmets so that they were just in view over the top of the bank, and apparently with the German's characteristic guttural chuckle awaited for our snipers to waste ammunition and give away their positions by firing at the steel helmets. But the Huns concerned lacked foresight, and forgot that there might be snipers at the bends—and there were!—and that he might be enfiladed. For a good percentage of the mischievous Huns it was a last prank. The hard lesson was taken to heart and the Germans did not again play that particular little game.

The following is an account which I received from a well-known officer sniping instructor, and a brilliant rifle-shot, who went out to Italy to put sniping really on the map. "I went off for a week with a couple of Scouts, snipers, to the American Battalion from whom we were to take over the line shortly afterwards on Mt. Grande, approximately 18 miles from Bologna. The line had been static for some weeks and it appeared as though the Americans had ceased to take any interest in the war at all! They nearly had a fit when I told them, with becoming modesty, that we had come hoping to snipe a few Huns and thus do a little to speed up the end of the war. Their attitude was amusing and is reflected in their comment 'Say you can't do that; if you shoot at them they'll shoot back at you!' We did not take much notice of this remark and went off to do our damnedest. One morning in the grey dawn we went off to one of their forward slit trenches with a guide who having shown us into the position beat a hasty retreat and left us alone in the middle of No Man's Land! And the relief never came! I learned a couple of tips in sniping soon afterwards—this slit trench which was intended for sniping work was (a) littered with 'C' ration tins thrown all round the front of it and (b) it was dug under the boughs of a tree. (a) Caused immediate 'stonking' when we arrived and (b) caused exceeding unpleasantness as any shell that might have hit the branches would have air burst right on to us. The American I had with me had a wireless with him netted to their 4.2 mortars, so we decided to have some fun and duly laid them on to a target. To cut a long story short they couldn't get within 800 yards of it, and I nearly passed out with laughter at the whole business! There was certainly no sniping from that post!

"Another day in the same sector I picked up with my telescope a whole bunch of Huns about 700 yards away on a mountain side who were digging like mad. The Americans had no telescopes and were not really bothering to use their field glasses—such is the ennui of war. And they certainly had no intention of doing anything about those Huns. Anyhow we decided to have a crack at them, much to our American comrades' amusement and amazement. We fired from a position in a house and hit at least two of the Jerries in the day. As usual Jerry produced the Red Cross flag to go out and collect the bodies, or the wounded men. We missed a couple too, but the expression of utter surprise on their faces as I saw it through my telescope at being sniped at by a single bullet from over 700 yards away was something I shall always remember. One was an Italian officer which gave us a clue about a change on the enemy's front—next day the Italians took over that part of the line. I came to the conclusions that where one could get no nearer than 700 yards across an open valley it was worth while sniping with a chance of securing an occasional hit; the telescope was invaluable where the field glasses were useless; Jerry did not like being sniped at (his reply of 30 mortar bombs round our house was quite ineffective, and expensive); we had got the moral benefit over him—his attitude after this bout of long range sniping was not half so cocksure and brazen as formerly. I must say that the Yanks were amazed at that which seemed to me to be just plain common-sense, and they regarded us as the heroes of the day!

"Jerry was very keen to find out exactly where we were; we knew that he could not see us. One day he put up a dummy target over his trench to draw our fire whilst he watched through a periscope situated nearby. Both the dummy and the periscope I picked up through my telescope, and so I am quite sure that he was most disappointed at the failure of his ruse. Next day we expected the obvious—that he would try a little bout of counter sniping. So at dawn we watched the only piece of cover he could get to during the hours of darkness where he could snipe back at us under 300 yards range. Like a good little German he had done the obvious and he was there all right. One burst from a Bren which had been lined up in readiness for him finished him off before he had time to become a nuisance.

"The moral to my visit to this sector was this:—sit back and nothing happens, but there are heaps of opportunities for sniping if one goes out of one's way—and one need not go far—to find chances and spend one's whole time to that effect looking for opportunities. To do so sends up one's morale by 100%, and not only the personal morale but the spirits of the whole unit in the sector.

"With the Lovat Scouts I saw little sniping; the lines were too far apart and there wasn't a stitch of cover between our lines and their's. We used to do a lot of sniping from hides in the mountains, sending chaps out to build

[109]

them at night some half a mile in front of our line, and then going to occupy them and snipe a couple of days later. But very often we drew a complete blank—Jerry never showing himself. From one hide which I went into myself we had a couple of shots at 350 yards, and followed these immediately afterwards by laying a 3.7 battery on to the post through the medium of a 48 set I had taken out with me. We certainly gave them hell. Once again the telescope was invaluable compared with the binoculars. That same evening after the two of us had been sitting in our trench-hide all day long unable to move I suddenly heard a couple of Huns making a noise about 50 yards below us on the same mountain ridge—how they got there Heaven alone knows. We couldn't see them, and they couldn't see us though having heard our shots earlier in the day they must have known that we were somewhere in the vicinity. Unfortunately we had made one mistake in the building of the hide—we had no covered withdrawal possible by daylight, and so could not move out of our hide to a position where we could have picked them off. It was a great pity. I must admit that our enforced inactivity and withdrawal back to our own lines that night was rather eerie!

"Another day we found an unsuspecting Bosche about 600 yards away from us, and we could not get any closer to him. So we lined up three snipers together and got them to fire simultaneously hoping that one of the bullets would hit. The hope was fulfilled! This is maybe an unorthodox way of using snipers, but for a long range shot the practice is more than useful.

"Our snipers were often used on moonlight nights, lying out in front of the line to await the arrival of enemy patrols. But the patrols very seldom turned up in the right place!

"In Italy there was a good deal of terrain in which there was no cover at all to render possible the exercise of daylight stalking. One was always under observation from one or other of the mountain peaks, and the result was therefore largely stalemate; but, once again, even taking into consideration the long ranges, it was possible to snipe provided one was keen and had initiative.

"One thing the Lovat Scouts did very successfully and that was doing all the observing for our Mountain Gunners; with their telescopes they saw more than the whole of one Division put together. There were over 140 telescopes in the Battalion and they were the best weapon they had; they always knew that they could see miles farther than the Hun could, and that certainly gave one confidence, especially when out sniping."

In the Middle East theatre the earlier models of the British telescope sight were often found to be unreliable, and until they were modified the zeroes and focussing of these models could not be guaranteed to stay put; considerable trouble was also experienced by the lenses of the sights becoming completely blurred due to the melting of the Canada balsam which joined both sets of the rear lenses—undoubtedly caused by the hot climate.

The standard of shooting in the hot climates was found, as always, to be lower than in the temperate fighting zones, and one of the reasons put forward for this was that it was impossible to produce a high standard of shooting when the men had to shoot in shirt sleeves, the causes being:— one's elbows must have a comfortable position on the ground; with only a shirt covering the elbows when crawling and shooting on hard and stony ground life, for the sniper, was not much fun; the rifle must have a firm bedding in the shoulder, and this can never be obtained with any rifle when there is only the thickness of a shirt between a steel rifle butt and the shoulder bone . . . with a sniper's rifle it is even more difficult since due to the height of the 'scope sight the firer's head is forced into a position high on the cheek rest and consequently the end of the butt is forced down into the shoulder that amount; this makes it difficult to bed the rifle securely in the shoulder even with a sufficiency of clothing; the method of using the sniper sling which is a great asset for steady holding causes a strain on the upper arm and without sufficient clothing round the arm a throbbing of the arteries will be set up and consequently steady holding will not be maintained—some form of padding where the sling bears on the arm is necessary.

The sniper smock was the answer to the above points in temperate climates. The sniping authority whose Italian adventures have just been recorded suggested that for the sniper in the hot climates a Bush jacket should be used with padding on both shoulders, and down the back half of both sleeves from the shoulder to the cuff; at the elbows and along part of the forearm an outside leather covering of thin flexible leather would complete the modifications. A "jacket" of some description was essential wear for the sniper—he had to have pockets for the carrying of his tools.

It was in Italy that one "sniping conscious" officer declared: "I had to bite the ear of an idiot who asked a sniper to shoot a Hun who was only some 50 yards away! The sniper is, or should be, the most highly trained infantryman, the most skilled specialist and he should not be called upon to do any everyday job that the ordinary soldier can, or should be able to, do himself."

In Italy one New Zealand private soldier had over 60 certified kills to his own rifle. A South African officer had more than 40 kills and got a Military Cross for his sniping, but was eventually killed himself.

JAPANESE SNIPING

The term "sniper" was as grossly misused in connection with the Japs as it was to the Russian sub-machine gunners and the German riflemen. The average Japanese sniper was a rifleman, and not always a good one, who had selected for himself an advantageous position from which to fire at his enemy. The true Jap sniper suitably camouflaged, specially armed and equipped with concentrated rations was responsible only for a very small amount of that which was so-often termed "sniper fire." It was noticed that these snipers seldom fired at parties of men larger than two or three along the jungle tracks because they feared detection by the remainder of the group, and parties of three and four men searching for these snipers by maintaining careful watch or by patrolling action had a deterrent effect.

The Japs in Malaya were certainly adept at camouflage and appeared to shirk no discomfort so long as their object of concealment was achieved. Their training had been thorough and resulted in the possession of an almost animal genius for melting into their backgrounds. In the early part of the campaign they were dressed in leaf-green uniforms which were a perfect match for their environment, the heads and shoulders being covered with green mosquito netting. Their helmets were equipped with wire with which to hold in place small branches and grass.

There are many stories which show that the Jap, although a tenacious fighter, was very much the automaton; he was slow to react to an unexpected situation. During the Kohima affair a British sniper in the half light of early morning, saw movement in a deep, narrow nullah which led to one of our forward localities. The range from his own position was only about 100 yards. With eyes riveted to the spot he saw a number of Japs crawling up the steep slopes of the nullah. This was certainly a pleasant job of work, and he immediately settled down with a stifled grunt of satisfaction, and proceeded to pick them off one by one. Immediately the first Jap had fallen to the sniper's first shot, the second man proceeded to crawl over his comrade's prostrate body. The sniper shot him, and the third man and the fourth and so on. The sniper was amazed to see that the Japs were apparently quite incapable of appreciating what was happening . . . they just continued to advance, crawling over the mounting mass of corpses. The sniper finally claimed 27 killed, and when daylight came the nullah was piled high with the dead bodies. (Had the Russians been fighting such an enemy their "sniper casualty claims" may have been accepted—but the wily Teuton was not the Jap!)

During this same operation Japanese snipers had caused a good deal of irritation to one brigade whose battalions were holding positions in the thick jungle at one side of a large hill. The best antidote to sniping activity being a vigorous counter-sniping, such an offensive was launched and each battalion swept its individual area with a section of *real* snipers. Keen rivalry developed between the sniping sections, and many good bags were claimed. One Battalion section claimed 35 kills in one day.

As opposed to "pukka" sniping the following is a good story. Two men belonging to one unit repeatedly asked for permission to go Jap sniper hunting, and finally they were allowed to follow their bent. Their technique was certainly unique—and rather dangerous, or, at least, it would have been had the Jap had real snipers in the area. Having treed or marked down their man this intrepid pair made preparations for his despatch to the heaven of his ancestors. One of the hunters, armed with a Bren gun, cautiously worked himself into a position where he could cover the general area in which the Jap was concealed with fire from his LMG; the second hunter, who, in peace-time regimental fairs had achieved notoriety by acting as "Aunt Sally," re-acted the part of "Aunty" bobbing up and down, now here now there, with skill born of long practice, in order to draw the Jap's fire. One ineffective shot from the Jap was usually sufficient to give the Bren gunner a clear enough idea of his position for him to search the Jap out in the undergrowth or trees with snappy bursts from the Bren. In one day this intrepid pair claimed 19 scalps.

In this theatre of war the essential use of our own snipers was fully understood, and it was repeatedly pointed out that it was useless employing as a sniper a man who was not a really good sniping shot plus an expert in fieldcraft. In slack commands there has always been a tendency to use snipers in a happy-go-lucky "must find him a job" role. So it was laid down that there must be a clear-cut object in sniper operations and that the object must be clearly explained to the sniper and his mate so that a correct selection of targets could be made. These targets were, normally, of the four usual types:—Officers, NCOs and signal personnel, in order to destroy control; crews of LMGs, MMGs and mortars, in order to destroy the enemy's fire-power; individuals moving along the lines of Communication, to compel the enemy to move in larger numbers and thereby weaken strength on the main front; *all* Japs, to lower general enemy morale.

Great stress was laid on the exercise of patience, and there can be little doubt that in this theatre, with its many natural discomforts, patience was the sniper's most important attribute. Hurried shooting was in many cases fatal, and the maxim that "the Jap you refrain from shooting to-day because it was an odds-against shot will turn up and give you a better shot to-morrow or the next day because he has not been scared" was wholeheartedly plugged. Particularly was this caution, this exercise of patience, necessary at dusk, when the light was going very rapidly and the sniper had not had the good fortune to have a shot all day.

Exercise of guile was not limited to the Jap—some people appear to think that cunning is the prerogative of the Orient—one of whose favourite tricks was to simulate movement in a neighbouring bush or tree to his own position by means of string. Simple British stunts for forcing the Jap to present himself as a target included the uttering of a sudden, sharp noise which very frequently caused the

Jap to incautiously sit up or start if in a hidden, lying position, or to "freeze" when moving. A piece of white material waving on a stick—rag and bamboo and a piece of string the only props for the "illusionist" on a flank—often resulted in an inquisitive Jap rivetting his gaze upon it, and then stalking it, and finding—death.

One report although unofficial but believed to be reasonably accurate states that in Burma two Brigades pooled their snipers, approximately 48 on paper, and in operations extending over two weeks were credited with 296 certain kills. British casualties were two killed and one man wounded in the finger.

AUSTRALIAN SNIPERS

Some of the Australian snipers were really remarkable shots, and probably the best of them were the kangaroo hunters. The majority of these men had been members of rifle clubs in Australia, where they used the .303 rifle with the heavy barrel which is so popular in that country, and which is very accurate over long and short ranges alike. Australian snipers were trained to engage targets at longer ranges than the British sniper.

Like all hunters for skins, European chamois hunters, Russian squirrel hunters and Canadian trappers, the Australian kangaroo hunters have to be extremely careful where they put their bullets. A hole in the centre of the back, though it would kill the animal, would certainly have an economic detriment to the pelt. A good hunter aims low, near to the root of the big tail, a shot which is nearly always certain to break the spinal cord, or high up under the forearms at the heart. Some of the best men prefer the head, maintaining that a brain shot is the most effective in bringing down the quarry, and despatching it humanely. Probably *the* reason why the kangaroo hunter made such a damned good sniper was that if he is to earn good money he must kill cleanly every time he fires. The kangaroo is not a nervous beast, and at the first few cracks of rifle fire a feeding herd will pause momentarily and then proceed with the important job in hand. The fact that one or two of their number collapse on the ground occasions no panic or concern since a kangaroo is an animal which lies down for a great deal of its time. The hunter is therefore at liberty to pick out his target leisurely, the big bucks and the other good skins. One hunter will frequently make a bag of twenty or more before the mob takes flight. But a vastly different story would be told if the hunter merely wounded with his first shot; a bucking, thrashing kangaroo would alarm the whole quarry, and the hunter would not be worthy of the title.

In Timor one of these kangaroo hunters had a great sporting time, and whether right or wrong, he played sportingly with the Japs, and never used his telescopic sight on his rifle when the Nips were at less than 300 yards range! He was credited with 47 Japanese killed but with characteristic modesty claimed only 25 certainties, remarking that "In my game you can't count a 'roo unless you see him drop and know exactly where to go to skin him."

Another 'roo hunter presented with a mass target of automaton Japs—the type of target which comes once only in the life of one sniper in a hundred—got twelve of the yellow-men in twelve shots in fifteen minutes. Some shooting!

PROTECTIVE CLOTHING

I was frequently asked if I considered that it would be a good thing if snipers were issued with protective clothing, in the form of a steel shield for the chest, etc. As is well known in World War I during trench warfare the German snipers used steel shields, and mention is made of these in Hesketh Prichard's book "Sniping in France." No doubt in static positions some form of protection would be of psychological value. But in a war of movement—and really most sniping is mobile, since even in trench warfare it was often necessary to crawl into a suitable position for the domination of a particular sector of the enemy's line—anything which hinders free movement is a serious handicap. A sniper in World War II who turned out with all the impedimenta as laid down at the sniping school, and although one may not agree with it one must admit that there was nothing in the schedule which was useless, was heavily laden enough being festooned as one sniper put it, bluntly but neatly, "like a bloody Christmas Tree"; had he been encased in a chest, pelvic and back steel shield he would have been like one of the Knights of old shortly after the advent of gunpowder when normal mail was rendered useless and suits of armour were made so heavy that once the gallant knight was knocked from his horse he could not get to his feet again. Russian "snipers" used special protective shields but there was nothing of the kind in the realms of British or German sniping in World War II.

I once heard about a German report which was said to have stated that certain of the Allied assault troops on D Day coming under heavy machine gun fire dropped to the ground by the impact of bullets but due to wearing steel linked jackets, or waistcoats, they got up again and carried on much to the consternation and sapping of morale of the German gunners facing them! My only personal experience of protective clothing was the three piece shield, chest, pelvic and back, with which certain ack ack units were issued in Normandy in July 1944. This "equipment" consisted of three 1mm thick, light, manganese steel plates and was designed in 1941 by the Research Council. The breast plate measuring 9" x 8" was to protect the heart and lungs; the 14" x 4" back piece was to cover the lower back and a large portion of the spine, and the third plate, 8" x 6" was to be worn over the upper and central belly. The plates were attached by web-straps and held away from the body by thick rubber padding around the edges. In 1941

BRITISH SNIPER IN SNOW SUIT

These snow suits were a winter issue to combat troops and snipers; worn a good deal in the Ardennes affair. Note the dark coloured buttons—a serious fault.

BRITISH SNIPER

This rifleman is in regulation sniper dress. Different views show the Hawkins position (upper) and the regular prone position (lower).

the first impressions of the body armour were favourable and optimistic. But scientific experts declared that it could save only between 2½ and 3% casualties, and when field exercises were held to see what effect the wearing of the armour would have on the stamina of the men the optimism changed to pessimism. Rapid and easy movements were seriously impaired, and men perspired so profusely that their powers of endurance were affected. I understand that some thousands of these suits were sent out to Normandy, but I never met an infantryman who had either worn or seen them.

It is certain that no body armour within reasonable weight limits is proof against the .303, .300 or the German 7.9mm cartridge at close ranges at which the infantryman is most likely to be hit. It would therefore have been bad tactics to burden him with extra weight which would have interfered with his mobility.

Just before I left Germany I found one of these shields and tested it. I put up the chest shield on the side of the range and fired three shots from a S. & W. .38 from five yards distance. Two of the cartridges were of normal British service type—R.L. jacketed, and the other a German cartridge, lead bullet. There was no penetration of the shield, and the dents were by no means severe. The lead bullet was almost completely flattened. At fifty yards bursts from a Sten carbine split the plate, and at 400 yards range every rifle bullet passed cleanly through; shots from a Mauser 7.63 pistol penetrated the shield at a range of 10 yards.

In writing of "protection" I am reminded of the story of an ack ack gunner who went into Normandy very early. He was a very fat fellow and about three days after landing the officer in charge of his section was making a round of the guns just after dusk when, as usual, all Hell seemed to be a-poppin. The previous night another gun crew in the section had been badly knocked about by anti-personnel bombs, over fifty per cent of the crew being down for the count. The fat one was on the gun, laying and the officer noticed that he had great difficulty in traversing. Hoping that he sounded very unconcerned the officer shouted "Brown, you are getting fatter than ever." In the light of flares and climbing tracer a sickly grin was his only answer. When the action was finished, temporarily, and Brown stood down from the gun, quite a laborious process, the officer could see that Nature never gave such a figure to any man. Closer investigation revealed that Brown beneath his greatcoat had two metal tins tightly packed with damp mud; one of the tins covered his belly, and the other was tied tightly around the waist to cover the vital spinal area. Brown never lived that matter down, yet, who knows, such a contrivance might have saved a man from mortal injury!

Although there were reports that in their Blitzkreig in Europe in 1940 the German Stormtroopers used a type of body-armour, and I remember seeing such suits featured in the graphic drawings of imaginative war artists at that time, I have never found confirmation of this, and having some experience of the later European campaign and compared certain incidents which I saw factually and then as conceived by war artists I am of the opinion that the armour I saw in the 1940 pictures was designed by the fevered flight of fancy of the artist concerned.

HISTORY REPEATS ITSELF

History certainly is repetitive and at one stage in World War II it again became necessary for those who fully appreciated the untold value of sniping to lay down the policy that each unit which was in contact with the enemy must dominate its area by the use of its own snipers. It was emphasised that every Battalion must have its own team of specialised snipers, that they must be "picked men, and fit men, and proud to be such; the best marksmen, skilled in fieldcraft, confident in their self-reliance, possessed of great courage and unrivalled patience." It was further ordained that the work of this section based on continuous detailed recorded observation must be directed by an officer of the Battalion HQ and carried on in every area by relieving units. One further point made was that the dress and equipment worn or carried by an officer or NCO should so clearly resemble that of the men that they should be indistinguishable through a telescope at 500 yards. But these excellent policies were not carried out to the letter by some units.

For some considerable time it was said that the Hun was still a more accomplished sniper than the British, and, curiously enough there is evidence to show that the Germans paid us the compliment of a like remark. During the campaign in N.W. Europe there is no doubt that we had the upper hand in the real sniping game.

Until the "officer and NCO indistinguishable from the men" policy had been adopted there were many leader casualties. In Italy during the battle for Carroceto a forward company of one of the Battalions in a Brigade had the Company commander, a subaltern and every sergeant killed by German snipers. These snipers worked well forward of their line and reserved their shooting for targets wearing field glasses, a soft cap, or carrying a map instead of a rifle or carbine. After this, orders were issued in many units that officers would not carry binoculars slung round the neck, and the majority of officers proceeded to carry rifles!

In many units the sniper rifles were in the wrong hands. In one company the new company commander, a pre-war rifleman, starting a blitz in the sniping department (there were two snipers in each company) found that neither of the then "snipers" had had any special training, and that the rifles were not zeroed, and were virtually useless. After asking for volunteers he picked out three good shots who were very eager to have a crack at becoming snipers, whisked them out of the line and with the aid of an armourer got the rifles in good condition again and zeroed into the men who were going to have a shot at the Huns.

On his first trip one of these fledgeling snipers had quite an interesting time. In the early morning he went out in front of the line to a position which had been suggested to him by the company commander, and kept close surveillance on a tank just forward of a ruined house. A Jerry suddenly appeared and walked into the house. The sniper put down his binoculars, picked up his rifle and waited for the Hun's re-appearance. Some time later the German came from the house and as he climbed up the back of the tank the sniper fired, and secured his first hit. Later in the morning he saw considerable movement in the tank, which ceased after he had fired through a convenient hole in the forward visor. A little later this sniper had more fun and gain at the same target. He watched a pigeon settle down on the roof of the house, and then fly down to the tank. One of the crew popped up out of the turret and stretched out his hands to take in the bird. The sniper fired immediately and was delighted to see the German's headgear fly off and fall to the ground as he slumped across the turret, where he lay until pulled inside by his comrades. On the following day the tank crew lay doggo, and no target was presented throughout the whole time the sniper observed.

There were units in which misuse, or no use, of the snipers abounded; and there were units in which the so-called snipers did not know their job. I have heard that the customary practice of one Battalion when facing the Hun was to send about twenty ordinary riflemen, the shooting standard of whom was low, out into No Man's Land after telling them to select single positions, and snipe the enemy. The net result of this grandiose practice was that the men got into what they thought a safe position, without any thought of whether they could observe or shoot from that spot, and lay there all their tour of duty hoping against hope that there would not be a "stonk" in their vicinity. These men were not snipers with all the attributes, and equipment, of trained specialists.

One of these men told me that being a fairly good shot he would have liked to have been a sniper but wisely he wanted some training first. He told me that some of the so-called Battalion snipers could not do so well in the shooting line as he could with iron sights, and that the standard of shooting of the snipers was matched only by their total unsuitability for their job. He expressed the opinion that very few, officers and men, in the unit had any appreciation or knowledge of the sniper rifle and telescope sight or of the sniper's job generally.

The method of observation prior to a unit attack in this particular Battalion was as unique as it was useless. Whereas in a unit which really appreciated and knew the worth of snipers it was the sniper's job to discover by careful and meticulous observation the strong positions and disposition of the enemy, the information garnered being of great help to Headquarters in formulating their mode of advance, and planning strategically so as to minimise the possible loss of life, the unit under review used to send out a couple of men, quite openly as though they were going on a pleasant stroll well behind the line, to "have a look round." The job was not relished by the men concerned, that is only natural, and therefore the job was not done as it might have been. Casualties to these "look-see" men were very slight; no doubt Jerry, who, despite all his short-comings was no dolt-head, guessed the idea, and therefore it was not surprising when the Battalion moved forward that they came under fire from LMG posts in houses which had certainly not been occupied when the two strollers had casually inspected such buildings.

An instance of non-cooperation with a sniper is shown in the following; the sniper, a colour sergeant in the Lovat Scouts, being given a lone hand expressed his intention of going out in the early morning, before dawn, to have a crack at some Huns who were known to be some distance away. The Company Commander in whose area he was operating decided that *he* would be helpful and ordered out a patrol in front of the Lovat, their job being to gain information as to the exact location of the Germans and on their way back to their own position pass this information to the sniper who was to wait at a given spot, impressing them with the fact that it was essential that the report reached the Scout well before daylight, otherwise it would not be possible for him to get out for a shot. The colour sergeant reached the given spot and waited—and waited. Finally he decided to push on himself just as dawn was breaking. He went out, saw nothing and returned. Due to the delay his time was limited and the country was very close. When he got back he was mortified to find that the patrol had located a Jerry platoon drinking tea in an orchard! The Lovat never discovered why the patrol did not contact him. Since this NCO was one of the finest sniping shots I ever had the privilege of meeting this lack of contact saved a number of Hun lives and, who knows, cost us quite a number!

Ideal Sniper Rifle

Military sniping is undoubtedly the acme of rifle shooting. Comparison of big game and target shooting shows that the former is carried out over indefinite ranges on poorly defined targets or partially obscured targets, which are frequently moving. The first shot being almost invariably the last it is clearly seen that of the two, big game shooting calls for more attributes than bull-plugging. The best possible sights, on accurate rifles, combined with the most accurate ammunition must be utilised to ensure success in such shooting where there are no such things as sighting shots—the first shot must be laid in, or near, the centre of the target. And sniping is big game shooting par excellence—more skilful, more cunning, more serious and more dangerous since the "game" has an equal retaliatory power.

Up to and including the present the basic requirements of military sniping have been considered met by a Service rifle of above average accuracy chambered for the service cartridge, equipped with a telescopic sight (TS) possessing deflection and elevation adjustments in fractions of minutes of angle.

For some considerable time I have firmly held the opinion that the ideal sniper rifle would be one of smaller calibre than .303, say .276, light—without impairment of basic accuracy—and mobile, using a high velocity cartridge, and allied to a simple, light telescope sight of about 4 or 5 power. I think the high velocity cartridge essential. The flatter the trajectory the more simple is the shooting; the simpler the shooting the better the sniping. Experimentalists in this particular field recognise that their main interest must be in flat trajectory. If one had a rifle that would shoot actually flat, one would never need to worry about how much to hold under or over. A second's thought will reveal how much time has been spent by people devising means of range finding and a common trick has been using the width of a post reticule in the hunting 'scopes as a means of computing distance. Even range finders have been taken into the hunting field—but that is not practicable for the sniper! There is only one answer and that is flat trajectory—to be able to shoot anything as far as the eye can see through a 'scope sight well enough to hit a known mark. The flatter the trajectory the less error, and from this, of course, comes the speed of the bullet and killing energy as a result of hydraulic bursting effect.

With a view to confirming my opinions, or having them shattered, I approached a number of experienced snipers and sniper instructors and asked them for their views. The result was heartening, for with one exception, and his sole argument "against" was the question of calibre and, as he put it, "the resultant loss of stopping power" (I cannot see that there could be much argument from a man hit by an h.v. .276), there was complete approval for my suggested ideal combination. One man, whose opinion I value highly since the sniper section under his leadership was probably the best sniper unit in the British Forces in N.W. Europe, stated quite simply that he thought the suggested weapon "absolutely ideal," adding the suggestion that the 'scope should have improved pattern of lens covers since he had found that on many occasions when crawling to a position through wet grass the present type of leather lens covers did not afford enough protection. The majority opinion was that a more powerful 'scope was needed, about four or five power. The authority I have mentioned above stated:— "I would like the sight to be made of light, but strong, metal, and not to weigh more than a half of the present sight. I favour the slide method of fixing; it is by no means so clumsy as the present screw-on method. I would like it to be more powerful than the present 'scope; taking everything into consideration I think it would be difficult to improve on the present type of pointer and hair line."

One of the best sniping shots in the British Army favoured the adoption of the German type of sight, with its higher power and type of mounting; with elevation drum mounted on the top of the 'scope, lateral adjustment by means of a screw plug on the rear clip of the block. To complete the general adoption of the German idea he plumped for the German type of reticule. He was one of the very few who expressed a favourable opinion about such a reticule. But since he was so good at the game, a first-class hunter and sniper instructor, his opinion is of value.

The one dissentient voice uttered the opinion that the present service rifle could be made lighter, being careful not to make it too fragile and susceptible to recoil and that an ideal would be such a lighter service weapon, plus a simple, larger scope, allied to my original suggestion of a high velocity .303 cartridge. The suggestion of a special h.v. .303 cartridge for sniping I put up some time ago, but the authorities turned it down on the grounds of difficulty of supply in the field. In connection with this it is necessary only to point out that if the sniper's job is recognised as it should be, the task of an highly specialised soldier, it seems incongruous that the authorities will not sanction the manufacture and distribution of a weapon which would give the best results in the hands of such a military crafts-man, or, at least, a special cartridge of high velocity for the present rifle. After all, there were snipers in World War II who were disconsolate if they could not have a particular brand of .303 ammunition. All snipers, if they are worthy of the title, show some discrimination in their selection of the normal service cartridge. At the sniping school before an operational tour all the students zeroed their rifles just prior to going off to the forward areas, and each carried 50 rounds of the ammunition—same manufacturer, same box— with which he had zeroed his rifle. By such attention to de-tail does one evade every possibility of the enemy one aims at being missed. If special h.v. ammunition were issued for sniper use and such cartridges were handed to the ordinary infantryman by mistake I am sure that, judging from the standard of shooting of the average so-called rifleman, there would be no tragedy—not even to the enemy!

The officer who expressed a preference for the retention of the .303 calibre thought that a lighter type of the 32 'scope would be nearer the ideal at which to aim, provided that the sight still retained its robust quality. He thought also that for an active service sight the present method of attachment was about the best that could be devised since the slide type of attachment has a larger area of contact and is therefore more liable to be thrown "off" by grit and mud. His general view of the No. 4 Sniper rifle was that although by no means ideal it was the best weapon possessed by any army—"It is weighty and is characterised by the ease at which the telescope is knocked off zero, but even so I con-sider the sight the best I have ever come across."

Arthur Fulton, member of the world famous gunsmiths at Bisley, a brilliant shot and himself a sniper in World War I writes:—"Such a rifle as you describe would be advisable, but I suppose the objection to it would be on the grounds of the difficulty of providing a comparatively small number of rifles and cartridges of different bore. I quite agree about the advisability of a simple 'scope sight allied to the high velocity cartridge."

Sniping Shot vs. Bisley Tiger

One often meets people who say that so-and-so is a good game shot but a poor target shot. This is difficult to understand since if a man is good enough to put his bullet where he wants it to go in the body of a stag at an indeterminate range in poor light he should be able to *place* his shots at a clearly defined "Bull" on a target at a known range under comfortable shooting conditions. But it *is* true that frequently one comes across first-class target shots who do not make good game shots, because they are unable to quickly pick up and clearly see a difficult mark, such as for instance an antelope often offers when perhaps only its head is showing from a bush the same colour as itself, because their judgement of distance is poor, or because they suffer from buck-fever and get too excited.

During the training of snipers there were many instances of men being excellent targets shots but failing in the role of sniping shots. When I mentioned this matter in the course of correspondence with an officer, a very well-known Bisley shot and a sniping instructor in England and Italy during the war, I was taken to task and my opinions rebuked in similar sentences to the following:—"In my experience, the lad who has shot at school or at Bisley has been streets ahead of anyone else, because he's been a better shot." Frankly I should have thought that anyone who had sniped and worked as a sniper trainer would have found instances qualifying my contention that many range and competition shots did not make the grade in sniping shooting. This was a point mentioned to us at the sniping school in Holland, not only by the chief instructor but by officer students on the course who had in their units some men who were very good target shots but who found that shooting under service conditions was a vastly different proposition. In 1943 I had a fellow in my own unit who was an ex-Army man and a range shot of considerable skill and experience. When I took him out on some elementary sniper shooting I was very disappointed. He was slow, and his shooting at sniping targets lacked a good deal. In other phases of sniper training he was useless.

I am not decrying the normal target shooting ability at all, and I wholeheartedly agree that it was good generally to have under instruction men who had been civilian rifle-men, because many of them were the answer to an instructor's fervent prayers, but my point is that it did not naturally follow that such good orthodox shots made snipers and applied their excellent marksmanship in the realms of sniping shooting with its individual and singular standards. During later sniper training I found cases of "marksmen" (men who had qualified for the crossed rifles badge under the old full war course standards) falling below the standard of sniper shooting of men who had not won the marksman's badge.

Psychologically the difference between resting on a placid firing point and shooting in war, even if one is in a comparatively safe position oneself, is the greatest possible contrast. The ice brain pack of the one does not come from the "frig" of the other, unless, of course, one has nerves of steel—the toughest steel. Even in hunting the difference is most marked and I have had personal experience of good target shots failing lamentably in the hunting field with its nerve tensions resultant of growing excitement. The basic shooting ability is there, but there are many other factors to be considered. A simple but interesting experiment is to take a "range" shooting man out into the open country and having previously measured the distances to certain prominent objects get him to judge the range to such objects, not only from the standing position but from the ground level. (Judging distance from the lying position should have been taught at sniping schools, but wasn't; this may have resulted in some German lives being spared!) Give him his yardage errors since he will be fully acquainted with the ballistics of the cartridges he uses and ask him what would be the result of such errors in judging the range. Again, place an object the size of a man's head about 650 yards away, and ask your companion if he thinks he could hit it with the first shot of the day. I have no doubt that many men won't even see the target head!

I repeat, I agree that every aid known to the civilian or range shooting man counts to good shooting, but I am firm in the opinion that it is far better to train snipers on hunting lines—"naturally" rather than by "range tiger" methods. I think the matter boils down to the old word "experience," natural or as near natural as possible, observing, stalking and shooting. I have met men, and trained men, who had never even heard of a minute of angle, yet they were magnificent shots in the field, and excellent snipers.

Frequently, in the sniping game, too much emphasis is laid on the shooting part to the detriment of the "whole" qualification. Do not misunderstand me—I know how important shooting is; but a man who was only a good shot frequently killed more, and certainly lived longer, than a brilliant shot who lacked prowess in movement, stalking and concealment—hence, again, the failure of some competition shots in the sniping field. I well remember the physical fitness fetish which was an integral part of so many musketry schools. Well, there are many men who have shot really well when not feeling by any means good physically, no doubt due to mental concentration, acute knowledge of the physical handicap—the triumph of mind over matter!

In the same way a man who does not consider himself capable of getting in a killing shot at 500 yards or 400 yards will get in a position nearer to his quarry, as a result of his stalking ability, where he is supremely confident of the result of his eventual shot.

My main criticisms of the training at the war-time sniping schools were:—a good deal of the shooting was not in the nature of an equivalence of field shooting, there was too much "range shooting" atmosphere about it; the qualifying standards were not high enough. If the qualification figure was 60% under almost ideal "range" conditions, up to 400 yards on flat, inanimate targets, it is easy to realise that a Jerry had at least a very fair chance of survival from some so-called snipers.

I have been rather surprised to find that one contemporary school is teaching wind allowances in minutes of angle for allowance on the deflection drum of the scope sight. It was always found that the hardest thing to get over to embryo snipers was the elevation table and anything which appertained to "minutes of angle." Whether it is due to a faulty educational system or not, the fact remains that to commence talking to sniper students, including officers, about minutes of angle was to completely enshroud them in a mental fog.

And I can see many snags ahead for men who endeavour to allow for wind by adjustment of the lateral drum. During training I stressed the great value of experience in allowing for wind, which is rarely, if ever, consistent over the total distance of the bullet's flight. There has been more poppy-cock talked of wind allowances than anything else in the shooting game. Surely anything which adds to the complication of a sniper's job is not to be encouraged. The less sight alterations a sniper has to make the better.

All this brings us once again to the word "experience." The more "observation, stalk and kill" practice a man gets, the more accomplished he becomes. By "seeing" the results of his shots on near-"natural" targets at varying ranges and under divers conditions he learns much more than he will by weeks spent in the "minutes-of-angle-theory-cum-practical" shooting at classification targets at known ranges. In other words he becomes a "hunting shot" which is the ideal for sniper training, and one for which we should earnestly strive.

I have been taken to task by the same Bisley man mentioned earlier for suggesting that a 2½" grouping standard at 100 yards was too big a group to warrant full points on sniper qualification tests, and told that "2½" was all that it was practical to go for with a No. 4 rifle. Yet the same authority had said that in Italy most of the sniping was done at small targets at 600 yards or more—this in support of the contention that the Bisley man was *the* man for a sniper. I think a very simple arithmetical calculation will prove the ambiguity of such reasoning. If one cannot reasonably expect more than a 2½" group at 100 yards from the No. 4 sniper rifle, then at 600 yards it is not feasible to suggest that the rifle is capable of shooting within less than a 15" diameter circle; therefore it is very problematical whether anyone, especially a good shot, could hit, say a Jerry's head, at that range with one shot!

I have approached a number of snipers and sniper instructors, all with war experience, on this question of target and sniping shot, because I think it is a matter of great interest and importance. All these men confirmed my own strongly held view that the best sniping shot was the hunting shot, the man who had shot game, no matter what its importance or quality, in short, the man who had shot at *live* targets. Each had evidence to bring forward to support the claim that some excellent target marksmen were of little or no use in the field, and had failed as snipers; and they could quote instances of brilliant performers on the range at normal targets failing to retain that shooting capacity on "live" targets—game in general, deer—and

Man! One of them repeated a story I had heard before—of how one of the best army marksmen who was travelling around units giving demonstrations of shooting was taken out to shoot deer one evening, at his own request, and not only did not shoot one but had to have the beasts pointed out to him—he couldn't see them. One target that he was put on he missed at a range of slightly less than 100 yards. He improved a lot after some experience, but he never attained half the standard of shooting he was capable of on the range at normal targets at known ranges.

During training in England just prior to D Day one sniping instructor had in his sniping section two exceptionally fine target marksmen. In his laconic report on them in France he said:—"Both failed to make the grade." The same authority stated that in nine cases out of ten, in his long experience of both peace and war shooting, a high percentage of brilliant target riflemen failed lamentably to retain their shooting prowess when the target was live game or Man.

There was one man who attended sniping school who was a very good shot on the type of targets then in use, but in the other elements of sniping he was poor, always doing in the phrase of his Scots instructor "Stoopid things." A report as to his unsuitability for the sniper's job was made, but on his return to his unit he was sent out to snipe; his usefulness was very limited—he was wounded and taken prisoner!

One officer instructor said that in the realms of the other ranks he had rarely had the experience of a good marksman being useless as a sniper, since the man who is a good marksman is generally above average intelligence and therefore has the makings of a good sniper. But he could envisage the "academic" type of marksman, especially officers, who would be perfectly useless at the sniping game. But this instructor held the view that no brilliant target marksman retained his shooting ability on live targets, on the grounds of nervous temperament which is present in all men to some degree; and that many cool target shots were anything but cold when sniping.

Teaching sniping on classification ranges, or stereotype sniping ranges, at two dimensional targets both "classical," and "modern" if any, is lacking in true values. Sniping shooting should be hunting shooting, and the real way to become a hunting shot is by experience—experience not based solely on a "mathematical alteration of sights" character.

Use of the "Hawkins" position was pushed a good deal in training at sniping schools. This is a splendid position for accurate shooting, but I personally cannot see that it is *eminently* and *frequently* useful on active service. It is a very low position and if the terrain is suitable for a long sight view from such a near-to-the-ground position it naturally follows that the firer to a certain extent is exposed to view. In grassy country such as N.W. Europe it was difficult to get such a sight view, and although I have been told that the "Hawkins" position was used a great deal in the desert and in Italy, I found that in sandy country—such as Sylt— the muzzle blast kicked up one hell of a swirl of dust and sand. I am quite aware that Hawkins won the King's Prize at Bisley; that his stance was barred from competition shooting, and that it is a position which ensures a very steady hold, but once again the old argument crops up —— Bisley is certainly not the battlefield.

In the schedule of practices laid down for sniping shooting, sighters were allowed. This I maintain is a travesty of sniping training and shooting. I agree that sighters are of great value to target shooters, but there are no markers in the field—and hitting assessment is by observation only!

❋   ❋   ❋   ❋

Some of the staff of the Sniping School, in Germany, during July-August, 1945. Author in center of back row.

BRITISH SNIPER

Two rather unconventional but very good shooting positions for the sniper. Upper is a sitting position well known to American shooters and often used. Lower is a variation of the back position (often used in British match rifle competitions), and a good one to drop into for a quick shot from sloping ground or to fit into a small shell hole or hide.

The opinion has often been expressed, not only by the British, that one of the main reasons why we beat the Germans at the sniping game in two wars was that our snipers very frequently worked in pairs—as a team.

The sniper has a most difficult job, and his battle is a personal, or near personal, one; his courage, and guts he must have, is of the lonely type; his life is dependent not only on his skill as a shot, but on his qualities of patience and self discipline, his fieldcraftsmanship, his confidence; and his burning, controlled enthusiasm. And he carries the terrific responsibility of knowing that he can be instrumental in saving the lives of many of his comrades, and he is well able to influence the morale of his whole battalion.

A *lone* sniper can do much—there are occasions when a sniper working entirely alone can do a more effective job than two snipers working together—but generally speaking the advantages of a sniper team are manifold. One of the salient advantages is elementary psychology—the presence of another man is a terrific booster of morale. Sniping is a nerve-wracking game; and the strain tells on even the toughest fibred of men, albeit unconsciously in some cases. Two pairs of eyes are better than one, and many observation reports handed in by sniper teams must have been more comprehensive, reasoned and clear than had a single sniper been out in front.

It was essential in the "team" idea that the two men forming it were not antagonistic, and possessed mutual understanding. To send out a sniper pair who were at loggerheads would have been fatal, not only to themselves, but to the job on hand. That fact was clearly understood by everyone.

The team, well equipped, could certainly travel lighter than the lone sniper, and a pair could be certain of their kills since the man who was not taking the shot could have the target covered and under the closest scrutiny either with binoculars or telescope. In certain cases it was possible for the second man, or observer, to put the rifleman on a target he could not really, strictly, define in his telescope sight; for example a Hun extremely well hidden in the shadow of bushes who defied the power of the TS but could be clearly seen through the penetrative telescope could be KO'd by "team work," the observer indicating the target to the sniper, giving him the fire order and watching for the result through the telescope. Snipers were trained in this work, and it happened!

In instructing I used to tell a "peaceful" story of such shooting co-operation; in Germany a colleague and myself spent many happy evenings seated on a balcony firing at rats which towards dusk frequented a refuse pile about thirty yards away from us. We used a .22 Winchester with telescopic sight and enjoyed some good sport. When it became too dark to see clearly through the 'scope sight, one of us using powerful binoculars would put the "firer" on to targets by "indication" methods and give the order to fire. Usually we placed a sheet of white paper on the pile to serve as a reference point. One evening when I could only just discern the paper as a light toned blob my colleague using the binoculars gave me a clear-cut indication "bottom right hand corner paper" a crisp, incisive "Now" and we went down to find a really big rat killed cleanly with a shot through the right shoulder.

I do not think that anyone can rant against the policy of snipers working in pairs and in complete unity. There were times when one met a tough, taciturn, hard-bitten case who preferred to work alone; such men travelled farthest and killed best alone, and a wise commander allowed them full rein.

Speaking of psychology it was stressed at Sniping School that if an enemy sniper was active in one's area the best policy was to have him labelled, or libelled, with an amusing, even rude and uncouth, nickname. By so doing the troops reacted in the right manner and the sniper became an object of derision, not fear. To have called him "Sure Shot Sam" or "Dead Shot Dick" would have been fatal to morale.

SNIPING OPINIONS

The ideal "Range" for sniping is not a range at all, but a tract of natural country embracing as many different types of terrain as possible. This becomes *the* working area whereon can be carried out observation exercises, stalking and, with the exception of the original tests of the man's basic marksmanship, all the shooting . . . at three-dimensional dummy targets, the only target worth anything for sniper training.

Such a range should be the exclusive training ground for the sniping school so that it is always ready for use—at any hour of the day or night. It is essential that snipers should be trained to do their job at all times—day and night. There are many nights when sniper shooting can take place—in the moonlight or bright starlight; when snow is on the ground, and at dusk and dawn.

It cannot be stressed too highly that anything in the nature of "regimentation" is utterly alien to sniping. Sniping is essentially an individualist job, and stereotype methods, usually a feature of a normal military training establishment, tend to detract from that atmosphere of "a soldier treated as an individual and a man" which is an integral part of the correctly run sniping school. In the war-time sniping school in Europe, situated within easy reach of the forward areas—a pattern for sniping schools in time of war—a man *was* treated as an individual. Shooting and stalking were taught as a game, the greatest sport of all.

In the course of a report of a sniping school activities I mentioned that training had been given with rifles rested on cover. This caused some adverse comment from one of my friends who is a well-known figure in the English shooting world—a former winner of the King's Prize. He wrote to me and said:—"Take every possible chance of using a rest, but the rifle itself should never come into contact with that rest—but in no circumstance rest any part of the rifle against anything hard. I jolly well mean this and when I read your notes about this I much wanted to smack you!" Now my notes stated that in a demonstration to the sniper-instructor-students on the course I had settled down with my old P 14 and proceeded to fire a five round group at a normal 2″ aiming mark (not set centrally) on a 4′ target from the 100 yards firing point, resting the forepart of the rifle, some six inches from the muzzle, on a hard surface, to wit, a sandbag. The result was a lovely tight 1½″ group central, 1″ above the aiming mark. And I don't think anyone will say that this is bad grouping with an old service rifle using iron sights. Nor was this just a flash in the pan. With this P 14, my own No. 4 rifle with iron sights, and a No. 4 Sniper rifle with TS, it was very rarely indeed that the five shot group exceeded 2″. The two best shots of the students also put up some excellent shooting with rifles rested in this way. And since previous experience in training men had borne out the same results I came to the conclusion that the talk of rested rifles spelling negation to good shooting was not entirely borne out in practice.

In replying to my friend I said that I approached the question of the "rested rifle" with some diffidence since I realised fully that he had had much wider and more vast experience than myself, yet I could only write from my own actual experience, and that I could assure him that which had been written was fact. I pointed out that in 1942 and early 1943 when weapon training officer to my unit I had a chap who was a brilliant performer on the range when left to his own devices. I had been trained in the usual orthodox manner and looked askance at any departure from the accepted canons of shooting. When I saw "W" resting his rifle, either on a sandbag or a piece of turf, I stopped such a practice and the result was that his scoring ability dropped from about 95% to something in the neighbourhood of 50%. After intensive coaching in the orthodox method of holding without any really decent result I allowed him to go back to his former style, and he celebrated the event by scoring 98% of the possible, and once more became the best scoring shot in the Squadron. Even on field firing he always appeared to find some kind of a rest.

During sniper training I considered it essential that the men should be exercised in shooting with their rifles rested, since on service there are times when a shot in that position is the only one possible. Curiously enough on the day that I received my friend's condemnatory epistle I was speaking to a World War I sniper who had been a pillar of strength to the local Home Guard battalion during World War II. Unprompted by me he brought up the question of rested rifles and said that he had never been able to understand why there should be a certain piety in musketry schools about this matter. During the last war he had always shot resting his rifle when possible and had been very successful. During Home Guard range work in World War II he had consistently shot better than anyone else in the Battalion, but, of course, he had been barred from competitions because of the unorthodox position he adopted. After the competitions he had much pleasure in shooting against the winners and beating them!

I do admit that on many occasions I found men, indifferent and bad shots, resting their rifles on cover and firing all over the place; and that when I had pointed out to them that they must have only the hand, or wrist, rested and not the rifle, they showed some improvement. My point can be summarised thus:—When a man knows what he is about it is possible that he can, on occasion, do some really good shooting with the rifle rested, and handling it in his own individual style.

It has been frequently asked:—"Was such training as that afforded by sniping schools successful in actual sniping in the field? Or had it to be modified?" A sniping NCO of great experience whose opinion must be highly valued said: "The training given at the sniping schools was first-class, but unless a man knew something about the greatest of games before attending the courses I doubt very much whether the course was of much value. It is impossible to train men to be snipers in the brief period of two to three weeks." My own opinion, although I thought that the training could have been improved in a number of ways, was that it depended mainly on the man trained. If the right type were sent to the sniping school they could, on completion of the course, go straight on to active service sniping and successfully practise that which had been preached to them. There was little need for any modification so long as the sniper combined a full measure of common-sense with the fruits of his training. Such a combination led to full success on numerous occasions.

Sniping officers and NCOs were all of the opinion that to have a team of successful snipers depended entirely on being able to get the right type of man for a start. It is not an exaggeration to say that not one man in a hundred possesses the qualities required to make a successful sniper, and therefore time spent in training many men was, to a certain extent, time wasted, except that very few men left a sniping school without having succumbed to the sense of enthusiasm always prevalent at such a school, and without being much more conscious of the deadliness of the rifle as a weapon of precision.

A sniper should be trained to such a pitch that he is so good, and knows it, that he has supreme confidence in his ability to hoodwink, outwit and kill any enemy. If *the sniper* knows that the odds are that the other chap is not so good as himself, then his confidence should be such that any insurance company could quite safely grant him a long life-policy. For the benefit of students when at the Training Centre I used to put on a demonstration of individual stalk and kill. The opponents were two Lovat Scout sergeants, both masters of the game. One of them, a very hefty fellow, would go down in grass about nine inches high some twenty-five yards away from the students, who remained standing, and on my signal he would really go to ground. He was not seen again until he chose to show himself. It seemed impossible that a man of his stature could hide himself away in such low cover, and move so fast without any perceptible movement of the grass; and the invariable comment from the students was something like:—"Blimey, he must have gone down a rabbit 'ole!" Thus they came to a full comprehension of the fact that once a man becomes so adept as that Lovat Scout undoubtedly was he is in a position to fear nothing, since he is supremely conscious of his ability to get anywhere without being seen.

Perhaps the product turned out by war-time sniping schools was not so good as he might have been in many cases; but ten or fourteen days is not a long time even to impart the rudiments of such an important job. On the other hand a considerable number of ex-students gave many Huns mortal headaches!

In the trench warfare of World War I the sniper and observer worked as a team, and it is significant that the same combination was eminently successful in World War II. It has been recorded that the Germans agreed that our successful sniping campaign was the result of this team-work, and that snipers working in pairs yielded vastly superior results than snipers hunting singly. But I am not alone in thinking that there are many situations in which the lone sniper would be worth his weight in gold. During World War II snipers were not used enough, and the real lone sniper was very seldom, if ever, used. Lone snipers could have been used in a deep penetrative role, well behind the enemy lines. Given guts, *absolute* fieldcraft ability, stealth, cunning, supreme confidence in his own prowess, and a splendid shot, the death and confusion that such a man could have caused in the enemy's rear is inestimable. There is an old maxim that he who travels alone travels farthest. It is true. And the sniper who travels alone can reach positions it is impossible for two men to reach, and get targets which no *team* could see. But the lone sniper must have longer and more arduous training than was the standard in war-time schools. The "team" idea was a good one, and I am sure that results were obtained just because two men were out together. Anything which added to the morale of men was of inestimable value in war.

Future of Sniping

What is the future of Sniping? This is not the difficult problem many people, including perhaps those in authority, think; in the British Army we have seen the results of the lack of regard for sniping and sniper training twice in one generation. In the 1914-1918 War we paid very heavily indeed for our lack of a sniper organisation, and it took many months of heavy casualties before anything was done to remedy the defect. And the remedy, when it appeared, was not derived from actual Army sources but was, in the main, the idea and inspiration of one man, Hesketh Prichard. Towards the end of World War I there was actually a standard British sniper rifle— the P 14 fitted with Aldis 'scope sight.

One would have thought that a most bitter lesson having been learned—so effectively that we beat the Hun at his own game—sniper training would have been part and parcel of British Army training. But no—when World War II started where were the sniping schools? They did not exist. Again it took many deaths before the Powers that Be sat up and took notice, and tardy action. Again, once the rusty cogs got moving easily, mainly by the sterling work of one or two men such as Major Tony Wills and Major Underhill whose efforts cannot be praised too highly, the Hun was trounced. But writing now, many months after World War II, I must confess that I should not be in the least surprised if sniping is again allowed to lapse, and sniping rifles and telescope sights relegated to forgotten armouries where they will become the delightful haunts of venturesome spiders.

During my last few months in Germany I frequently heard the remark "Oh, there cannot be any sense in training snipers now." To say that remark was facetious is gross under-statement. My idea is, and I will readily admit that many who passed the remark quoted above have since agreed with me, that the day of the trained rifleman, the expert *service* shot, will never pass. In the future there may not be the call for so many riflemen, but the expert "cheap" killer will always have a place in the scheme of war. And an Occupational Force in a country which is still, and I think may be more so in the future, hostile has an essential need for sniper trained men. There can be no doubt that a cold and calculating German armed with a rifle, and surely none of us are going to be so damned silly as to think that *all* German weapons have been surrendered (would we so easily give up our beloved rifles and guns?), can still be much more than a nuisance to the authorities. And in the forest areas of Germany a man knowing the country like the back of his hand could add many scalps to his totem and escape the dragnet which would be set sweeping against him. One can bring tanks and flame-throwers to bear, but what use are these against a single resolute individual who has the backing of almost every other German? Send a section, a platoon, a company, even a battalion to bring such a man in—I am quite willing to wager that it would be a waste of time. To get such a killer there is only one remedy, and that is to send a similar type of individual against him.

There is only one effective measure against sniping and that is counter-sniping. There is only one type who will account for an intrepid hunter, and that is a person of the same calibre. This is just one instance why it should be considered essential that sniping training is carried on at properly established sniping schools both in England and abroad. Taking into consideration the fact that the men who had been snipers during the War would probably all be leaving the forces I considered it was very important that new men should be available for the sniper's job. And since the sniper might be called upon in his true capacity in, and over, German terrain then his training, or some part of it at least, should actually take place in Germany. This factor, quite apart from hunting being the nearest peace-time approach to sniping, was taken into consideration when I fought on every possible occasion for the inclusion of hunting trips in the sniper training schedule.

Superficially I suppose it may sound a trifle curious, or idle, to mention sniping and rifle marksmanship in an atom-bomb age. But one is not going to use atomic energy to do the job that one small piece of cupro-nickel covered lead will do just as effectively, quickly and probably more humanely. Apart from the question of snipers' use in the occupied countries there is also the point that in many areas which are subject to American and British law and order there is ever present the threat of insurrection and strife. In such fields a few teams of snipers will do the work more expeditiously, and at far less risk of life, than a garrison battalion or more.

In peace-time, not the least important of the manifold reasons for the retention of sniper training is that such training is really enjoyed by at least 95% of the men who undergo it. At heart every normal man is a hunter. That inherent instinct is thrown to the surface after a few days, or hours, at a sniping school. He is indeed a dull dog who has not at some time in his life been thrilled to the heart by stories of Red Indian stealth and cunning. The individual training a soldier receives at a sniping school is always pleasing to his ego. No matter how regimented he may have become by years of the strict routine of Army existence he takes on a new lease of life when he goes to such a school and is treated once again as an individual, and is taught that he alone, for this set job, counts. I am quite definite in my opinion that should the British, and American, army authorities allow sniping training to fade into Oblivion it will be a damned bad thing. I have met many men who said that their time at sniping school was the golden period of their service life. I fully and whole-heartedly endorse that sentiment.

"If the rifleman is to be retained, at all, in the composition of the Armies of the future, it will only be by virtue of the fact that he can and will conscientiously and ably deliver an accurate and effective fire upon single, individual targets."

Some years ago McBride penned the above trenchant words, ("A Rifleman Went to War"—Capt. H. W. McBride) and since then another great struggle has come and gone. Perhaps he visualised that the next war would be much later than 1939. In World War II the rifleman, except as a sniper, did not occupy a prominent niche. I know of a rifleman in a famous Regiment who fired his rifle once only from D plus 3 to April 1945! Certainly there was nothing in this war to warrant comparison with the epic stand of the British riflemen at Mons in 1914 when by virtue of their *accurate rapid* fire they stemmed the German hordes to such good effect that the Huns thought that every man in the British force was equipped with a machine gun. The regular British Army, small though it was, of 1914 was without doubt the finest rifle trained body of men the history of War has known; and this was due to the foresight of one man, Brig. General N. R. McMahon, DSO. and the fact that the British Government in office previous to 1914 would not sanction the purchase of machine guns. McMahon, realising that the machine gun would play a prominent part in any future struggle, and that the British Army was not going to be well equipped with them, decided to train the British Infantryman to such a standard with the rifle that the lack of machine guns would not be so badly felt when the struggle dawned. Proof of his foresight came at Mons in 1914; this stopping of the Huns marked the beginning, albeit it took a long time, of the end. Many Germans have admitted that it was at Mons in 1914 that they lost World War I.

But McBride's statement I think can now stand in its succinctness, and read it as you will there is no getting beyond the fact that it is a splendid argument for the retention, and expansion, of sniping in military training.

McBride's Book "*A Rifleman Went to War*"

For two or three years I had endeavoured to buy a copy of McBride's "A Rifleman Went to War" but without success. When I heard the CI of the sniping school, Major Underhill, most warmly praise the work I decided to make another effort to at least *read* the book and finally the well-known gun people, Parker-Hale of Birmingham, kindly loaned me their sole office reference copy.

The book arrived one day in early April shortly after my second crossing of the Rhine; we were static—under canvas —just awaiting events. Once having started the book I cursed the fates that had sanctioned the breaking of my small paraffin lamp, which had been sent out to me from home and which had rendered yeoman service during the long winter nights in Holland, for my reading had to finish with the passing of daylight. I *devoured* that book and, in many respects it might well have been written of World War II. There is no doubt that McBride's book should have been in the library of *all* training establishments, not only sniping schools.

McBride *knew* the sniping game from A to Z; he was trenchant and militant, a keen observer and knowledgeable of the wiles and cunning of the Hun, and I have frequently contrasted his practical knowledge, gained from true war experience, with the anaemic pseudo-ability of training personnel who have never been to war. McBride would have been a terrific power in a sniping school. He may not have been very popular with the authorities on account of his frankness but he would have been a great instructor.

On page 144 of "A Rifleman Went to War" there occurs this passage:—

"A man may know all the text books by heart and be able to repeat them forward and backward, may be an expert rifleman and all that, but it is only in actual combat that he can *find* himself."

This should be emblazoned in letters of gold across the gateways leading to all training schools. It is one of the most profound passages in a book which abounds in sage utterance and counsel. I copied it in my diary and before one of my lectures at the Training Centre I always printed it on the board. The students were mainly veterans of more than one campaign and they fully appreciated the truth. I shall never forget the expression on the face of a Warrant Officer instructor, just out from England, when he looked into the lecture room one morning and saw the passage standing starkly on the blackboard. In a way I felt rather sorry for him and I have always imagined that he was of the opinion that I was hitting at him and had set down the passage solely for his benefit. He knew the pamphlets by heart; he was an excellent weapon handler and shot—but was entirely lacking in experience of *War!*

Without doubt McBride's book was of considerable help to me and to instructors who shared my opinions. I have always considered it something of a tragedy that it was not readily available to us at this side of the Atlantic.

BRITISH
WEAPONS AND EQUIPMENT

RIFLES

S. M. L. E. · No. 4 · No. 5 · Ross · P. 14

SNIPING RIFLES

SCOUT REGIMENT TELESCOPE

Swift Training Rifle · .22

S.M.L.E.(Short Magazine Lee-Enfield). Mks. III and III*.

ALTHOUGH the No. 4 Rifle had for a year or two been
the standard service arm of the British Forces it was still
possible to meet thousands of men, many of them old
soldiers, who regarded it as being of small worth, and who
swore by their S.M.L.E.s. Their great regard for the
Lee-Enfield was such that they never really bothered to
try to shoot well with the No. 4. I had in my platoon an
old soldier who, for some months after joining us, shot
quite indifferently with the P 14 with which we were at
that time armed . . . it was in the early days. His actions
on the firing point were a delight to watch, his position,
his bolt manipulation a glorious series of examples for
the rest of the men to follow. But his scores were never
good. When I tackled him about it he said that he could

[149]

never shoot with such a rifle, he wanted an S.M.L.E. I told him that anyone who could shoot with the S.M.L.E. could do better with the P 14 providing that he was a fellow who could use the long butt—and I knew that during his earlier Army career he had used the long butt S.M.L.E. since he was a long armed individual. I allowed him to use my own S.M.L.E. one day, and he put up a really good score. On the following day when we were again on the range I borrowed the range-warden's S.M.L.E. which was fitted with a Parker-Hale aperture sight, and after imploring him to use the sight properly allowed him to fire the same practices as the day before. He improved his previous score.

On the next visit to the range he used a P 14 and having settled down beside him with my telescope, he once more fired the practices. He scored a possible. And from that day on he became one of the best shots in the Unit. He was a convert to the P 14, and when some time later these rifles were handed in, and we were equipped with the No. 4 he was very loath to part with the '14. But he took kindly to the No. 4, and continued to shoot exceedingly well. There is no doubt though that for ease of bolt manipulation and rapid fire the S.M.L.E. was and is, the finest rifle in the world, and in the trench warfare of World War I it was the ideal weapon. To elaborate this statement, if elaboration be needed, it is necessary only to point out the following:—

The locking lugs on the Lee-Enfield action are at the rear of the bolt. One lug bears against the resistance shoulder on the right of the body, while the other rides up and bears against the rear wall of a cam slot on the left side of the body. There are advantages and disadvantages to this system of locking, but from the point of view of rough usage such as is obtained on active service the former far outweigh the latter. The principal disadvantage to the system of locking is that super-accuracy is difficult to obtain since the bolt and the major portion of the body is

BRITISH SNIPING RIFLE

The standard No. 4 (T) sniper rifle.

BRITISH SNIPING RIFLE

A modified No. 4 Sniper rifle, with pistol grip and cheekpiece style of butt of Canadian make. Has thick rubber pad in place of metal butt plate.

BRITISH SNIPER TELESCOPE

This is the Scout Regiment telescope, a three-draw, bulky, clumsy and heavy glass but a splendid instrument in the hands of a skilled observer. It magnified about 20 diameters, with a field of view of but $1\frac{1}{2}°$, and if properly used could penetrate deep shadows, show up enemy camouflage and reveal badges of rank with ease. Under suitable conditions of light it would show up troop movements to a distance of ten miles. Generally, this big telescope took over when the lower powered binoculars "gave out."

in a state of compression when the shot is fired. *Super-accuracy*, however, is not needed by the big majority of service men—indeed the bulk of riflemen are incapable of getting the best out of an extremely accurate rifle since their shooting prowess leaves so much to be desired. Only the sniper requires such accuracy, and late in World War I the sniper's need was catered to by the introduction of the P 14 with telescope sight. This one drawback is amply compensated for by such advantages as simple and sweet bolt action which could not be bettered for rapid fire. There is no abrupt turn over of the bolt lever as is necessitated by forward locking lugs. The action functions well in conditions of sand, mud and dust which spell trouble to other types of bolt action. And the action is certainly easier to clean than in types in which there are forward locking recesses in the body.

❀   ❀   ❀   ❀

No. 4

This rifle differs little from the S.M.L.E. of which it is really a modern copy; in fact, when it was first produced it was known as the S.M.L.E. Mk. VI. The Lee-Enfield, as is generally known, was not designed for modern mass production, having been born years before such things were thought about. The Rifle No. 4 was designed purely from the point of view of mass production, and the number of different types of steel and of difficult machining operations was reduced to a minimum. At the same time certain improvements were incorporated such as:—

Slightly heavier, sturdier and "floating" barrel which is not in direct contact with the woodwork.

Improved stocking up arrangements.

A machined surface for the bolt head to ride upon inside the body.

A smaller and more compact bolt head resultant of the feature immediately above.

A new type of bolt retaining arrangement.

Aperture instead of open sight.

A few thousands of these rifles were made for troop trials round about 1930–1931. The trials proving satisfactory the design was approved and laid aside for use in an emergency, since, as usual, financial stringency precluded any more positive action, or production, at that time. When the second World War broke out this rifle went into production.

Many of the early rifles were very poor and had many faults, and at one stage opinion was dead against the model. Bolts needed a lot of work before they functioned decently; rear sights had considerable lateral play; magazines were faulty; the bores were poorly finished due to lack of machine operations, and there was great tolerance and allowance manifest when passing the bores for gauging— anything from .301 to .305 was passed as being fit for use. Some of the rifles were terrible.

I remember one afternoon in late 1942, I was in charge of a party firing on a 30-yard range using No. 4 rifles. One of the men had fired three shots and scored three bulls on the miniature target; I noticed that he was taking a long time to get his fourth shot away and asked the reason. He said that he could not see his foresight. He was quite right— the barrel had bent so much! The later No. 4s improved a good deal, and I have fired hundreds of such rifles and very rarely have I come across a real "rogue."

War production, in which time is a most vital factor, resulted in dispensing with a number of the peace-time gadgets which were incorporated in the original design of the rifle. Certain of these modifications were:—

Omission of the cut-off; piling swivel and butt disc.

Simplified design of foresight protector.

Radically simplified backsight.

Simplified bolt retaining arrangements—explained in more detail below.

And, a matter which does not really concern the rifleman, a circular spike bayonet vice the cruciform.

The new backsight arrangement was very simple, although to a musketry instructor taking new recruits it was far from easy of explanation; it consisted of two aperture battle sights set at right angles to one another. The shorter range one was calibrated for 300 yards with the bayonet fixed, and was correct for 400 yards with the bayonet unfixed. The longer range aperture was correct for 600 yards—without the bayonet. The method of use supposing that the normal practice of fixing bayonets when within 300 yards of the enemy was adhered to, was as follows:—

At 300 yards use the 300 yards aperture with the bayonet fixed and take normal aim.

At 400 yards use the 300 aperture without the bayonet fixed and take a normal aim.

At 600 yards use the 600 aperture, obviously without the bayonet fixed and take a normal aim.

Up to 300 yards aim down a little using the 300 aperture. The maximum aim down at any intermediate range should not exceed eight inches.

At 500 yards use the 600 aperture and aim down. The aim down at 500 yards is at most two and a half feet.

The rules were certainly simple, and ensured that a man always kept his target in view. But in actual practice with men of little intelligence the flip sight was something in the nature of a severe headache. Despite the oft-repeated injunction, on the firing point at range practices, to the firers that they watch that they use the correct sight one would always find some chap whose shots were going high say at 200 yards, the result of his firing with his 600 yards battle sight! And a great number of the rifles tested as they were received from the factories revealed that those responsible for the calibration of the two battle sights were hay-wire. There was more criticism of this sighting arrangement than anything else connected with this rifle.

One peculiar feature was that we were told that all the rifles were zeroed at the Ordnance Factories without the bayonet, and yet immediately they were received by units they were supposed to be zeroed with the bayonet fixed. To a zealous and enthusiastic rifleman such orders were the cause of much heartburning; especially so when once after making application for enough foresights for the re-zeroing I was curtly informed that "foresights were not available for the zeroing of rifles," and that the number of foresights I had demanded (70) was more than enough to *maintain* 2,000 rifles for 12 months!! I cannot forget my reactions when that illuminating message was read me by my CO.

Later in the war this flip sight was replaced by a tangent backsight, the first of which were made of thin metal, using a spring clip method of fixing the sights and looked exactly what they were—a very cheap job and virtually worthless.

A few months later these in turn were replaced by a much more solid finger screw type of backsight, similar to the tangent sight used on certain LMGs.

Although the majority opinion of the flip sight was that it was very poor I personally did not mind it in the least once I had become used to it; if a man knew his rifle intimately he could shoot well even with this sight. It was certainly of a rigid type, vastly different to the first issue of tangent sights mentioned above where one fixed the setting at 300 yards, fired a shot and then found that the clip had slipped down to zero.

As a rifleman I detested the business of bayonet fixing, and would have none of it. In a mobile war when troops are constantly on the move, climbing into lorries, etc., it was essential that the No. 4 rifles should be checked frequently.

It is my considered opinion that the No. 4 did not stand up to the wear and tear of active service conditions as well as the S.M.L.E.

The simplified bolt retaining arrangements mentioned previously consisted simply of the abolition of the bolt-head catch and the substitution for it of a small cut-away in the bolt head runner in the body. The bolt head would only come out of the body when strictly coincident with this cut-away. Even if the bolt is manipulated deliberately with the object of trying to make the bolt-head jump out it will not do so.

❊   ❊   ❊   ❊

No. 5

The need for a lighter rifle for the troops in the Far East theatre became apparent in 1942/3 when the jungle troops in Burma found the No. 4 too heavy and slow to bring to the shoulder, and the airborne men too expressed a desire for a rifle easier to handle but just as effective as the standard service rifle. In my opinion a carbine similar to the Winchester would have admirably filled the bill, but the British brought out the No. 5 rifle which is merely a lightened version of the No. 4. Six inches off the barrel, a machining-off of the side of the butt, and the insertion of a rubber pad for the shoulder and the No. 4 became almost the No. 5.

I say almost since there are one or two differences. Naturally shortening of the barrel results in increase of flash, so a flash eliminator was introduced, and the muzzle flash on the No. 5 is now less than that on the No. 4. The weight of the No. 5 is 7 lbs., or something like 2 lbs. less than the No. 4; the maximum effective range is 1,000 yards, and a new eight inch steel blade bayonet was introduced for this rifle.

One interesting point about the No. 5 is that it can be used as a light mortar, hurling grenades a distance of about 250 yards. When used in this role the launcher is attached to the flash eliminator and a mortar sight fastened just above the breech. A second rubber pad is slipped over the butt. For high angle fire the butt is placed on the ground in the same manner as the now old-fashioned discharger cup for 36 grenades and S.M.L.E. combination. Low angle fire takes place from the shoulder, and up to ten grenades can be fired without undue discomfort.

With this rifle was introduced a cleaning "compact"; in substance much after the German cleaning outfit idea. The cleaning materials, pullthrough, flannellette, oil bottle, gauze and cleaning brush, are all neatly packed into a tin similar to a two ounce tobacco tin.

❊   ❊   ❊   ❊

Ross

When going to pre-Octu early in 1942 I was surprised that we were issued with the Ross rifle with its straight pull bolt action, and we used them for about a month. Some of the rifles were not too hot, but the one issued to me was quite a good shooting job, and I did fairly well with it although our shooting practices were very limited. There is no doubt that the Ross is a good target rifle—the King's Prize was won with a Ross in 1913 at Bisley—but it is hopeless for active service work; its complicated bolt renders it susceptible to interference from dust, grit and sand. Readers of McBride's splendid book will recall that the Ross rifle was issued to the Canadian Expeditionary Force in the early stages of World War I, but was almost immediately found unsuitable for trench warfare and discarded in favour of the S.M.L.E.

One of the most interesting features of the Ross to the accuracy loving rifleman was the backsight, which appears at first to be quite a comprehensive and intricate piece of work. It is a rather sad commentary on the methods used at pre-Octu that the backsight was never explained in detail to the embryo-officers. Maybe there was no instructor capable of the exposition! Such a sight goes some way to make extreme accuracy possible, but there were no fire-

[156]

arms fanatics amongst the instructors, and the rifle was mainly a tool necessary to drill with and with which to indulge in bayonet fighting. I must admit that with the short bayonet I found much pleasure in bayonet fighting with the Ross.

One or two of the fellows who had heard a little about the dangerous "straight pull bolt" actions were a little sceptical about using the Ross but, like McBride, I had never heard of a Ross bolt flying back and hitting anyone in the face; on the other hand I am told that there have been such accidents in America. I don't think that anyone at pre-Octu ever took the risk of stripping and re-assembling the Ross bolt; any accidents which may result from the use of the Ross are due to incorrect assembly of the bolt. When the breech is open the rear of the bolt-head should be about one inch from the sleeve. If it is only about $\frac{1}{4}''$ the bolt has been wrongly assembled and the rifle should certainly not be used.

❋ ❋ ❋ ❋

P 14

Of my beloved P 14 which accompanied me on the Great Adventure on June 5th, 1944 I can speak with a real affection, tempered with a great regret that orders being such as they were I could not find it possible to bring the rifle back with me when I left Germany in late January 1946. I would willingly have paid £20 or £30 for it, but there was no chance of purchase. Even in England, in 1943, when I wished to purchase a service rifle no one, and I contacted many parties, appeared to have any idea whatsoever of the method of procedure necessary for a serving soldier to purchase a service rifle, and I was looked upon in the light of an eccentric for having the temerity to make such a request.

Throughout, and particularly after the cessation of hostilities, I was greatly incensed by the way in which any man being a red-hot firearms enthusiast was looked upon as a potential criminal. Surely in an assessment of whether a man is a fit person to possess firearms (no matter how great the number) that man's service record should be a reliable, and indeed the sole, guide. But everyone was treated alike and, as is the way in these matters, one can safely wager that the "suspect" types were they who got their weapons home, and the real firearms-conscious, reliable people were unsuccessful. To ban all firearms because it may give rise to "murder potential" is ridiculous. Men, or women, seeking to murder will not stop because there are no firearms handy. One may as well ban all knives, table and otherwise, and pokers—and string!

My only criticism of the P 14 was the length of the butt; it was too big for a little fellow, and had I been lucky enough to retain it the shortening of the butt would have been the first job—because that rifle certainly could shoot!

Some P 14 rifles were fitted with a fine adjustment backsight, and these were used for sniping purposes in the 1914–1918 war before the advent of the telescope sight. Such rifles were denoted by the suffix F instead of T; the F, of course, denoting "fine adjustment." Other than the fine adjustment sight there was nothing special about the "F" rifles.

The P 14 was a conversion of the design of the .276 calibre weapon which was under consideration for the re-arming of the Forces prior to the World War I. A change of calibre on the outbreak of a war which would necessitate the complete change-over in the factories—not only those concerned with the rifle itself, but the ammunition—was entirely out of the question, and since it was thought the factories turning out the S.M.L.E. could not cope with the demand the British Authorities were forced to approach the USA as an additional supply source, and the American factories proceeded with the manufacture of the newly designed rifle in the .303 inch calibre.

❋   ❋   ❋   ❋

Owing to the fact that the locking lugs on the bolt are forward and therefore the bolt is not in a state of compression when a shot is fired, and that the body is stronger and the barrel heavier, accuracy at short ranges with the P 14 is much superior to that of the S.M.L.E. For this reason this rifle was, towards the end of World War I, fitted with a telescopic sight. When so fitted the designation of the rifle was Rifle No. 3 Mk. 1*(T). Fittings to take the telescope were fixed to the front of the top of the body and the left side of the backsight bracket. The telescope was fitted by means of two legs which hook under the front fitting of the rifle. The rear fitting on the telescope has a single leg, the squared end of which drops into the rear fitting on the left side of the rifle body, and is secured by a swing-over locking bolt. The telescope is sited centrally over the axis of the bore.

Particulars of the telescope. Pattern '18.

Magnification x 3.

Field of view $7\frac{1}{2}°$.

There is a focusing adjustment, and lateral adjustment is catered for optically. The reticule consists of a cross wire and a pointer. There is an adjustable range drum; the three adjustments to be made are:—1. Focusing: 2. Lateral: 3. Vertical.

✽ ✽ ✽ ✽

RIFLE No. 3 MK. 1*(T)A.

This is a P 14 rifle fitted with an Aldis 'scope sight. A small number of these attached by permanent fixings to the rifle were issued at an early stage of World War II. The telescope is similar in appearance to the P 18 but it has no optical lateral adjustment. This is catered for mechanically in the fitting which attaches the telescope to the rifle. Focusing and range adjustments are carried out in the same manner as for the P 18 'scope sight. The telescope is attached to the rifle on the left side and slightly above the body, not vertically above the centre line of the bolt as is the case with the combination of the P 14 rifle and P 18 telescope. This offset position is certainly not the most suitable place for a telescopic sight. In view of this telescope position a detachable cheek rest was made for use with this rifle and telescope. This, when attached, allows the firer to maintain a firm pressure on the butt with his cheek in the normal manner. The cheek rest issued with this rifle was shaped to the butt and attached by means of a single screw. It is rather interesting to record that once a cheek rest had been evolved for this rifle it was realised that the same, or a similar, rest would be of great assistance both with the normal equipment of both P 14 and P 18 telescopes, and also with the No. 4 rifle, for which a new sniper's telescope sight was in process of being. And, therefore, the cheek rest has become an issue for all sniper's rifles fitted with 'scope sights.

In my experience there were quite a number of snipers, and sniping instructors, who did not like the cheek rest at all. One Lovat sergeant maintained that he shot better without the cheek rest, and proved his point to his own satisfaction, and mine. But, generally speaking, if one has not got the cheek rest the majority of men must contort not only their face but the whole head, and maybe the shoulders, in order to get a correct view through the 'scope sight. And apart from the discomfort inherent upon such a procedure there is the added danger of any undue movement giving away one's position.

✤   ✤   ✤

Origin of the P 14

It may not be considered irrelevant here to very briefly sketch the evolution of the British Service rifle. The first service breech-loading rifle was adopted in 1864. This was the Snider. (Joseph Snider's breech action used in the

Enfield which had appeared in use in 1853; this had three grooved rifling and fired cartridges similar to the "Boxer".) The Snider, which had an external hammer, was of a calibre of .577 and revolutionised service shooting and may well be considered to have initiated musketry training. It was soon superseded by the Martini-Henry, a single loader rifle of .450 bore and hammerless action. (Martini breech action—Henry rifling.)

The .303 calibre was adopted in 1889 and a magazine rifle used for the first time. The magazine action, selected after many trials, was that designed by Lee (an American) and the rifling selected was designed by Metford, hence the rifle was named the Lee-Metford. The magazine held seven cartridges only.

The original .303 cartridge was designed for black powder and the rifling was of the shallow groove type. When cordite took the place of black powder it was soon shown that the shallow rifling did not give the barrel a long life owing to the increased wear caused by the hotter powder gases and higher velocities. After much experiment a deeper grooved type of rifling was adopted in 1899, and this was known as the "Enfield" rifling. It was married to the Lee breech action, and the new rifle was known as the Lee-Enfield; this rifle we refer to as the "Long" Lee-Enfield.

After the South African War a short rifle was adopted for all branches of the British Army, and this was the well-known Short Magazine Lee-Enfield, considered by many authorities as the finest "active service" rifle ever produced.

Round about 1911 the authorities decided to adopt a new cartridge which would give higher ballistics than the .303 which was, of course, designed in the days of black powder propellants. After much experimenting a bottle necked cartridge of .276 calibre was accepted; the bullet weighed around 130 grains and developed a muzzle velocity of 2,800 f.p.s. The authorities wanted 2,900. The pressure generated was much higher than that given by the .303 and it was considered that the Lee breech action was not strong enough to withstand the pressure of the new cartridge; the Lee action bolt having no forward locking lugs. An entirely new breech action was adopted, very similar to the Mauser action with its forward locking lugs. A number of these new rifles—they retained the Enfield rifling —were made at Enfield in 1913, and they were known as the P (attern) 1913 Enfield. They proved to be excellent shooting rifles, and when Britain entered the first World War in 1914 large orders were placed in America for this new rifle in the normal British service calibre of .303. (It was considered doubtful whether the S.M.L.E. factories could turn out sufficient quantities of the well-known, tried S.M.L.E., to equip the rapidly expanding Army, and in the stress of war it was not considered expedient to manufacture two calibres of ammunition.)

In the .303 calibre the new rifle became known as the P 14. Actually the Enfield people turned up trumps and produced enough S.M.L.E.s to cover all requirements and therefore when the shipments of the P 14 came over they were not issued to the "active service" forces, but the Home Defence organisation were armed with them. A number of P 14s—the quality of their accuracy being well-known—were used by snipers in World War I, and in conjunction with telescopic sights mentioned elsewhere it became the official British Army sniper rifle, and remained so, on paper at all events, until World War II, being finally superseded by the No. 4 Sniper rifle.

No doubt in the period between the two World Wars the thousands of P 14s were stored in armouries. (I have met many Territorials who had experience with them; and the P 14 has always been a big favourite with civilian service-riflemen.) They certainly saw the light of day again at the start of World War II, and particularly after Dunkirk when our fortunes were at a very low ebb many units of the British Forces were armed with them. They were withdrawn gradually as the No. 4 rifle appeared in ever increasing quantity. Ack ack units in England were armed with the P 14 throughout World War II. Odd P 14s were met in N.W. Europe; I should imagine that such rifles had been taken across because they were tried and trusted good shooting jobs as was the case with my own sterling Pattern 14.

The M 17 is, of course, the P 14 chambered to take the American service cartridge and was manufactured in thousands when America entered World War I in 1917. A large number of these rifles were shipped over to this country in 1940 and the Home Guard were armed with them. In England this rifle was widely, and erroneously, known as the P 17. In a way the man who uses the correct nomenclature of M 17 is recognised as a true knowledgeable rifle fan.

❋   ❋   ❋   ❋

No. 4 (T) Sniper Rifle

This sniper rifle, the standard sniping weapon of the British Army, was a selected No. 4 rifle of above average accuracy on factory test, fitted with two metal plates to take the telescope sight—No. 32 TS—a cheek rest and a special sling.

The 32 telescope sights were "paired" with rifles and were not interchangeable. The focus could not be altered, and the power of the 'scope was 3. The elevation drum mounted on top of the TS was graduated from 0 to 1000 yards and adjusted in 50 yards clicks in the case of the Mk. 1 sight, and in one minute clicks with the Mk. 11 and 111. Lateral adjustment was obtained by turning the deflection drum situated on the left side of the 'scope. Provided careful maintenance was observed the TS could be removed from a sniper's rifle and afterwards replaced without alteration to the zero being greater than one minute of angle—for practical purposes (i.e. at the ranges to which snipers were trained) almost negligible.

There were many snipers who thought that the No. 4 (T) was an extremely good and accurate rifle but was too heavy and clumsy when fitted with the 32 telescope sight. Ex-hunters thought that a rifle designed on the lines of a sporting rifle would have been much more useful, and one of them expressed the opinion that the leather sling with the sniper rifle was worse than useless, in fact, a positive hindrance, and that a broader, softer sling was required. A new, simpler sling of broad webbing was introduced after the war. This gave more support than its leather predecessor, and was not inclined to slip. It was a great improvement for wet weather—a leather sling was a damned nuisance when wet, and dried hard and stiff. The new sling required a keeper band for the loop and then it would have been quite good. I tried such a sling, along with a couple of Lovat Scout sergeants, and firing from about 120 yards at a Hun Head target which was difficult to pick up against its background on a wet morning, each firing five rounds, we scored fourteen hits.

Late in 1944 one or two modified No. 4 Sniper rifles made their appearance with a new style butt of Canadian make and, in place of the normal metal butt plate, there was a thick rubber recoil pad. I do not think this experimental job was given any special designation or modification number. Some of the reports on such rifles submitted by sniping instructors were laudatory, some adverse. To me these rifles appeared to be heavy and more clumsy and unwieldy than the normal butt type. But, as a small chap, I could shoot comfortably only with the smallest size of butt, and I much preferred the ordinary type of butt plate to the rubber pad. I found that the small of the butt of a service rifle in almost every case was much too thick for my right hand. Particularly so was this in the case of the No. 4s. I never came across a single rifle of this type with a small so slim that I could get a really comfortable grip with the right hand. My old S.M.L.E. was a very comfortable "small" and this, allied to a short butt, renders the rifle a delight to use.

When going down to the sniping school during its sojourn in Europe it was requested that the sniper, or sniper student, bring his sniping rifle with him. The condition of some of these rifles had to be seen to be believed; they were in a damned disgraceful condition, and, fired in such a state, would have been about as much use as an air rifle. There can be no greater proof of the lack of knowledge and crass ignorance shown in many units of the value of snipers, sniping and the sniper rifle than the woeful shape of some of the rifles I saw when I was at the school in Holland in March 1945. Some of these rifles were painted green, and it seemed that so long as the rifle was painted that colour the unit responsible thought that the rifle was O.K.—it had been camouflaged! In some cases the sights were useless; in others there were mechanical defects which rendered the weapon valueless for the normal rifleman's job, let alone the precision art of the sniper.

If the snipers' rifles were in such a condition, I shuddered to think of what the ordinary rifles were like! Small wonder that thousands of men never looked upon the rifle as their best friend. In any case this remark was overplayed by irritable NCOs in the men's recruit days; it was very rare that one came up against such an NCO who knew a great deal about rifles and shooting, and there was an almost complete lack of contagious enthusiasm. If an instructor is not a rabid enthusiast himself his activities will not yield any good results. To an ardent rifleman who venerates firearms it was sheer agony to see such maltreatment of weapons—and such a lack of appreciation.

Occasionally, at sniping school, one stumbled across a "rogue" rifle. The rifle I was first issued with there was of this type. With it I got two consecutive 1½" groups at 100 yards, and it was eminently capable of 100% on application of the zero at the same range; (6″ Bull) although I scored only 96%. But at 200 yards and beyond it became something of a scatter-gun. My performance at 200 yards at application and snap practices I considered woeful, and I was feeling terribly discouraged until I saw one of the Lovat Scout instructors, a very fine shot, take ten shots to get into the bull when he got down to test the rifle. In disgust he looked down at the number of the rifle—swore—and said that it had been condemned some time before and should never have been issued to me!

❊   ❊   ❊   ❊

TELESCOPE AND BINOCULARS

Part of the equipment for each sniper team was one Scout Regiment telescope, or, at least, it should have been. Opinions differ on the utility of the Scout Regiment telescope, but I lean towards the view held by the majority of the Lovat Scouts with whom I worked. Now these men, or many of them, were unexcelled in their use of the telescope; as deer-stalkers their job depended to a large extent on that ability, and they brought to the sterner game of war all the skill at observation they had gained in the wild hills and forests of the Highlands. The majority of them found the three-draw Scout telescope too bulky and clumsy, heavy and badly packed, and many went to the length of saying that it was entirely unsuitable for use by snipers. They preferred the two-draw Ross telescope, but said that it was high time a really good, light and smallish telescope appeared for service purposes. On the other hand some authorities still swear by the Scout Regiment telescope, maintaining that if one is to have a field of view, clarity and magnification, a large 'scope is inevitable. These people are against the introduction of the Ross (x 15) for the above reasons. (The Scout Regiment telescope magnified 20 diameters and had a $1\frac{1}{2}°$ field of view.) It was most important that every sniper became an adept with the telescope, which could penetrate deep shadows, show up enemy camouflage, and reveal such important details as badges of rank with ease.

One of the most difficult things in training men in the use of what might be termed precision instruments is to get over the fact that they are delicate and must be treated gently, with care, and that they must be fully maintained. Far too many men subscribed to the idea that weapons and war instruments were Government property and therefore needed no careful handling . . . that they could always be replaced! In my experience I saw really beautiful and extremely good binoculars ruined within a period of weeks by gross handling and lack of normal care in their use.

In the British sniping game much use was made of both binoculars and telescope; used side by side they formed a perfect observation team. As pointed out previously the sniper's telescope was the Scout Regiment, and although considered too bulky and unwieldy by some authorities, and archaic by others, there can be no doubt that it did a grand job of work in the hands of men who could use it, and get the best out of it. The stalking telescope is not an easy instrument to use, and use-perfection can only be obtained by long, constant practice. Some of the Lovat Scouts, ex-deer-stalkers, were experts with this telescope and quite frankly I was amazed by the ease in which they picked up camouflaged and hidden objects at long ranges. (I was told by one Scouts deer-stalker that it took a great many years' experience before one possessed even the rudiments of the usage of a stalking telescope!) It was essential that despite any initial difficulty a would-be sniper found in the handling of the telescope, he should become a master in its use. The telescope could find a well concealed man invisible to binoculars, and in good light it was possible to see troop movements well in excess of ten miles. Whether the Scout Regiment telescope was old-fashioned or not is really beside the point; the fact remains that it was a darned good instrument capable of sterling work.

The lenses in the telescope were of very soft glass, highly polished and easily scratched, and the cleaning of them called for great care. Stress was laid on the "flicking off" of dust, and polishing lightly. Greasy lenses were cleaned with methylated spirit. When damp the lenses fogged easily, but this was remedied by removing the object glass and eyepiece and placing them in a clean, dry place. Some lubrication of the draws was necessary to prevent sticking; grease was never used for this purpose. I always found that a very fine film of *thin* oil did the trick better than anything else.

One common fault found with men using the telescope was that they drew and closed the instrument quickly and roughly. Care was necessary in its carriage. One very useful tip to facilitate quick focussing was to mark the individual focus with a ring scratched on the rear draw. Many men, after using and closing the telescope, failed to adjust the eye-shutter and thus allowed dust and dirt to settle on the eyepiece.

Unless a man held the telescope correctly he could not hope to do good work with it. It must be held comfortably and still, and therefore rested on something. There were many ways of achieving this comfortable, rested position and one or two are shown in the photographs and illustrations. One very useful tip when using the 'scope was to sight the object desired to be scrutinised along the top of the telescope, and then without moving the instrument drop the eye to the eyepiece.

To avoid eyestrain it was essential that both eyes should be kept open; to many this was not an easy matter at first but came with practice. The power of concentration necessary in the full use of the telescope was very tiring, and in the field it was the usual practice for each man in the sniper team to use the telescope for about twenty minutes, and then pass it over to his companion.

I have used a Scout Regiment telescope as a "spotting" 'scope on indoor ranges under artificial lighting conditions, and have found it to be better than any normal "spotting 'scope." Many .22 riflemen using such ranges have been amazed at the clarity of this telescope.

Binoculars were, of course, much easier to use (yet it was astounding how many times they were misused) and at dusk, or on moonlight nights, with their power of illumination they were extremely useful. The average pair of binoculars used had a magnification of 7 diameters (my own were x10) with a field of view of some 7°. It was surprising to note how many men were unaware of the most elementary facts of focussing. I too must quite frankly confess that it was only at sniping school that I became fully aware of the full potentialities of fieldglasses and commenced to really *enjoy* using them.

A sniper team trained in observation—knowledgeable of the system of search and knowing what they were looking for—and equipped with a pair of binoculars and telescope had no excuse for missing anything on their particular sector from zero to miles back. What the naked eye saw but could not define could be confirmed by the binoculars, and that which could be discerned but not delineated by the fieldglasses was capable of clarification by the penetrative power of the telescope. Undoubtedly in the hands of men who were capable of getting the best out of them the binoculars and telescopes issued to snipers were a magnificent combination and worth their weight in gold.

❋   ❋   ❋   ❋

SWIFT TRAINING RIFLE

Fairly early in the War there came into being a monstrosity called the Swift Training Rifle. This was a device for teaching marksmanship in a small space indoors, or out, *without expenditure of ammunition and without noise or any danger.* I *underline* the farcical attributes! It consisted of a rifle which was similar to the service rifle in weight, shape and balance, and trigger pull, and had a breech bolt that had to be handled in the same way as when loading the normal rifle from a magazine. There was a target stand to which the rifle was fastened when in use; this stand moved freely so that it adjusted itself to any movements of the firer when he was taking up position, either prone, kneeling or standing. The target marker was a rod which was projected a short distance from the muzzle of the rifle, being propelled and almost immediately drawn back, by the action of springs. The rod was provided with a double marking end; one was sharp pointed and marked the actual impact of the "shot" and the other was lance-shaped, and hit below the aiming mark showing, if the paper was cut or distorted, that the rifle had been moved during the "up-the-barrel" period. Also, if the lance-mark was out of the perpendicular as regards the hole made by the *bullet*, it showed that the rifle, and therefore the sights, had been canted.

It was about this weird and wonderful invention that the leading shooting magazine in England said:—"With this ingenious piece of apparatus the whole of rifle training can be taught." To read such a eulogy of what the majority of riflemen surely thought a useless toy was enough to make one despair forever of the future of British shooting. I maintain that the use of the Swift training rifle was that it might possibly be used as a rather uncomfortable drawing-room game. And yet, in 1942, NCOs of my Regiment travelled hundreds of miles to take a *24-hours'-"course" on this "weapon,"* and I never knew one who did not come back to treat the matter as a huge joke.

In Feburary 1942 I was at the R.A.F. School of Musketry which was run by Flt. Lt. Hanson, probably one of the best all-round shots in the world, and an ardent enthusiast whose keen exuberance was contagious. The Swift Training Rifle was supposed to be one of the weapons we "took" —we saw it and immediately forgot it. It was clearly apparent that none of the instructors had any time for it. And I certainly had not! I have been amused many times by laudatory references to the weapon in the one or two magazines devoted to shooting in this country. Read this:— "The Swift Training Rifle is a rifle and target combined. It has the same weight, holding, balance, sighting, trigger release and bolt action as the Service rifle. It is a psychotechnical method of synthetic training which, besides training men to aim correctly, teaches them to effect subconsciously and automatically with a rifle having the characteristics of a Service rifle, the series of movements necessary to make a good marksman." (The Rifleman. June 1942.) In the same journal in March 1943 there appeared in the Correspondence Columns a letter from a Brigadier in which this extract appeared:—"It does great credit to the R.A.F. that they were first to clearly understand the immense advantages of musketry training's mechanisation aid to the self defence of their airfields by making their ground staffs excellent shots in the quickest and most economical way by using the Swift Training Rifle." My comments on this are brief since I know a good deal about the ground staffs' excellent shooting—the majority could not have hit a haystack at 100 yards; and I think it is to the eternal credit of the British Army that they had little to do with this, to me, idle toy.

I never came across an Army man who knew anything about the Swift. Any instructor knows that rifle shooting can be taught successfully *only by shooting*, and that the so-called "psychotechnical" method was entirely lacking in elementary psychology. The user of the Swift rifle knew that there was to be no noise, no "bang" and no recoil, and it is this noise and kick of which the recruit, who is at all nervous, is most afraid.

Three men whom I had for shooting training in 1943 were all gun shy, and, as a result, all were putrid shots. All three were inclined to be real nerve cases, and consequently I had plenty of patience with them. After the first time on the miniature range, firing the service rifle—.303— I talked to them quietly and seriously, and they settled down again on the firing point and fired a second time. The results were not much of an improvement—all three were flinching badly and their rifles were shaking all the time they were holding. I packed them in for the day, and the same evening I took them out with me, rabbit shooting, after borrowing a couple of 20 bores along with my single-barreled 12 bore. Rabbits were scarce that night and we did not get a shot, but on the way back I put up a couple of bottles on a fence and each one of the chaps had a crack at them from about 15 yards range, starting first with the 20 bores and then having a final shot with the 12. Naturally, at that range, they all three walloped the bottles, and I could see that despite being a little afraid of the loud report and the "seen" violent recoil when their companions fired, they were very pleased with themselves. I told them that compared to a shotgun the service rifle was a wee timorous beastie and so on.

The next morning I took them on to the short range again, and this time let them fire with a .22. Frankly, their shooting with the .22—it was not a particularly good specimen, but was the only one available—was more deplorable than with the service rifle on the previous day, and therefore I was not really surprised when he whom I had considered the most nervous of the bunch asked could he fire his service rifle again, since he did not like the .22; he said that the plop of the .22 put him "off" more than the roar of the .303. (Curiously enough I have the same experience—I cannot become accustomed to the noise of a .22; the pip and squeak always puts me off, and I somehow always wait for the plop rather than concentrate on

[172]

my aim and release!) All three men did much better with the .303 rifle, particularly when I and my sergeant were down alongside them. To cut a long story short all three men passed out as second-class shots a week or two later on the open classification range, and one of them eventually merited first-class qualification.

Mention of .22s reminds me that in 1943 I endeavoured to purchase a .22 rifle for training purposes, and was offered one by a leading British Miniature Rifle organisation on the condition that my unit became affiliated to the organisation and paid the membership fees. Since I required the rifle solely for service training purposes and was quite willing to pay £10 or so out of my own pocket for it, and we were at War, I took a very poor view of this organisation's attitude, and naturally refused to accede to such a condition.

A further illustration of the big part played by nerves in a man's shooting was shown when my CO ordained that every man in the Squadron should shoot for his pay; that is, unless every man qualified as a second-class shot at least, there would be a rigid adherence to the classification rules and a man would come down and lose pay in consequence. At the end of these practices there were nine men in the Squadron who had not qualified as second-class shots, and in their midst there was much wailing and weeping and gnashing of teeth. The CO was very decent about it, and told me to take these chaps up to the range as often as possible, and afford them every chance of qualifying. This went on for a couple of weeks and still the nine did not make the grade. In the end, on one particularly fine morning, I took them on to the range again and said:—"Now, look here! This morning you have to qualify, and I, personally, will see that you do—understand!" The substance, and tone, of the speech was obvious, and they settled down quite happily on the firing point. They were, in effect, shooting that morning without the nerve bug of "loss of pay" predominant in their minds. You may guess the result. There was not a single fellow in the nine who did not pass the second-class shot qualifying standard by at least ten points, and one of them actually put up first-class shot scoring! And the practices were at 100, 200 and 300 yards ranges, and included snap and rapid!

*　　*　　*　　*

The 10-Shot Magazine

Many riflemen hold the opinion that one of the blessings of the British service rifle (the S.M.L.E. or the No. 4) is the 10-shot magazine, and one of the questions I have been asked frequently is "How did you find the ten-round magazine?" I think the majority of men who fought in N.W. Europe will agree that it was not a rifleman's war. It *could have been;* the fault lay in the fact that far too much emphasis had been laid on firepower, and the average man armed with a rifle as his personal weapon did not fully understand its powers nor was he capable of using it as it should have been used. There were very few riflemen in the full, acute sense of the word. But having this "fire power consciousness" when rifles were loaded they were filled to capacity; any man would get more of a psychological kick out of having ten rounds in his rifle than five. It is no exaggeration to say that the *true use* of the rifle was mainly restricted to snipers and sniping.

In many cases in actual practice I personally doubt whether this magazine-filled-to-capacity fetish was a good thing. The magazine springs in the No. 4 were notoriously fickle, and at a critical moment it was quite likely that there might be a "jam." In rapid fire practices on ranges in England there were very frequent cases of sticking magazine springs, resulting in many "hot and bothered" shooters. (It was surprising how many men suffered from a mild attack of nerves similar to "buck fever" when on the firing point!) There was much swearing as the individual saw his chances of winning the inevitable sweep fade as the result of getting away only a couple of shots instead of ten. (The magazine springs of the S.M.L.E. were good, but then this rifle has always been regarded as a true craftsman's job.)

Many range rapid fire practices were a waste of time and ammunition since a large number of men were of little use in normal slow firing practices. But, on the other hand, there were occasions when men put up better scores firing rapid than when firing normally. In some cases this brought to light the fault with the individual—dwelling too long on aim. Many of the rapid practices were fired at 300 yards range and I have had examples of men putting eight or nine shots in the bull and inner rings (bulls and inners together counted the maximum points in rapid shooting) when they could rarely do better than magpies in application shooting from that range. Taking far too long on aim was a common fault, resulting in high nerve tension and unsteadiness and in many cases men I trained improved 100% when the fault was pointed out to them.

Unless there was a collective target it should not have been necessary for a sniper to use a number of cartridges—the first for the individual target should have been the last and only one! In the case of a surprise patrol target at short range the sniper was told that the quickest, most effective shooting might be done by using iron sights, but that, of course, was impossible if the TS was always carried fixed to the rifle. And that was a matter for the individual sniper; some preferred to carry the TS in a pocket of the smock until they reached their position, and then fix it, carefully and without undue movement; others much preferred to fix the 'scope before setting out. When the telescope sight was fitted, cartridges were loaded singly; the number loaded were varied according to the ideas of the individual sniper.

A rifle loaded to schedule capacity had nine cartridges in the magazine and one in the breech. In rapid practices on the range the usual procedure was for the rifleman to have four cartridges in the magazine, one in the breech, and a clip of five rounds by his side; this necessitated a reload during the practice and it was amusing to see how many times men failed to count the number of rounds fired and therefore "fired" on an empty breech; their frantic haste in reloading the clip which often caused a jam and their erratic, uneven bolt action which frequently resulted in two rounds seeking to enter the breech at the same time! Rapid practices to some men were hell, and no amount of instruction got them out of the habit of "erratic rapidity."

There can be no doubt that on such occasions as that at Mons in 1914, when the highly trained regular British infantrymen halted the Hun hordes with accurate and devastating rifle fire, the ten shot magazine was a blessing. In service training it was laid down that it was the duty of the rifleman on active service to ensure that his magazine was kept fully charged, hence when an action was finished he should have known how many rounds he had expended and thus replenish his magazine to capacity. In actual practice I always thought that to keep nine rounds in the magazine for any length of time was courting jam trouble, but, in all fairness, I must say that a good deal of magazine and loading troubles was occasioned by the rifleman himself; if he lacked "touch" there was trouble. If a man drives a car without that same fine touch he never gets the best out of it; a rifle is a wonderful piece of mechanism and to give of its best it must be handled with thought and understanding.

*　　*　　*　　*

FOREIGN WEAPONS

Mauser Kar 98K · *German Sniper Rifles and Equipment* · *Gewehr 41* · *Gewehr 43* · *German Automatic Rifle Sniper* · *Austrian Steyr-Mannlicher 8mm* · *German Machine Guns MG 34 and 42 Schmeisser* · *MP 44* · *.22* · *Sporting Rifles and Shotguns* · *Mannlicher-Carcano 6.5mm* · *French Rifles American Weapons*

During my time in N.W. Europe it was but natural that I should take every opportunity of using the divers types of weapons with which I came into contact. Many had the same idea, but in the majority of cases it was from sheer idle curiosity, and not from a *real interest*. Probably the enemy weapon which was used most by Allied troops was the German Mauser rifle, and it was astonishing to hear how many men thought this rifle to be superior to the British and American service rifles. I write "astonishing" but that is a mild term, since at least 95% of the men who uttered such statements hardly knew from which end of a rifle the bullet appeared; most certainly they couldn't *use* a rifle of any type, so their complacent verdict just arose from that queer foible which is so prevalent of extolling anything which is thine enemies and slinging mud at that which is thine own.

Once, for a joke, I took a man who had been talking a lot of rot about the superiority of the German weapons compared with our own down on the 25 yards range we had built when static in Holland in the winter of '44-'45. We carried a No. 4 rifle—belonging to the culprit—a Kar 98K of mine (which was a good shooting job at short ranges), a Walther pistol, my S & W .38, a Sten carbine and a Schmeisser. I told the chap that I looked forward with keen interest to his substantiating his deprecatory remarks about our weapons by putting up some excellent targets with the 98K, the Walther and the Schmeisser. I fired the No. 4, the .38 and the Sten. My targets were not bad, and malicious though it may appear I found the green and yellow jaundiced appearance of my companion's face pleasing. Anyhow he proceeded to do his best with the German weapons, and a damned poor best it was too. At twelve paces he never once hit the standard pistol target in six shots with the Walther; anyone standing in front of him at 25 yards when he was using the Schmeisser would have escaped unscathed, and with the Mauser he had only four shots on the Hun Head target at 25 yards! He then used the British rifle, Sten and pistol and although his performances were really shocking by all shooting standards he certainly improved on his showing with the German weapons. He returned to his section in very chastened mood, and never again was he heard to speak glowingly of the Huns' armoury!

I fired a good deal with the Mauser Kar 98K which was given to me by an officer in the Belgian Maquis in September 1944. (Kar 98K—a carbine model of the normal Mauser M 98, with a barrel length of 23½″ against the 29.15″ of the M 98; a great number of these carbines were in use in the German Army.) This rifle or carbine was almost new and, apart from the barrel which was typical of practically all weapons which the various Allied Maquis possessed in that it had never been cleaned at all, it was in very good condition. At ranges up to 300 yards I found this Mauser to be accurate, and the open sighting was, in my opinion, a more accurate form of sight than that of the old S.M.L.E. the heavy, broad-based tapering foresight dovetailing into the V notch much more *easily* than the thin blade foresight which was a feature of the standard, earlier British army rifle. But to anyone familiar with the crisp, clean and easy bolt action of the S.M.L.E. and the No. 4, the Mauser bolt was nothing but a headache, and absolutely hopeless for anything in the nature of rapid fire. If one filled the magazine and fired the five rounds fairly quickly it took quite an effort to open the bolt for the last round. The furniture of these rifles—of 1940–1942 vintage—was very poor and on more than one occasion I saw definitely warped butts. Another feature of the normal German service rifle, to many, was the almost vicious kick which every rifle of this type possessed. Personally I never really noticed this unpleasantness, probably due to the fact that my favourite No. 4 rifle which I picked up out of the sea on D plus 1 had itself a very hefty recoil, a feature which was remarked upon rather ruefully by everyone whom I allowed to use it. Having got used to this more than average kick I, unlike the majority, was never really acutely conscious of the recoil of the Mauser.

I always considered the Mauser to have unpleasing lines, and in assessing its capabilities as impartially as possible I place it a long way behind the No. 4 and the Springfield. The safety catch on the Mauser was a clumsy contrivance, and very awkward of manipulation. But I do grant that it was a "mobile" weapon.

✻   ✻   ✻   ✻

There was not as much standardisation in the German sniping equipment as in the British. The German sniper

[179]

rifle was the normal Mauser service weapon, 98, or Kar 98K, equipped with fittings to take telescopic sights; the telescope sight was by no means standard, and although the number of sniper rifles with which I came into contact was comparatively small I cannot recollect seeing two 'scopes of the same make. One can say roughly that they fell into two classes—small and large.

One of the telescopic sights was very small, little thicker than a man's finger and about 6″ long. This was fitted to the rifle slightly forward of the point of balance, and in some theatres was found more frequently than the larger type. The field of view was small and there were many who thought that it was almost useless for practical sniping.

The large types of telescopic sight were roughly the same size as the British 32 'scope. In some cases they were 4 or 5x hunting 'scopes, with large objective and ocular lenses which were superior in light transmission and resolving power than the British equivalent. On the majority of these German sights the method used to alter deflection was by moving the forward end of the sight sideways in a dove-tailed bracket fixed on the rifle. This to many was a most unsatisfactory method since it was almost impossible to make a really fine adjustment. Both small and large sights were, generally speaking, good from the point of view of clarity and power, but some British authorities held the opinion that they sadly lacked a practical range or deflection adjustment. Personally I do not altogether share this view since it will have already been apparent that I favour the cause of the simple TS. I hold that if the German sniper were good—and there is no doubt that the true German sniper was a master of his art—and knew his rifle and 'scope intimately the apparent "no-practical-adjustments" would make little difference to his shooting, and his killing!

The field of view and the clarity of all the telescope

sights I examined and used were extremely good. Many
people have expressed the opinion that the reticule arrangements on these German sights were poor, mainly consisting as they did of thick cross hair and central pointer,
the latter meeting the cross hair base at the point of
interruption as shown in the sketch. I am quite aware of
the antipathy both in England and America to this type
of sight (the type is shown as a "poor reticule" in Whelen's
"Telescopic Rifle Sights" page 5; the same classification
is accorded to the type of reticule in the British 32 TS),
but I have found it to be really good, and one of these
sights allied to my No. 4 rifle, even with a temporary,
and ill-turned, mounting resulted in, to me, the finest
shooting combination I have ever handled. If I were handi-
capped in the manner which so-called authorities say
that I must be, namely the thick cross wires obscuring
the target and cutting out a certain amount of light, then
I was not conscious of the fact. And once having found
by experimental, and practical, shooting the true zero,
and the working of the elevation and deflection adjustments, I was quite prepared to tackle anyone armed with
the normal British sniper rifle and 32 TS on any form of
true sniping target at any range up to 500 or 600 yards.
This combination allied to a h.v. .303 cartridge would
certainly give me a very fine sniper's rifle!

The method of attachment of the German 'scopes was
quite simple and did the job effectively. Many regarded
it as much inferior to our own screwed arrangement, but
personally I have not a very high opinion of either the
British or the German method but would much prefer a
mounting such as that on the Springfield sniper rifle.

Although the normal type of 'scope on the German
service rifles had reticules similar to that shown in the
sketch I frequently met another form of reticule which was
mainly found in TS mounted on hunting rifles, but was
occasionally found in sniping 'scopes. This type shown in

the sketch found many detractors; I found it satisfactory myself, but must admit at once that I never used it in anything but good light. One of the finest sniping shots in the British Army however has expressed a decided preference for this type of reticule, comparing it favourably with the British type saying that it was easy to lose the

"A"   Form of reticule found in many German hunting telescope sights, and the type frequently found in the TS mounted on German sniper rifles.
"B"   Form of reticule found in many German sniper's TS.
"C"   Most popular form of reticule in British sniper Telescope sight.

British pointer in failing light against a dark background, and he would have incorporated it in his ideal telescope sight. German sniper rifles in Italy were frequently found with this reticule.

Another point to the detriment of the German service rifle often put forward was that it was on the heavy side. The weight difference between the German and British service rifles was a matter of only a few ounces, but since the Mauser was more clumsy in appearance and handling properties it seemed to be much heavier.

One thing which struck me as being very peculiar was that, on occasion, we came into contact with 3-barrel guns (rifle-shotguns) fitted with large telescope sights. The rough details of one of the best of these sights are:—Make: "Ebra." Power:—x8. Type of reticule:—as normal Army TS (see sketch). Length:—14¼ inches. Diameter of eye lens:—1⅜ inches; field lens:—2⅛ inches. This sight has a focusing device in the form of a knurled ring around

LATE MODEL OF GERMAN SEMI-AUTOMATIC SNIPER RIFLE

Upper: THE GERMAN MAUSER RIFLE fitted with light telescopic sight which has exceedingly long eye relief and can be mounted well ahead of the action, permitting normal manipulation of bolt.

Lower: THE BRITISH No. 4 RIFLE—Sniper—fitted with their 32 telescopic sight. This rifle is specially stocked for sniper use.

the body, similar to British binocular focusing, and the normal German ungraduated range drum. Alteration of deflection is obtained in the usual German manner by turning a key operating on a dovetail joint on the rear point of attachment—rather like the way an ordinary rifle foresight is held in place. We also found ordinary, double barrel shotguns fitted with telescopic sights.

Gewehr 41

I had a brief acquaintance with the German semi-automatic rifle, the Gewehr 41, and found this to be quite a fair weapon of sound basic design. But it was not so handy as the Garand; it was heavy (nearly 11 lbs.) and, to me, clumsy, and anyone familiar with the Garand would regard the GW 41 as being unnecessarily complicated. One interesting feature was the method of gas operation; the barrel was not "tapped" as in most gas-operated weapons. After firing the expanding gases were trapped in a cone attached to the muzzle, and drove back a floating piston which operated the rifle. The magazine capacity was ten normal German 7.9mm service cartridges.

The Gewehr 43 was a later model of the 41 and more mobile, with a length of 43″ against 45″, and a comparatively much lower weight, approximately 9 lbs.

The German automatic sniper rifle was the Gewehr 43 plus a telescope sight, and some examples of this late-in-the-war developed weapon were extremely shoddy; one officer has gone so far as to say that the rifles of this type were made of the poorest materials he had ever seen used in any firearms. Certainly the finish bears no comparison with the first Hun semi-automatic rifles. The telescope sight mounted on this rifle, although similar in many ways to the normal German sniper rifle 'scope, is inferior in others, and altogether the composite job is suspect from the point of view of utility and service.

Details of the sniper semi-automatic rifle shown:—

Markings on rifle:—K 43. "45." Number.

Telescope sight:—"GW Z F 4" plus a series number which does not correspond with number on rifle. Length. 6½" approx. Power not specified but taken to be approximately 3, or 4. Range drum on right side of body, graduated in 100 metre clicks from 0—800.

The somewhat primitive deflection drum on top of body has a removable dust cover; this, in common with most German 'scope sights can only be adjusted by means of loosening three screws. The sight has a leather protector similar to the British type except that one end is formed by a rubber eyepiece about 2" long which can be removed from the protector and fitted to the sight before firing; this is a good idea since the sight itself is rather a long way from the eye in the normal firing position.

❋   ❋   ❋   ❋

To anyone who knows the sniper ropes as they should be known it is almost sacrilegious to talk of an automatic sniper rifle! Once again we have the onus of "lead spewing" ascribed to sniping. Talk of the Garand being used for sniping has always been cacophony to a true sniper's ears, and it is my fervid hope that the British authorities will never contemplate the use of an automatic, or semi-automatic, sniper rifle. Automatic rifles mean weight; the tendency for the ideal sniper rifle should be less weight, not an increase. We must not lose sight of the fact that the rifle is but part of the sniper's make-up and must be carried as an accessory only in the preliminary part of the sniper's action—he has to get to places before he can use it.

There were many men who could distinguish semi-automatic rifle fire as distinct from normal rifle fire. I have heard it described as a "thump-lash"—like the bull roar of an elephant gun to the delicately tuned ear of the fire-arms expert.

If a man is given an automatic rifle there is always the

danger of his blazing away indiscriminately. And to the argument that with an automatic rifle the sniper will not be subjected to movement of reloading the answer is that there is more actual "firing movement" with the automatic.

And where is the automatic rifle which has the basic accuracy of *the sniper rifle?*

No—the ideal for the sniper remains the selected hand operated rifle, firing the one true shot which counts for everything—the killer!

✳   ✳   ✳   ✳

AUSTRIAN STEYR-MANNLICHER 8MM

My first acquaintance with this rifle in World War II provided another example of firearms ignorance displayed by members of the British forces. When I arrived at Fassberg in Germany in April 1945 I was met by an excited NCO who told me that he had found a German armoury which contained about 150 French rifles and a good deal of ammunition. I asked him what model they were, but could get no satisfactory answer. Within an hour I had been told about these French rifles by two of my brother officers, and then another officer produced one of the rifles, again with the remark that it was "French" and a "Lebel." I recognised it immediately as an Austrian Steyr-Mannlicher, 8mm, with the straight pull back bolt action.

On the following day I went along to the German armoury and selected a really good specimen from the rifles remaining there and about 100 rounds of ammunition. The barrel length of this rifle was about 30 inches, and the total weight 8¼ lbs. The S-M is the official rifle of the Austrian and Bulgarian armies and many thousands were used by the Italians in World War II, presumably part of the booty taken from Austria after World War I.

Having heard at some time or other that it had been claimed that this type of rifle was capable of firing 35

unaimed shots in the minute I decided to try it out at the
first opportunity, and must admit that I was very sceptical
about the efficiency of the straight pull backwards and
forwards bolt action to go through such a test without
jamming. I was conversant with other types of the straight
pull back action; the Ross and the Swiss Schmidt-Rubin;
which I had found to be sadly lacking in rapid fire qualities
when compared with the slick S.M.L.E. of the sweetest
bolt action in the world. I managed to get off ten rounds
with growing difficulty in bolt manipulation before the
use of a mallet became necessary! Only slight practical
knowledge is required to see why this type of bolt action
has never achieved wide popularity. Theoretically this
bolt is much faster to operate than a turning bolt, but
factually the S.M.L.E. and the No. 4 can be operated faster,
due to the fact that in the turning bolt the primary extraction of the fired case fitting tightly in the chamber is
brought about by the direct leverage of the bolt knob in
its upward movement. In the straight pull through type
such leverage is not present. I found the Steyr-Mannlicher
quite accurate up to the limit of the ranges fired—300
yards—and there was little kick and the rifle handled quite
well, except, of course, that my lack of stature did not lend
itself to the usage of such a long rifle. The ammunition
used, though of the same make and from the same box,
showed a good deal of variation in elevation.

✻   ✻   ✻   ✻

Machine Guns MG 34 and 42

No one who heard the angry "drrrup" of a Spandau
can ever forget it. Both these machine guns were marked
by a beautiful simplicity of design, and once one had
fired them and become used to their high rate of fire, one
was certainly filled with admiration for them. But I still
adhere to my conviction that in the matter of machine
guns during a hot attack, or at any other time, nothing

would have been so effective as a twin .303 Browning had a suitable ground mounting been devised for them. Statistics may prove that the Spandaus were high in the table of lethal weapons, but personally I doubt it. Their terrific rate of fire was a doubtful advantage, and as has been shown elsewhere there was late in the European campaign in certain areas some attempt at conservation of ammunition by interspersing the much maligned wooden-bulleted cartridge in the Spandau belts or saddle type drums.

But there was certainly one thing in which the Spandaus stood supreme. Morally they were the most devastatingly effective ground weapon of the war!

❋   ❋   ❋   ❋

THE SCHMEISSER

This was a thoroughly well designed weapon for its job, and although inclined to be heavy it was delightful to use even if only on account of its finish. Frankly it was no more destructive than its most humble progeny, the Sten, which the British produced when a machine carbine was needed most urgently.

In general the design of the German weapons was good, and the workmanship in all early models was excellent, but this tailed off progressively as the war continued, and towards the end it was possible to find certain German weapons which fell below the danger point. But the Schmeisser continued to be a perfectly well turned out job right to the conclusion of the war in Europe.

On June 7th, 1944 I picked up a Schmeisser carbine and a Walther pistol, and it was interesting to see the difference in the steel of the two weapons. The Walther was, or had the appearance of, a very new job, and yet although it had lain on the side of a ditch probably for only a matter of a few hours the barrel was in poor state, and did not respond at all well to cleaning; but the Schmeisser which bore signs of hard usage on June 6th, was in perfect shape despite having been in a similar spot, and cleaned up as bright as a new penny.

❊ ❊ ❊ ❊

MP 44

The MP 44, an improved type of automatic machine carbine made its appearance in N.W. Europe rather late in the campaign, and it is a fact that many men who saw the carbine never saw the ammunition it used. I remember accompanying an officer on an inspection of a German ammunition dump just after the War and finding some thousands of rounds of this special cartridge, which is of the same calibre as the normal German rifle and machine gun ammunition—7.9mm—but whose length is only48mm against the standard's 80mm, and my companion remarking that although he had seen many captured MP 44s he had not before come across the ammunition.

The Huns were very proud of this automatic carbine with its rate of fire of 456 r.p.m. and, according to their reports, it proved to be very successful in battle on the Eastern front, and it was commented upon very favourably by many German commanders. So effective was it considered that it was officially decorated by Hitler who bestowed upon it the title of "Sturmgewehr"—assault rifle.

It was this weapon which came very prominently in to the military, and general public (who like to read of something sensational even though they know nothing about it) eye when it was fitted with a novel curved barrel attachment which swung a bullet through an angle of 32° and therefore made it possible to fire over cover, and around corners, and to hit targets out of visual sight of the firer.

This "round the corner" weapon was one of the secret weapons destined to hold up the Allied advance, but it was produced too late for general use, and there are no instances of it being used against British or American troops, although there are Russian reports that it came into action against them being used by German tankmen to kill tank destroying units. Tank crews could fire it from the inside of a tank against close-quarter attackers.

A number of these weapons were issued to the forward German elements in Europe but these were captured before they had been used. When the British experts first saw these many of them laughed, and thought it a waste of time and money to test such a grotesque weapon. At the same time the opinion was current that the man who attempted to fire it would certainly be seriously wounded if not killed. But the weapon worked and was found to be effective at ranges up to about 100 yards. The working explanation is simple. A small explosive charge forces the bullet up the barrel to the curved attachment, and the ten small holes bored into the curved barrel allow the gases to escape and so reduces the velocity of the bullet as it rotates through the remainder of the barrel. A periscope sight fitted to the front of the attachment enables the firer to look along the carbine, and out of sight of the enemy, see and engage any target within 32° of his line of sight. By tilting the carbine on to its side it is possible to fire around left and right hand corners, if the firer and weapon are supported by sandbags, but this is not the purpose for which the weapon was designed. Firing in this way would certainly cause some discomfort on account of recoil, and thus impair accuracy. The original idea of the carbine was to fire from beneath cover. One remaining feature is that the end of the curved barrel is straight so that the bullet continues its flight on a straight course when it leaves the barrel.

Once again the popular press reared its unknowledgeable head and talked about a weapon which could be used for "sniping"!

The general opinion of the straight MP 44 was that it

was an interesting experiment, but that, as one officer put it, it was neither "fish, flesh nor fowl." I did not come across many examples of this weapon, but those I saw were poorly made throughout, and bore little resemblance to the excellent craftsmanlike jobs we had come to expect from Jerry at the beginning of the War.

❁ ❁ ❁ ❁

.22 RIFLES

There could be no doubt about the quality, the finish and the accuracy of the German .22s. There were a large number of the normal German service Mauser with .22 barrels, and these I found excellent for both target and rabbit shooting. The German .22 ammunition however was vastly inferior, in my experience, to the American and British type.

I was privileged to use only one or two German sporting rifles, but these too were wonderfully finished weapons, and extremely good to fire. I used a large number of German shotguns of all gauges and found them all excellent. They were good killing guns; even one ancient, but well preserved, pin-fire weapon did everything one asked of it. It was interesting to see that the 16 gauge gun far outnumbered the 12 bore. One double-barrelled 16 bore-cumrifle (3-barrel gun) had a most interesting gadget. When the slide which brought into action the rifle firing pin was pushed forward, a V notched rearsight was raised towards the breech-end of the twin barrels. The foresight was a white enamelled barley-corn.

❁ ❁ ❁ ❁

MANNLICHER-CARCANO 6.5MM

I used an Italian service rifle on ranges once or twice but had a very poor opinion of them. I reckon that it is about the worst service rifle I have ever handled.

❁ ❁ ❁ ❁

There were a number of French rifles left behind in the beach-head area in Normandy, together with a large quantity of French ammunition. These were the Lebel M' 16, 8mm; the Mas M 26, 7.5mm and the Lebel M 34, 7.5mm. I never had the opportunity of *seriously* trying these rifles, but I fired the Lebel M 34 without being enamoured with its capabilities.

✻   ✻   ✻   ✻

AMERICAN WEAPONS

Frankly I have nothing but praise for the Winchester Carbine M 1, and my enthusiasm and regard was shared by many other British officers and men. It was light, handy and stood up to really rough usage.

My own carbine had had a chequered career. Who used it first I know not, but I do know that it came to me via the Wilhelmina canal and a Canadian. It had apparently been used during the early fighting in the Dutch salient since it was recovered from the canal, at that time dry in the particular vicinity in which it was found, in late October 1944 by the man concerned in its sale to me, along with a Garand, cleaned up a little (but not much) and used later in more than one tour of the forward areas. I finally got it for the meagre sum of 60 marks (30/-), my bid being 10 marks more than the next would-be purchaser, when the Canadian was leaving Germany for repatriation. The carbine was in good condition, and by the time I had spent a number of loving hours cleaning and crooning over it, the barrel was brilliant and unblemished and the whole shone like something good out of a gunsmith's catalogue.

The first time I fired the carbine was at about 100 yards range at a Hun head-type target. The first five shots made quite a good group on the target, MPI being just topside centre. Two other officers who were on the range with me also fired five rounds, and nine more holes appeared in the target, the tenth shot being just above. One of these officers had used a Winchester before and spoke enthusiastically about it; the other whose first experience it was immediately became a fanatic, and I understand did not rest until he became the proud possessor of one. Back from the 200 metres firing point using the same sight it took me about three shots to get into the bull, the first being low inners. Once in the bull there was no difficulty in keeping the score at possible, and I remember one morning taking the carbine down to the range when we were putting a course through normal grouping and application practices with the rifle, and astounding the chaps by plugging bull after bull with the carbine from 200 yards, putting up a score which equalled the best of the riflemen there; from the 300 yards point I was not good but even so scored higher points than many of the men with the rifle.

For handiness, mobility and ease of shooting from any position this little carbine was certainly the finest weapon I have ever handled. My usage of it later was great, indeed it was limited only by the scarcity of ammunition. During my time at the Training Centre I forever plugged for its use by the second man of the sniper team. It seemed to me to be the ideal weapon for the sniper's mate, since it was capable, in the hands of the right man, of almost sniper-like accuracy up to 200 yards. When running the Sniper instructor's course for NCOs of my Regiment I introduced the use of the carbine in this role, and made quite a number of converts. During the sniper team stalks one of the men was armed with the sniper rifle, and the second man carried the carbine. Once they had got into a position for a "kill" on the dummy targets used I allowed the second man to have a "go" with the carbine, and two of the NCOs shot as well with it at ranges up to 150 yards as they did with the rifle.

I used this carbine for hunting, and found that the cartridge was, on occasion, powerful enough to drop roe deer at ranges up to 150 yards. I know that many people, including American service men, expressed, forcibly, the opinion that the carbine was of little use for hunting purposes, and that, as issued, it failed on small deer. One man reported to me that he had hit a roe at about 70 yards and that the deer just bounded away wounded, and not seriously at that! I heard of other similar instances, but such incidents as these do not constitute proof that the carbine was of no use for small game. More than once I saw deer hit by .303 British service cartridges, and bound away—and not to die within a few yards of being hit. And when reading of such incidents one must remember that the British service cartridge is supposed to be far too powerful for the biggest of red deer. Is is not a matter of hitting but where one hits. And I am quite convinced that any one using the Winchester carbine, and *being able to use it*, on a small deer at ranges of from zero to 150 yards would bag the animal providing the hit was in the heart or lungs region. Such a hit is well within the prowess of anyone who *can* shoot with the carbine. With the service cartridge as issued it was possible to put five shots into a 6″ group at 150 yards, and even when the service cartridges were "treated"—made into expanding type by filling and drilling cavities in the nose—a similar group was obtained. Incidentally such expanding cartridges were a little suspect by some individuals since they thought there was a danger of losing the core, but I never heard of a case where a jacket had become lodged in the bore. These impromptu hollow-nosed bullets certainly resulted in a higher percentage of clean kills on deer than the hard-nosed service cartridges. But one of my students in January 1946 secured a lovely roe with one round from my carbine at a range of about 80 yards; it was a killing shot in the right shoulder the animal not moving more than a yard.

I understand that amongst American service men there was some agitation about the carbine being uncomfortable in all positions, due to the protruding magazine and short pull, and that confusion was caused by mistaking the safety and the magazine catches. The latter I think was a justifiable complaint, and a fault in the design. But I certainly do not agree that the carbine is uncomfortable in all positions. In fact, I think it lends itself admirably to any position. I know that I have never been very much good in the off-hand position with a rifle, but with the carbine I shot quite well in that position, especially when using the thin sling, which with me, being a small, short-armed fellow, was probably used in an unorthodox manner and one for which it was not designed. Really my only serious criticism in relation to the Winchester carbine was the varying quality of the ammunition. When putting on demonstrations of shooting with this weapon I had always to go carefully over the ammunition available and make a serious selection. There were a large number of defective rounds, and I should say that many showed lack of stability to weather and storage conditions.

It was amusing to read in one journal that the Germans were developing a carbine after the style of the American Winchester, a carbine which would, however, be much heavier and firing a new and very powerful bottle-necked cartridge, a shortened version of the normal German 7.9mm rifle cartridge, with a powder capacity of 32.0 grains, and a pointed bullet which would almost have the same muzzle velocity of the standard rifle cartridge—2,700 f.p.s. This carbine turned out to be the MP 44!

Some time ago I asked a former colleague for his opinions on American weapons. He said:—

"The Winchester carbine is an excellent little trick. I can claim to know this weapon fairly well as you are aware. I carried one for a long time as my personal weapon, and it gave me every satisfaction, particularly on patrol and close quarter work on which we were primarily engaged. I found it extremely accurate and hard hitting up to 250 yards; it may be more though I have never tested it for longer ranges than 250; however, I should say that its velocity, with all that that implies, falls off pretty rapidly above that range. Its lightness and robustness make it well suited to active service. In view of such praise it appears a little hard to put forward any faults, but I have three 'grouses' as follows:—

"1. The return spring is inclined to be weak, though this may be inevitable.

"2. Partly as a result of (1) the action is rather prone to become stuck when fouled by sand or other foreign bodies under service conditions and usage.

"3. Extraction is not as good as it might be, due I think to a weak extractor spring."

(This report struck me as being a very fair summing-up of the weapon's capabilities; as to the faults I never experienced them myself with my carbine. During sniper training, at Sylt particularly, my carbine was subjected to really hard usage in sandy country—no one can stalk through sand for four or five hundred yards and keep a weapon free from the element—and it never ceased to function admirably when used by any of the six people who carried it at one time or another. The extraction was always good.)

"The Springfield is a good shooting rifle; there cannot be two opinions about it. But the bolt action is clumsy to us who have become accustomed to the easy bolt manipulation of the S.M.L.E., No. 4 and the No. 5. And to me the whole rifle does not seem so 'handy,' and suggests largeness, unwieldiness and unbalance when compared with the British service rifles.

"The Garand is an excellent shooting job, but in my opinion it is too heavy and clumsy for a personal weapon. I have yet to be convinced of the desirability of an automatic rifle for general issue until its weight and dimensions can be brought down to, or *below*, that of the contemporary service rifle. I am not so well acquainted with the Garand as with the Winchester carbine so am not qualified to discuss its mechanics in detail. However I would suggest that the same objections with regard to the fouling of the working parts on service applies to the Garand as to the carbine since, superfically at least, they are similar."

(Although the weight of the Garand is given as but 9½ lbs. this officer's opinion as to the heaviness of the weapon is shared by most British officers and men who have used it. To me it appeared clumsy, and never seemed to "come" to the arms and hands as did my S.M.L.E. or No. 4. And, although this may sound a little ridiculous, it was an *impersonal* weapon; certainly *I* could never have thought so much about a Garand as I could about a normal service rifle. Many men too, complained of the kick of the Garand but, as I have mentioned earlier, such a thing never troubled me. One thing was noticeable though to a trained observer and that was it was much easier to see the muzzle flip and set-back of a Garand than that of a normal rifle; even when held by men possessing a vice-like grip that muzzle lift was clearly apparent, and a trained sniper, once he had picked up the general direction of the shot might easily locate the exact position of the automatic rifle by that one feature. There were many men too who could easily discern the different toned "crack" of an automatic rifle.)

"It is apparently laughable for me to attempt to criticise the Colt .45 automatic after all that has been written and said about it. It is undoubtedly a very fine handgun and a hard hitting job. But in my opinion it is on the heavy side for a handgun, and I think the 9mm equivalent, say the 9mm Browning, can do the job very nearly as well, whilst being much handier from the points of view of carriage and actual firing. Both types however, like most of the automatics of similar design become very easily fouled by sand, etc., due to their working parts being comparatively exposed during firing."

(It is this susceptibility to fouling of the automatics which adds power to the opinion held by many that for service purposes it is impossible to improve on the revolver or pistols of the type of the Enfield and the Smith and Wesson. Certainly the action and the structure of these weapons stand up to the wear, tear and stress of service usage better than any of the normal automatics. And once again I say that I would infinitely prefer to have my old S. & W. than any automatic pistol, the much over-rated Walthers and Lugers included, for a combat weapon.)

My colleague closed his brief commentary on American weapons with:—

"Relevant to the issue of sniping and small arms or not I feel that I must put in a word for this delightful pet and very dear friend of mine—the Browning .5 machine gun. Once you have mastered their individual idiosyncrasies, and believe me each one is a bit different, they are extremely reliable weapons. Stripping is exceedingly simple for a weapon of this kind, in fact I always reckoned to be able to teach a man all he need know about them in less than an hour. They are very accurate up to long ranges when on a good mounting, and that hell's brew of tracer, incendiary and AP like our own Besa ammunition, is something to be reckoned with by any up to the largest tanks, let alone men! I really take off my hat to that wonderful weapon—the Browning .5!"

❊ ❊ ❊ ❊

SPRINGFIELD. CAL. .30. M' 03. A 1.

This Springfield rifle is seldom seen in England, and my personal knowledge of it is not extensive. But I have used it enough to know that it is a first-rate rifle, and allied to the M 1 or M 2 cartridges it is accurate up to ranges exceeding any other service rifle with which I have shot. To the all-round rifleman, as distinct from the service rifleman, the sighting arrangements are of primary interest, and although in my view all service rifle sights bear super optimistic maximum range settings—surely there is a good case to be made for the limiting of sights to 1,000 yards or less on *service* rifles—it is interesting to see that the Springfield has a maximum sight range of 2,850 yards by using the open notch in the upper end of the leaf. Having something like an ever-present and vociferous bee in my bonnet re h.v. cartridges and resultant flatter trajectories, I am enthusiastic about the cartridge for this rifle; I am sure that if we had a .303 cartridge which would develop similar ballistics it would be a very good thing.

❋   ❋   ❋   ❋

M 17

The M 17s which I used in England in the years 1940–43 were really splendid weapons; I never came across a bad one. In certain quarters they were not popular, but that can be primarily and summarily dismissed with the one word "ignorance." There is in England still a certain prejudice against the aperture sight, and it is always possible to meet some fellow who decries the aperture sight and says that he could shoot much better with the open V, such as that on the S.M.L.E. If I heard that assertion once during my years as a Weapon Training Officer both in England and overseas I heard it a thousand times. In 90% of cases the claimant couldn't shoot anyway! My answer was a stock one—"If a man can shoot well with the open V he's going to shoot better with the aperture when he becomes used to it." And if the grumbling one could shoot at all, so it proved!

Many of the Home Guard in 1940 did not like the M 17; usually these fellows were veterans of the first World War and the word rifle to them meant only the S.M.L.E.

Upper: THE BREN GUN, one of the best light machine guns and one of the most mobile.
Lower: GERMAN LIGHT MACHINE GUNS. "Once heard never forgotten."
(Left to right:—'42, '34 and '15.

Upper: THE PIAT—(Projector Infantry Anti Tank) with bomb in position for firing. In the hands of the right man, this weapon was capable of knocking out tanks—and it did KO tanks too! Because of its great work in the hands of determined, courageous men it became known as the V.C. weapon. *Lower:* THE TEMPERAMENTAL STEN GUN.

It was sometimes very amusing to hear many such men, who had never actually stirred out of England during 1914–1918 and had never heard a shot fired in anger, prating at great length on the subject of musketry and shooting; many of them were physically incapable of hitting a haystack at 50 yards, and mentally incapable of appreciating the true worth of a rifle. The higher velocity .300 cartridge gave slightly improved ballistics than the .303 cartridge in the P 14, and I should say that the M 17 was probably the most accurate rifle I have ever used. My only criticisms against the rifle were the lengthy standard butt, and its slightly less mobility than the British service rifles. But for the *riflemen* of a platoon or company who could have been formed to provide a kind of reserve (and only slightly less effective) body for the sniper section the P 14 or the M 17 would have been the ideal rifles.

❋ ❋ ❋ ❋

PISTOLS

English Pistols · Luger and Walther · Browning 9mm M 1935 · Czech M 1938 · Russian Tokarev · Italian Beretta · Austrian Steyr 9mm · Spanish Astra 9mm. · 7.65mm. Pistols—Walther and Mauser

Many Englishmen appear to have a great distrust of all handguns, and it was amusing to see how some men handled a pistol or revolver for the first time; gingerly, as though the barrel were made of some plastic substance which would playfully curl up and come to rest in their direction when fired. It may appear a rather curious innovation, but I maintained that it was part of a sniper's training to become familiar with the handgun—one never knows when such a facility will be needed—so familiar indeed as to be able to draw with speed, and shoot with either hand with a certainty of hitting a man at ten or twelve yards, not once but two or three times in the most brief space of time.

The British for a long time used the .45 revolver; in tribal warfare this weapon fired the .45 manstopper cartridge, with its heavy bullet squared at both ends; only a bullet of this type was thought sufficient to stop onrushing natives! It came as a surprise to many handgun enthusiasts that the type of handgun which was to the forefront in World War II was a calibre of .38 or thereabouts. Many people have expressed the opinion that nothing less than .45 calibre was a "stopper." But the British started experiments with the "Pistol No. 2 calibre .380" in the year 1928. This pistol, developed at Enfield, and variously known as the "Enfield" or the "No. 2" is a six shot hinge-framed revolver closely resembling in exterior appearance the old "Pistol No. Mk. VI calibre .455"," in other words, the .455 Webley. The Enfield was primarily designed to permit quick pointing and rapid snap shooting, since it was thought, (and future events showed the quality of the thought) that the main use of a service handgun was for combat work; the general balance of the Enfield was designed to help the *average* man to instinctively point, and hit, his opponent. The authorities were not concerned with whether a man could hit a revolver target bull six times in six shots at a range of 12, 15 or 25 yards, but they wanted a pistol which, in the hands of the average soldier armed with it, was capable of being pointed at, and hitting, a man in the least possible time. The whole pistol training, in the proper combat schools, was to that end. The weight of the Enfield is about 28 ounces, some 12 ounces less than the Webley. The barrel length is five inches, and the cartridge is the standard British .380 service cartridge, which to all intents and purposes is the same as the reliable .38 S. & W. Super Police cartridge with the 200-grain bullet.

Just before moving off into concentration area ready for D Day I managed to secure for practice shooting for the men in my unit armed with the Enfield and the S. & W. .38 (in our designation the "S. & W. Pistol No. 2.") a few hundred rounds of Western .38 Super Police, 200-grain Lubaloy coated bullet, nickel plated case, which gave such excellent shooting that I carried a plentiful supply throughout the campaign.

One feature of the Enfield was that the detachable side plate gave easy access to the mechanism for cleaning. The light weight and less recoil (and many men who had known only the .455 Webley were very surprised when they fired the .38 Enfield for the first time) resulted in the average man putting up a far better performance than he did with the heavier calibre weapon, and after a little practice it was good to see how these men so rapidly brought their guns into play, and with instinctive pointing sense and quickness on the trigger secured hits on man-size targets at anything up to 15 yards. And it was later proved a hundred-fold that the 200-grain bullet moving at a velocity of about 650 f.p.s. had quite an effective stopping power when compared with the heavier calibred brethren.

When War broke out British factories could not turn out the Enfield fast enough, so the Smith and Wesson people were asked to augment the supply of .38 pistols. I used a Smith and Wesson pistol for nearly four years and I have nothing but praise for it.

So much has been written about the Luger and the Walther 9mm pistols that I consider it unnecessary to add much to the ever-growing volume. Maybe there are some people who are not aware that the Walther was originally designed to take a cartridge of roughly .45 calibre, but was finally adapted and put into production as a 9mm weapon. I found the hang, balance and grip of the Walther to be better than the Luger, and have nothing but admiration for the craftsmanship of these German pistols, but I am still a sworn adherent to the standards of the Enfield and Smith and Wesson for a sturdy, reliable combat job.

I know there has been a good deal of discussion and comment in America about the Walther P 38 and its "safety." Such interest in weapons is almost unknown here in England; we are by no means so firearms conscious as the Americans—our rigid firearms laws see to that! My view on this safety matter is that only a dim-wit will ever allow the hammer to slam down on a loaded cartridge. Surely everyone must realise that no gadget is entirely fool-proof, and that wear and tear will eventually render any "safe" contrivance suspect? Subject to normal handling, that is safe handling which is an integral part in the make-up of all firearms conscious individuals, the Walther is certainly not a sly rogue.

The Huns used the Browning 9mm M 1935 quite a bit—there were a large number taken from them, and one could always find these pistols in any captured arms dump. My experience with them was not extensive, but one owned by a brother-officer was extremely accurate at long ranges, and we had great entertainment, at least he did since my pistol shooting has always lacked a good deal, shooting at tins floating down a fast running stream. Some of these Browning pistols owned by the Belgian Maquis people were in a shocking state, and I considered that the firing of such weapons would be a far greater hazard for the firer than the fired-at!

The Czech M 1938 is probably the smallest service pistol and fires the 9mm short cartridge. In certain areas in Germany there were large numbers of these pistols picked up, and I found them to be really sound and good looking little weapons. Accuracy was good, and they were really delightful to handle. The short 9mm ammunition was, however, difficult to find, and consequently my own shooting with the Czech pistol was limited.

The Russian Tokarev pistol was very similar to the Colt .32 automatic. The calibre was 7.63mm and the cartridge closely resembled the famous Mauser 7.63, but had a lighter load, which resulted in the bullet having a velocity of about 1,000 f.p.s. compared with the Mauser's 1,392 f.p.s. A sound workmanlike weapon, with an accuracy far greater than any other .32 automatic I have ever handled, the Tokarev was more sought after by souvenir hunters rather than by shooting enthusiasts, mainly because of the terrific difficulty of securing the necessary ammunition.

My acquaintance with the Italian Beretta was very

brief, but it was enough to show me that this was a simple, sturdy pistol excellent in use and performance, and an exquisite little job which I would have given pounds to possess.

The Austrian Steyr 9mm automatic pistol was an interesting weapon, and in the areas of my pilgrimage there were very few found. But several times I came across large stocks of the special 9mm ammunition for this pistol. The cartridge is longer than the Parabellum, the overall length being 1.37″ compared with 1.14/1.16″. This ammunition rusts very easily; the bullet is lead with a steel jacket, the latter being plated over very thinly. The cartridges are clipped, the clip holding eight rounds, and since the magazine of the Steyr is located in the butt, but not removable, the cartridges are stripped into it from the top of the pistol, the clip being inserted into a clip guide, and the cartridges pressed clear by exerting firm downward pressure, after which the empty clip is pulled out. The recoil of this pistol was hefty and I found it much more difficult to hold than the majority of handguns.

One of the most interesting pistols I had in Germany was a brand new Astra 9mm; this was one of several found in a German airfield armoury. A Spanish arm, it is about the best hand weapon which comes out of that "copyist" country. It has pleasing lines, incorporates the Colt grip safety, and is unique by being chambered with sufficient tolerance to take .38 or 9mm ammunition; both these calibres were stamped into the barrel of my pistol. I had seen a little data regarding this weapon, one remark being to the effect that it would take most brands of 9mm ammunition, although in Spain the Bergmann type of 9mm ammunition was given as the standard for the pistol. I found that it was most difficult to find 9mm ammo which could be used in this particular weapon, and only the very few rounds of the Bergmann type, of slightly longer case and thicker base than the normal Parabellum, I was fortunate enough to obtain, gave me the full advantage of perfect firing, ejection and feed. The normal types of 9mm sat too close in the breech and consequently the striker could not reach the primer. I tried all types including the GFL M 38. and occasionally it was possible to fire a couple of rounds consecutively. One day noticing that a number of rounds of WRA 1942, which was used by my NCOs for their Stens, appeared to have slightly convex primers I tried these in the Astra and found that this very slight primer curve was just enough to allow the striker to make contact with the cap, and operate the gun in grand style. But there were very few of these rounds, and I never came across any other WRA of varying year which would fire in the Astra. The pistol fired the normal British rimmed .38 cartridge, but these had to be fed into the breech singly since they would not go into the magazine. I filed one or two of these cartridges down, and with this treatment the pistol functioned perfectly.

When lecturing later on elementary identification of firearms this little dodge provided a good practical illustration of the point that a revolver cartridge can be fired from an automatic pistol. The Astra, although looking hefty, it was 8¾" overall, with a barrel length of 5½", was not uncomfortable to use. With the Bergmann cartridge it was a terrific hitter, this cartridge giving a muzzle velocity of about 1,200 f.p.s. and a striking energy of 400 foot pounds. When these pistols were found they were in extremely cheap canvas holsters which gave little indication of the quality of the contents.

The action of the Astra is plain blow-back, but even with the most powerful cartridges I experienced no discomfort due no doubt to the strength and heaviness of the weapon. The recoil spring, which is around the barrel, is one of the stiffest to be found in any self-loading pistol, and considerable effort was required to retract the breech. Stripping the pistol was one hell of a job, and I well remember sit-

ting on my bed one very hot afternoon in May 1945, clad
only in P.T. shorts, tackling the job of dismantling the
barrel. Before I jockeyed the barrel free from the grooves in
the action body in which sit the segmental lugs of the
barrel, and the double collar with milled outer ring, etc.,
I was perspiring freely. And then, the pistol having suddenly burst asunder, I spent some minutes on the path
outside my room—the window being open—searching for
the spring! If the stripping was difficult it was child's play
compared with the assembling, where great strength was
necessary to manipulate the recoil spring. I made a vow
that the pistol would not be stripped again unless it was
absolutely necessary!

Some time after the end of the war in Europe the most
popular calibre of handgun was the 7.65mm. This was
understandable since all troops were ordered never to walk
abroad without being armed, and the possession of a small
7.65mm pistol which would lie snugly in the pocket was
the ideal, and much better than carrying a rifle, a carbine
or even the standard .38 pistol for those who were fortunate
enough to be armed with such a personal weapon.

Of course in certain units of the British Occupational
Force there had been orders issued to the effect that every
enemy weapon must be handed in, and failure to carry out
this order, if detected, carried with it the penalty of court-
martial. Despite the order there were thousands of troops
walking about armed with captured pistols. Personally
I held the opinion that the most sensible idea would have
been to have gathered in all weapons on the understanding
that every man who wished to have a pistol for personal
protection when walking out could obtain one on signa-
ture. Had such a scheme been formulated there would have
been many more weapons surrendered, and a census, and
a record of their distribution, could have been taken.
And men could have been trained in their use, since there
is no doubt that hundreds of individuals were carrying

handguns who had not the slightest idea of how to use them.

No one could have wished for a nicer little handgun than the Walther 7.65 double action automatic. The one I picked up in Germany was absolutely new and unused, and when I first fired it I was astonished to see such a good target. Despite its 19 ounces weight there was no trace of discomfort in firing, and the weapon handled beautifully.

The Mauser 7.65 had the reputation of being a dangerous weapon, but I carried one about with me for a long time in Europe and found it extremely useful and reliable, and in its compactness and ease of handling, I ranked it with the Walther 7.65 as the best pocket automatic I have ever used. I thought it a good idea that such a weapon should be part of a sniper's equipment since it could be carried easily in one of the many pockets of the sniper smock, and there can be no doubt about the psychological value of possessing a handgun. The safety catch on the Mauser was really "easy" and simple, and came naturally and automatically to the thumb. The "danger bug" comes from the fact that when the action is open and a magazine, whether loaded or not, is inserted the slide runs sharply forward immediately the magazine is seated, and should the loader have his finger on the trigger there is every likelihood of the cartridge being fired. If the chamber is loaded but there is no magazine in the gun the trigger cannot be pulled. The Mauser has no hammer, but has a spring-driven firing pin and when it is cocked an extension of the firing pin protrudes from the rear of the gun to indicate that it is cocked. Some authorities hold the view that this makes the Mauser a very dangerous weapon because if it is dropped so that this projection strikes a hard surface it is possible that the firing pin may be knocked off the sear and the gun discharged. My view on this matter is that much can happen to a lot of weapons if they are carelessly handled and dropped on hard surfaces!

MACHINE GUNS

Sten Carbine · *Bren LMG* · *Lewis* · *Vickers*
Browning M 1919 · *Browning Automatic Rifle*
Twin Browning .303

THE STEN CARBINE

This was the weapon the pedigree of which was known
to wags as "By Marks and Spencer out of Woolworth." It
was generally acknowledged to be a makeshift weapon; the
British wanted a submachine gun in a great hurry, and
there was not time to design and turn out meticulously a
high grade article. We wanted a killing weapon—at once;
and we got it; but during its lifetime its killing propensities
were not wholly confined to the enemy!

The Sten certainly became notorious for the number of
shooting accidents in which it played the central character. If there was a round in the breech it was eminently
possible for it to "go" if the carbine was laid even lightly
on the ground. No prima donna, ballerina or tennis star
was ever more temperamental than the Sten gun. Sometimes
a Sten would fire single shots whilst at "automatic," or
automatic when the catch was at "single." But it was more
than a useful weapon and must have written "finis" to the
earthly career of many Germans. It was copied from the
German Schmeisser, and since the copying in no matter

what primitive form of an enemy weapon was abhorrent to many Britishers, the Sten had the distinction of being talked about in Parliament!

The Sten enjoyed quite an amount of fame with the Hun, and I shall never forget the look on a German pilot's face in Normandy—he had just baled out of his ME 109 after having been accounted for by a Spitfire—when the savage threatening of a Sten in the hands of a sergeant who hated all Huns, adequately checked this particular Jerry's rapid movement in the direction of his Luger. The Stens were no things of beauty; they were no respecters of persons be they friend or foe, but they did that which was asked of them in no uncertain fashion. As regards accuracy they varied a good deal. I remember handling one in 1942 which was capable of really good shooting at 100 yards. Certainly no Thompson I saw and handled could approach this particular Sten for accuracy.

In connection with the Sten it is perhaps interesting to record that some of the later issues of Sten gun ammunition were loaded so as to develop higher ballistics than the 9mm Parabellum pistol cartridge, and that the resulting pressures were appreciably higher than the normal pressures developed by the Parabellum cartridge. It was unsafe to use such ammunition in self-loading pistols since both pressure and recoil were excessive for a pistol, but I am quite prepared to wager that it was used! I never heard of any accident as the result of using Sten ammunition in such pistols as the Walther or the Luger.

* * * *

THE BREN LMG

There can be no doubt that the Bren light machine gun was a really good sound weapon, but I do not think anyone will seriously contest that it was as mobile an LMG as could be devised. The early models were extremely accurate, and I heard many decry this accuracy as being the greatest defect of the gun. I well remember a sergeant of a well-known Regiment telling me in the summer of 1941—he had had considerable experience, being a survivor of Dunkirk and Narvik—that had there been in Norway only one quarter of the machine guns and those guns had been Vickers instead of Brens it was his considered opinion that we should have held a footing in that country for some considerable time. He told me that after one or two successful actions he had seen dead Germans with three or more bullets in them, the result, he claimed, of the too accurate fire of the Bren. I don't think there can be any doubt that the early Brens were lacking in cone of fire properties. I tried quite a number of Brens out on the ranges at various times, and with the Mk. 1 of early vintage it was easy to group at less than 4″ with five shots at 100 yards and, fired in short bursts, the grouping capacity was extraordinarily good. With the later Brens it was difficult to obtain one which would put five single shots in a 4″ circle at 100 yards, and in bursts-firing there was definitely a greater "spread" than had been the case with the earlier models.

Personally my favourite was the old Lewis. And curious though it may sound this opinion of mine was shared by many, both officers and men. One great fault which many people found with the Lewis was that it was more liable to stoppages than the Bren. During the time I was an NCO I proved that this was a fallacy; my section at that time, 1941, was equipped with a ground Lewis, and it was fired very frequently. That Lewis went on the range, and a very sandy range too, many times without a single stoppage. I put this good performance down to the fact that the ammunition loaded into the pans, or magazines, was examined round by round, and *cleaned* if necessary. And anyone who used ammunition on service ranges in 1941 will not need to be told that there was a great amount of ammunition which required cleaning! Once the section had been instilled with pride in their LMG never jamming, or going wrong, there was never any need to drive them to select or clean the ammunition. And I always enjoyed firing the old Lewis much more than I did the Bren gun. I freely admit that the Bren was more mobile, or portable, but when I look back on training days in 1941 and 1942 and recollect that we often did route marches of 20–25 miles carrying platoon weapons, in those days the Lewis in our case, I think that the old Lewis guns must have been fairly portable. The men evolved the idea of two of them carrying the gun, especially suitable since we almost always marched in aircraft formation in single file on the sides of the road, and the scheme of one man holding the muzzle end and another the butt worked all right. But, of course, such a practice was not possible when it came the turn of the enthusiastic platoon commander to hump the weapon, and I must admit there were times when round about the 20th mile and I took the Lewis it made my shoulder ache. The big trouble however was not really the gun itself but the magazines or "pans" as they were more popularly known. They were heavy and by no means so handy as the Bren magazines. In the early days of the war the main defensive armament of some of our airfields was the single stripped .300 American Lewis. It was certainly light and easy to handle, and when firing at a drogue towed by aircraft there was no doubt about its cone of fire! Although looking like a toy it can be safely said that such weapons did a magnificent job of work.

Of the Vickers machine gun I will say little. My experiences with it have not been extensive, but I share the opinion of many who claim for it the title of the world's best MMG. Once one has tap-traversed on the Vickers the fascination of the weapon remains for all time, and I am quite sure that it has administered the knock-out drops to thousands of Huns in the two Wars. The Vickers in conjunction with the Mk. VIIIz cartridge was possessed of really long ranging power.

The Englishman's contact with the Browning M 1919 A 4 was almost solely restricted to Home Guard activities, and even there the experience was limited, especially in the early days of that force, since .300 ammunition was scarce, and with the threat of invasion imminent there was every necessity to conserve the meagre supply. But later I heard nothing but praise for the weapon by the men who had been chosen to use it, and I can assure everyone that to be a machine gunner in the Home Guard in the early days was a position which many coveted. Whether it arose from a basic desire to be at the back of a weapon which ejected more lead than any other, or a determination to have the weapon which presumably might spell death to more Germans I cannot say.

The above remarks can also apply to the Browning automatic rifle which became a weapon personal to the Home Guard, although I believe that certain Army units were equipped with it in the dark days of 1940. The allotment of this rifle was one per platoon, and in the Home Guard, on account of its weight, it usually fell to the lot of the heftiest fellow in the unit to hump it along!

In 1942 and 1943 there was a surplus of twin Browning machine guns; these had either been taken from, or manufactured for, aircraft, many of which turned over exclusively to 20mm cannon. Thousands of these twin Brownings on appropriate mountings were used for anti-aircraft work; in some cases they were mounted in lorries which became "flak" wagons. With the terrifically high rate of fire these twins had I have always maintained that I would rather have been behind them if attacked by low flying aircraft than behind a 20mm or even a 40mm gun. In 1943 we experimented with them for ground to ground use, and I personally thought the idea a good one. Had a satisfactory *mobile* mounting been forthcoming I am quite certain that they would have been extremely popular with the men using them, and just as highly unpopular with the Hun.

With their angry chatter and high rate of fire their effect on the enemy would have been something in the nature of the respect given by our men to the Spandaus.

I know that there were a number of these twin Brownings in Europe which were never used. On the morning of January 1st, 1945 when Jerry launched his all-out attack on the airfields in France, Belgium and Holland, I was on an airfield not far from the German border. We were fortunate, since all the guns on the airfield were on the alert as a result of one of the Bofors having gone into action against a German jet plane—an ME 262—at about 0840 hours. The plane was at a fair height, but the shooting was good, and the brief action resulted in every gun crew being on its toes, and in a state of vital awareness.

About ten minutes later there came a terrific roar and a FW 190 swept into sight going all out across the airfield with the whole wings ablaze from tip to tip with the flash of his guns. Without any exaggeration he passed within fifteen yards of the spot on which another officer and myself were standing, and he was flying lower than I have ever seen a plane fly, before or since. Some idea of that height can be gained when I point out that he had to lift slightly to get over a Bofors barrel which was at an elevation of less than 30°. The pilot was certainly a brave fellow, but his action was suicidal. His run carried him over three Bofors guns, each of which knocked hell out of him, and pieces of his wings and fuselage were clearly seen hurtling skywards. He crashed about 400 yards beyond the airfield, and there was very little left of either pilot or plane. A squadron of Tempests were taxying up the perimeter track preparatory to taking-off on the runway, and they were in the direct line of the FW's attack; by a miracle not one of them was touched, and none of the ack ack crews was hit.

There was a good deal of fun that morning, but that particular airfield was fortunate. No planes were hit or damaged in any way, and only one man was wounded. Vastly different tales were told elsewhere! I learned later that there were a number of twin Brownings complete with ack ack mountings in a store on the airfield. The HQ staff felt very sore about this, since had one of the twin Brownings been set up on the HQ site, well hidden and in direct line of flight of the first FW, they would have been able to join in the fun and they certainly could not have missed that Hun.

❖　　　❖　　　❖　　　❖

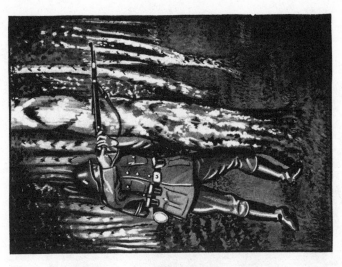

FIRING POSITIONS IN THE GERMAN ARMY

Standing positions as taught by the German Training Manuals. Note that they make use of available trees as a rest for the rifle and as cover, whenever possible to do so.

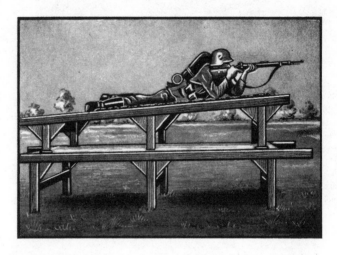

Prone position as taught by the German manuals. Note that the left arm is not extended to any degree.

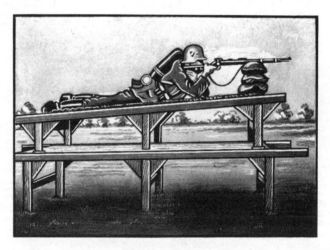

Another prone position utilizing sandbag rest for the rifle. Note the position of left arm, with hand grasping the butt of the rifle.

AMMUNITION

Frankly I was surprised that a large portion of the German ammunition salvaged from the battlefields and which had been subjected to damp, exposure and heat, was still absolutely serviceable when used months later. I was surprised, since a good deal of the later German ammunition, manufactured in the years 1942–1944 had a very poor appearance originally, and it was quite apparent that Jerry was finding a shortage in many metals.

We heard a lot about the danger of using certain brands of 9mm ammunition in pistols like the Luger, but very few people took much notice of such warnings. I found some specimens of the 9mm Parabellum proof round which was manufactured especially as a high pressure test cartridge; pistols after assembly being tested with such cartridges fired by remote control. I understand that only one round of such ammunition was used in the German pistol factories to test, or *prove*, a pistol. Such proof cartridges were identified by the fact that the whole of the base of the case, including the cap, was painted a bright green. I was told that someone had picked up a number of these proof cartridges in 7.65 calibre, but I never saw them.

In the later stages of the campaign most of the 9mm ammunition I came across was steel-cased. I have been told that the German Ordnance authorities found that steel-cased ammunition did not function very well in the Luger and Walther pistols, and that in 1943 an order was published reserving all stocks of the brass-cased 9mm ammunition for use in these pistols. If such was the case the order was not observed very rigidly since nearly all the Parabellum ammo I picked up in N.W. Europe was of the steel-cased variety. Only once did I find a quantity of brass-cased 9mm; this was of Geco manufacture, characterised by the red primer cap and red band at the base of the bullet. This was excellent ammunition and much sought after; as a matter of fact, I found all "Geco" ammunition to be really splendid, from 6.35mm to 9mm.

A late type of 9mm pistol ammunition made by the Germans was the "Pistol patronen o8 Sinter Eisen" (Pist. Patro. o8. S.E.). This was designed as a result of material shortages, and no high priority materials were used in its manufacture. In this bullet there is no core, sleeve or jacket; the whole bullet is homogeneous and composed of an iron powder which is first formed in presses under very high pressure and then heated to a degree less than the melting point but sufficient to make the compressed powder adhere into a solid mass, in other words "sintered." The Germans claimed a fairly high velocity for this bullet, in the neighbourhood of 1,400 f.p.s. I was given to understand that this bullet had one great drawback—it was extremely severe on barrels. After firing quite a number of such rounds in a Walther I can quite believe this; I found the recoil set up by this cartridge to be much more violent than the normal 9mm. The distinguishing feature of this "sintered" bullet is its dull grey colour. I found this cartridge rusted easily.

As we have seen, the Germans utilised a great number of foreign weapons. In the same manner they used extensively the ammunition of many other nations. I believe however that the bulk of the 9mm ammunition used by the Germans, other than that produced in their own factories, was Italian. In northern Germany I found a tremendous amount of Italian 9mm Parabellum. This can usually be identified by the letters "G.F.L." or "Fiocchi" stamped on the base of the cartridge case, followed by "M—38" which distinguishes it from the 9mm short (equivalent of the .380 Colt) used in the Italian Beretta pistol. The cap on this cartridge is covered with green lacquer.

One of the most interesting of the German 7.9mm cartridges was the black bullet with the copper point, used mainly in aircraft machine guns. This was both explosive and incendiary. The whole bullet was contained in a steel envelope, the envelope being coated with a deposit of copper gilding material. (The black colour of the larger portion of the bullet was obtained by oxydising this coating.) Inside the envelope there was a lead core which, in turn, contained an incendiary compound and an appliance which amounted to what might be termed a percussion fuse. The incendiary compound, usually phosphorous, was carried in the head of the bullet; the fuse was a large steel capsule, coppered over, closed at the rear and open at the front. The front end carried a capsule of very thin aluminum which was filled with a detonating explosive compound and this capsule rested on an aluminum disc which was supported by a shoulder in the steel capsule. The space in the rear of the steel capsule was occupied by the striker and a spring sleeve which was the safety device. This spring sleeve which was a small cylinder with a slit down one side to permit its being opened out or closed in the safe, or forward, position gripped the striker and had its front end resting on the aluminum disc. As the rear end of the striker was forced by the spring sleeve against the end of the capsule there was no risk of any movement of the striker. But when the cartridge was fired the bullet was suddenly propelled forwards with great violence when the inertia of the spring overcame the strength of the spring and the whole sleeve set backwards until it was stopped by the base of the capsule. In this position it fitted the body of the striker tightly and the two formed a single unit as it were which was free to slide up and down in the steel capsule. As long as the bullet was in flight the striker was kept resting on the base of the steel capsule, but directly the bullet hit there was a change of velocity and then the striker flew forward, the point struck the aluminum disc and capsule and the explosive compound was detonated. This detonation at least partially opened the bullet and thus the phosphorous was ignited to burn with a great violence.

Of course, there was much more of this special German ammunition that I did not have the luck to encounter.

❖ ❖ ❖ ❖

BULLETS FOR SHOTGUNS

To the hunting enthusiast it was interesting to see the large amount of "Brenneke" bullets in Germany. These were made extensively in Germany, prior to 1939, in both 12 and 16 gauges as well as smaller sizes. The purpose of the bullet was to provide a missile for use in shotguns against big game. Windage (loss of gas) was prevented by the base wad and the narrow ridge round the lead base of the bullet was compressed to an adequate degree during the passage through a full choke. Nose-on flight was maintained by the helical ridges on the outside of the parallel part of the bullet which helped to give the projectile a spin. A felt wad was screwed to the base of the bullet, and this separates from the bullet during flight. Although of undoubted use against such game as wild boar, I cannot see that this Brenneke bullet has any advantages over spherical bullets of the Contractile or Lethal types.

❖ ❖ ❖ ❖

[218]

The German "Wooden Bullet"

Specimens of the 7.9mm "wooden" bullet in my collection of small arms ammunition vary considerably in shape and size of the "bullet." In Germany I picked up a large amount of "wooden-bulleted" 8mm cartridges for use with the Austrian Steyr-Mannlicher rifle, a weapon which was used a good deal in certain areas. There was also large quantities of similar ammunition in 6.5mm calibre for use with the Mannlicher rifle M'95 with which I had a little experience in Holland. In July 1945 I found some of the 7.9mm ammunition which had been manufactured as early as 1928. In these early types the "bullet" is not wood (some authorities always term it Papier-mâché) but cardboard. One peculiarity is that this type of bullet weighs twice as much as the "wooden" variety. The propellant charge is not so great. When fired the "wooden" bullet disintegrates almost immediately, and sometimes it is possible to see the fluffy, harmless residue falling like snow a few inches from the muzzle. *But* there are times when slivers of the "wood" can be picked up a few yards from the muzzle. In German Army training pamphlets it was laid down that because of possible hurt by "fragmentation" such ammunition would not be fired once the "exercise enemy" were within a range of 25 metres. Knowing how malignantly the "safety" bug bit the German Army authorities it is safe to say that this range could have been halved without hurt to anyone. I fired scores of these cartridges at a target at ten yards range without once finding any impression upon it, and in the majority of cases no sliver of "wood" touched a target at five yards.

There can be no doubt of the great uses in training such ammunition affords. Whereas in English battle exercises, early in the War, LMG and rifle fire was produced by such expedients as rattling stones in a tin, or whirring a gas rattle, the Germans with Teutonic thoroughness used the "wooden" bullet for such training; it produced noise and afforded *real* handling training, particularly to machine gunners, since on firing enough gas was provided to drive the recoiling portions of the LMGs to the rear. The value of such training is inestimable. This unique innovation was not confined to small-calibre weapons. I had examples of 20mm "wooden" shells in the normal case. Having had some experience in 1943 in training men on Hispano 20mm guns I realise what a tremendous help such practice ammunition would have been in giving men "practical firing" experience with this gun. Later in the N.W. Europe campaign a good many Spandau belts and saddle type magazines were found with the 7.9mm "wooden" bullets interspersed with normal types of ammunition. The most likely explanation of this was that with the very high rate of fire of these guns—no one can forget the characteristic, short, sharp chatter of the Spandau—such an introduction conserved live ammunition without detracting from the potential killing power of the weapon. At one time dead men were found in the battle areas with four or five bullets in them. Three "wooden" bulleted cartridges to one normal type would give an equally good lethal result in such a high rate of fire weapon, conserve ammunition, and be a saving in weight—and, at the same time, there would be no impairment of the automatic efficiency of the weapon.

Details of 7.9mm German "wooden"-bulleted ammunition:

> Weight of case...... 169.75 grains
> Weight of bullet.... 6.75 grains
> Weight of propellant
>   charge.......... 20.00 grains
> Total weight....... 196.50 grains

Wooden-bulleted ammunition varied in the filling; in the majority there was just the propellant charge of the special powder, but, in others, there was, between the powder and the base of the hollow bullet, a little powder-impregnated wool which was slow burning.

BRITISH SMALL ARMS AMMUNITION

I think that every credit must be given to the small arms ammunition manufacturers for their consistently high standard of production during the War. Decently stored and maintained, ammunition very rarely gave any trouble, and with such material misfires were extremely rare. But there appeared to be a tendency to use old and much misused cartridges of all types—Ball, AP, Incendiary and Tracer—for rifle and LMG range practices and although the pantomime-like appearance of tracer always appealed to the average soldier (a child at heart) and I must confess I always got a kick out of it too, it spelled negation to a man's grouping capacity. There were times when I got a decent group firing a clip containing AP, English and American ball and Tracer, but more often than not there was a wide divergence in elevation of the various types. Practice groups fired with all tracer, or all AP were nearly always good, which showed that a high standard of manufacture was maintained. I used a good deal of American .303 (particularly WRA) and this gave consistently fine shooting.

An excellent shot with a good rifle, iron sights, and standard Mk. VII ammunition would put up *consistent* five shot 3″ to 4″ groups at 100 yards. And that speaks volumes for the man, the rifle and the ammunition. Lest anyone thinks that that shooting with a service rifle is not so hot, let me say that I am by no means alone in maintaining that a man who is capable of *consistently* (*every time he shoots*) putting up *five* shot 2″ groups at 100 yards with a *service rifle equipped with telescope sights* is a superb shot.

For a long time now, as a personal foible, I have meticulously cleaned and polished all my ammunition before use. This probably has not made any difference to my at times mediocre shooting but I have always thought that a rifle cartridge was a thing of beauty; and somehow it has always pleased me, and put me in a good frame of mind, when I have seen the cartridges gleaming brightly in the magazine and transmitting shafts of silver and golden light on their journey into the breech. And such a frame of mind is perhaps an unconscious aid to one's shooting. At first the men used to find this highly polished ammunition of mine something of a joke, but later I found a number of them, a bit shamefacedly, following my example.

In 1943 I had some experience firing with the old Mk. VI service cartridge. One day on a range in the north of England the range warden, an enthusiastic rifleman and a former county champion shot, asked if I would like to try the old Mk. VI service cartridge. Naturally I jumped at the chance. He told me that one day a Northern rifle club had run out of Mk. VII ammunition, and had used a considerable amount of the Mk. VI which had been stored in the clubhouse for a very long time. And once having settled the difference in elevation given by this type by a number of experimental shots they proceeded to put up some really creditable shooting. I fired quite a number of rounds that day with a like result. Taking into consideration that these cartridges were of 1910 vintage, and therefore 33 years old, the consistent shooting I got from them was an excellent reference for the manufacturers. There were no misfires and later when I stripped a cartridge and examined the cordite sticks they burned easily and evenly. The Mk. VI has the blunt nose bullet, which is heavier than that of the Mk. VII, with a muzzle velocity of 2,000 feet per second, and cordite propellant, and is the cartridge which many service so-called experts could not recognise and glibly termed "dum dums" when I showed them examples of the type.

The Mk. VIIIz .303 British service cartridge has a streamlined bullet and was used in the Vickers machine gun for long range work. The propellant charge is nitrocellulose (41 grains); the bullet weight is 174 grains (the same as the Mk. VII, the cordite charge weight of which is 37 grains; the Mk. VIIz uses nitro-cellulose, 41 grains, and has the same bullet weight as the Mk. VII—the suffix "z" on British service cartridges denotes that the propellant charge is nitro-cellulose); overall length is the standard 3.05″ and the bullet has a muzzle velocity of 2,525 feet per second. (The standard Mk. VII has a muzzle velocity of 2,440 f.p.s.)

There are two opinions on the merits of the streamlined bullet, with its tapered base as well as tapered head. It has a greater capacity for overcoming air resistance, flatter trajectory and higher striking power at long ranges, and greatly increased ranging power. One school of thought maintains that the streamlined type is the last word in bullets; the other holds the opinion that it is far easier to make a square based bullet and therefore the *standards* of manufacture are more easily maintained and a consistent, accurate bullet produced. Badly designed or manufactured bullets may wobble seriously or, in technical terms, give rise to oscillation. (The oscillation of a bullet may be termed a slight tendency to unsteadiness during flight.) And one of the great difficulties in making a streamlined bullet is to make it so that it will be free from abnormal oscillation. It has been suggested that the streamlined bullet may be more sensitive to disturbance by blast on its exit from the muzzle than the square based type, but close range target tests have shown that oscillation was negligible and spark photographs did not reveal any signs of wobble. During war-time, mass production is at its peak and it is quite likely that streamlined bullets manufactured under such conditions lack something of that careful finish necessary to guarantee accuracy for the medium.

[223]

The Germans were great believers in the streamlined bullet and I, along with many other interested people, came across specimens of German bullets the tapered bases of which were definitely lacking symmetry. Such a bullet might oscillate comparatively violently and the deviation of its axis from the direction of flight tend to deflection when striking penetrable objects, and result in an almost "keyhole" type of wound. The modern pointed stream-lined bullet spinning about its axis of symmetry must always be sensitive to any slight divergence of the point of impact.

There can be little legitimate antagonism against the school of thought which maintains that the streamlined bullet is not necessary for the sporting rifle with its com-paratively short range type of work. And since most battle rifle shooting, excluding sniping, was done at very short ranges the same remark can be applied to the service rifle. I used the Mk. VIIIz cartridge in a rifle (many people deplored the use of this cartridge in a rifle maintaining that it was harmful to the bore) and found that the additional velocity gave no appreciable advantage over the standard Mk. VII or Mk. VIIz. But, giving long ranging power, it was certainly just the type of cartridge for use in the Vickers machine gun.

.38 Pistol Ammunition

I found that the British .38 ammunition was consistently good and dependable, and this reliability was maintained throughout the war. For a long time this ammunition was in short supply and it was very difficult to obtain any for practice purposes. In the last year or so of the war the bulk of the .38 ammo I came across was of Canadian manu-facture, and this was quite good material. But I found that my best shooting (and again I must say that I am but a mediocre performer with a handgun) was done with West-ern 38 Super Police (200-grain LUBALOY coated bullet, nickel plated case) of which I obtained a supply in early 1944 when it was given out for practice. A number of officers who used this type did not care for it, since it left a copper coloured deposit on cylinder and bore which appeared to be quite difficult to clear by normal service cleaning methods and equipment. Since I always carried "civilian" cleaning outfits for both rifle and pistol—much more comprehensive than military cleaning tackle—this characteristic never worried me in the slightest degree, and I liked the ammunition.

9MM AMMUNITION

Taken all round the 9mm ammunition manufactured for the Sten machine carbine was dependable and stood up to its job in admirable style.

SOME FACTS REGARDING BRITISH .303 SERVICE AMMUNITION

Ball. Cupro-nickel envelope. Lead and antimony core. Muzzle velocity 2,440 feet per second. Annulus: Purple.

AP. Steel envelope coated with cupro-nickel. Lead and antimony sleeve. Hard steel core. Muzzle velocity 2,390 feet per second. Annulus: Green.

Tracer. Bullet similar in composition to Ball. Tracer composition in base. (Various types of "range of tracer burning.") Tracer composition ignited by flash from main charge. Muzzle velocity 2,300 feet per second. Annulus: Red.

Incendiary. Bullet stepped; of individual shape. Muzzle velocity 2,580 feet per second. Annulus: Blue or Black.

The extreme range of .303 Mk. VII cartridge is 3,700 yards. Terminal velocity of a dropping .303 Mk. VII bullet is 315 feet per second—striking energy of about 40 foot pounds. (60 foot pounds is the theoretical minimum to ensure lethal effect, but at 315 f.p.s. it would be dangerous.)

✸   ✸   ✸   ✸

GERMAN WEAPON TRAINING

It has been pointed out previously that the safety-bug, a parasite which was prolific and widespread amongst the British, also apparently stalked rampant through the august body of the German High Command. All German ranges showed the utmost regard for safety. I never saw a German classification range extending beyond 300 metres and on the majority of these ranges there was evidence that very little shooting had taken place beyond 200 metres. Most of the classification ranges were banked on either side to a height of 20' or more, and the butts were extremely well-built and solid; it may be irrelevant, but it is fact, that all these German butts seem to have served very usefully as latrines for both the retreating Huns and the advancing British and Allied troops!

Nowhere, better than on ranges, could one see that painstaking Teutonic thoroughness and attention to detail which is so much a part of the German make-up, and is both their strength and their weakness, for undoubtedly they lack improvisation ability. This thoroughness was exemplified by the small machines they had in the range butts for the pasting up of targets; a neat little contrivance of rolls of lightly joined circular pieces of paper, black and white, passing through rollers on to good quality sponges moistened with adhesive. This fine equipment was totally dis-similar to the British method of flour paste—notable for its entire lack of adhesive properties—made in a bucket, and applied to almost any type of paper by a hairless brush or a piece of stick! The latter is not an exaggeration of the "pasting-up-targets" facilities found on some British ranges during war-time!

The Germans used many different types of targets on the classification ranges, but the most common was the circular type, with the bull or highest scoring ring (12) set centrally in a silhouette head, or head and shoulders (German) as illustrated.

On one range I found a number of large targets, the central figure of which was a Jager set against a woodland background. At 100 metres this figure provided a "difficult-to-see" target. On the same range I came across, for the first time, the German "stone-wall" targets; the figure, superimposed half-over a stone wall which was central on the target, was that of a British Tommy; the background to wall and figure was a wood. A further large figure target, showing a British soldier running, was printed in many varying colours, the idea being to tone with various backgrounds. The "wall target" idea appears to have been approved by some British schools, and examples of British targets of a similar pattern are shown in the accompanying photographs.

German weapon training and classification range work appears to have been very much curtailed when compared with the British type of training. The Germans had a tendency towards putting their recruits on the field firing ranges as quickly as possible, in fact, after only the rudimentary classification range work had been done. I don't think anyone can dispute that the vast training area in Westphalia was the finest the German Army had, and therefore it is logical to see in it something approaching their ideal. And there, after giving the recruit the bare bones of shooting on the normal ranges they turned him loose on the many and varied field firing ranges with which the training area abounds, and upon which practically every manner of shooting could be practised within restricted limits. Throughout, the Hun seemed to pay very little attention to anything in the way of long range shooting; 300 metres appeared to be the limit, and this fact may be why there is so little evidence of any long range sniping.

Their policy certainly seems to have been to merge weapon training and fieldcraft into its tactical application on the ground at the earliest possible moment and to allow the two to go, or run, hand in hand, instead of separate entities as was the British policy. There are many British officers who once having caught the idea of this type of training are most enthusiastic about it, and wish to incorporate much of the Teuton idea into present and future training. That it has excellent points cannot be denied, and because of my experience in sniper training I am all for "natural" training. But to my mind field firing as practised by both the British and German armies does not warrant the term "natural" in its fullest sense. From what I saw of the German field firing ranges in the training area in Westphalia it was immediately apparent that they were "ranges," and situated so that the fire from all ranges fell into a "cauldron." In other words there was present the blasted "safety-bug" and the ranges were made to conform to that ideal. The targets, too, were not natural; I never saw a three-dimensional target on a German range, but all targets bore a very close resemblance to those used on British ranges. The silhouette targets were head, head and shoulders, trunk and full body, and paired head and shoulders symbolising a machine gun team. They were all capable of appearing and disappearing being attached to a network of wires running into control bunkers. These dugouts were solidly constructed of thick concrete, and again one was impressed by the safety measures that the German always adopted when indulging in shooting, and which many of us considered alien to a truly militarist nation such as Germany.

This question of field firing brings out an interesting point about targets. On such a range I think it is essential that the base of any stereotype target (I am not speaking of *the* sniper target, the three-dimensional dummy) should be of material which will emit some noise when struck by a bullet; again, targets which are constructed so that they fall when hit afford much more natural practice and give greater enjoyment to the shooter.

Many of these ranges in Westphalia were long, dreary flat stretches of country with little or no relief. But there was one "natural" thing about them; during the months of August and September they were damnably uncomfortable as the result of ceaseless attacks by millions of particularly hostile horseflies which alighted so softly on the flesh that one did not realise that they were there until they had bitten! And to stalk and lie in the heather pursued by about two hundred of these brutes was in many ways worse than running the gauntlet of enemy bullets.

One of the most interesting spots in the training area was that upon which had been built a model Russian village. It was perfect, and as one stood on a slight hill and looked down at the village there was undoubtedly the mantle of the Slav upon it, and, at any moment, one expected a typical Russian peasant to wander down the street. We were agreed that having such a training ensemble it would be eminently possible to devise, and execute, all possible methods of attack on such a village, and reach a stage so that when an actual "village assault" in Russian territory was imminent, all that was necessary for the commanding officer to say was "Plan 1 or 2" or whatever number had been given to a certain assault, and then he could sit back knowing that the plan would go as smoothly as oil spreads on water.

❊ ❊ ❊ ❊

Basically, German rifle training differed little from our own, but on normal German ranges many of the practices were fired from wooden platforms, or trestles, covered with coconut matting, which leaves one with the idea that the rifleman was a little pampered.

One or two of the positions taught to the young German rifleman were singular when compared with British training. For instance, in one position the recruit lay prone on the wooden platform with the forestock of his rifle resting on sandbags "midway between muzzle and forward sling swivel." He was given alternative methods of holding: (a) normal, left hand forward; (b) left hand placed under the rear of the butt. In the training pamphlet illustrating such a position no mention was made of the effect of a "rested" rifle. It is amusing to read that the breath should be held until the order "fire" is given. No doubt this was used as a means of torture by inquisitorial range officers and responsible for many purple-faced Teutons! This position was stated to be one "mainly for defence." The "attacking" prone position was the standard lying, without cover or rest.

More training in the kneeling, sitting and standing positions was given than in the British Army. Throughout rifle training, emphasis was laid on the fact that it was the right hand pulling the rifle back into the shoulder which produced the main gripping force.

When speaking of the sitting position the German manuals stated that this was used mainly when the firer was camouflaged, and suggested that more accuracy would be obtained if the soldier's back was against a tree trunk, and maybe the rifle rested on the very low branch of a tree! Comfort was apparently a fetish!

The stance for the standing position was conventional, and emphasis laid on the fact that such a position was for near engagements, and for shooting at fast moving, side to side targets. In firing standing behind trees, it was

Upper: GERMAN CLASSIFICATION RANGE

These were well constructed and entirely "safe" but they gave clear evidence of "safety bug biting," being too artificial and sheltered and certainly not "military" enough. Those white squares at top of backstop are not the targets but are target numbers, the actual targets are well below these designations and rise out of butts.

Lower: GERMAN FIELD FIRING RANGE

Note the rail tracks; along these they ran dummy tanks. Area in the background was known as the "cauldron," into which fell the fire from many other ranges.

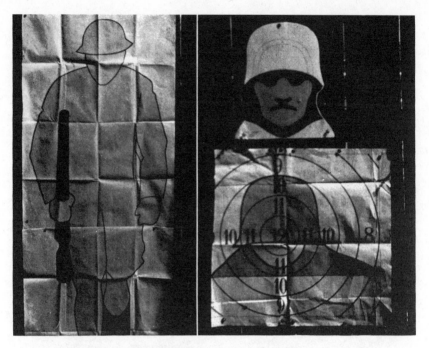

EUROPEAN RIFLE RANGE TARGETS

Left is a German silhouette target of a British "tommy" running. These targets were found in many different shades of colouring.

Right shows two different targets; top is a British "Hun Head" type of target; bottom is the center section of the German range classification 300 meters target.

Sitting position, as given in the German manual, and a very poor position according to American teachings and practice. Note in all these illustrations that the Germans teach the recruit to lay his thumb across the grip of the stock and not alongside of it.

ordered that as much leg and arm support as possible should be obtained from the tree trunk.

Included in the riflemen's manuals were photographs of German riflemen in trees—the latter always conveniently bare of all foliage. It was made quite clear that as secure a position as possible should always be obtained, whether lying or sitting, and that the rifle should have a solid foundation, rested on a branch or in the crook of branch and trunk. And, in this case, warning was given that rifles rested on wood had a tendency to shoot high.

✿   ✿   ✿   ✿

MAINLY IN ENGLAND

Home Guard · Ranges · Days of Days · Near
Shaves and Two Hits

HOME GUARD

THE weapons with which the Home Guard, or L.D.V. (Local Defence Volunteers) as the body was originally known, were equipped were many and various. I remember most vividly that night in May 1940 when Mr. Anthony Eden appealed over the wireless for recruits for the Local Defence Volunteers. Things were pretty grim—everyone in England knew that; and thousands of men who had not really thought themselves cut out for doing ambulance, ARP or fire service work, said "Here, at last, is something I can do." In the company in which I found myself, we started arms drill with dummy all-wood rifles. Some of the instruction was as archaic as the "rifles."

We went on guard duties immediately, taking with us the weapons we owned, or those which were loaned to us. In the first flush of enthusiasm many men spent all night watching and waiting for German parachutists without a thought for bed or work on the following day. But soon, wiser counsels prevailed, and the guard duties were put on a roster footing, and everyone got his share of sleep. On my first night's guard the total armament between nine men consisted of three shotguns, two double barrel and one single barrel (two of which were mine) 12 bores, one Savage .22 rifle and one Browning pistol, the latter very rusty and I should imagine more of a menace to the firer than anyone else.

Gradually we obtained more weapons, many not so lethal as shotguns, but it was some time before we received our first consignment of rifles, M 17s. Personally I spent many happy hours as a most willing volunteer cleaning the M 17s; they were certainly a tough proposition being more swamped in grease than any rifles I had seen before—or since. But it was good to feel a real rifle, and the time could not come quick enough when we took them out on an improvised range; the butts were perfect, or, I should say the butt-stop was perfect—a 100 feet high slag heap near a local colliery! These rifles certainly handled well, and in many ways I could not have wished to use a better or a more accurate weapon than the M 17. Unfortunately ammunition was very scarce, and we could not have the practice we all wanted—and needed. There was some exceedingly queer shooting to begin with, and it was surprising to see that some men missed a large improvised target at a range of 100 yards. But what such men lacked in accuracy they made up for in their keen enthusiasm, and once a miniature range was going well and the men got some rudimentary knowledge of holding and aiming their next visit to the "big" range yielded much better results. I do not think there was any occasion when we were allowed to fire more than five rounds in a day. And range days were very few and far between.

Quite a number of people held the opinion that if the Hun did arrive and perforce landed in wooded areas where he would probably escape detection much more easily, and where it would certainly be better for him to hide-up, then the shotgun would be a better weapon than the rifle. There is no doubt that for very close quarter work the lethality of the 12, 16 or 20 bore cartridge cannot be dismissed lightly.

Two of the most interesting characters in the company were the company commander, who had won the Military Cross as a very youthful subaltern in World War I, and who led his men with great dash (and, for many of them, too much vigour) and an old sergeant-major who had been a sniper in the 1914–1918 clash. His bag had been something like 50 Huns, and apparently he had been one of the very few snipers in his Brigade to come through unscathed, and had collected a Distinguished Conduct Medal and a Military Medal in the interim. He had many good stories to tell, and it was certainly good to see him shoot, on our much too infrequent excursions to the range.

Some of the shotguns we used in those early days were weird and wonderful instruments, though we never saw ancient muskets and blunderbusses such as at least one member of the German counterpart of the Home Guard was equipped with over the Rhine in March 1945. Our tour of duty usually finished at dawn, and since one or two of our guard areas were situated in really good shooting country, I, at least, made full use of the opportunity and I often returned home to breakfast with something for the pot. This "pot-hunting" became rather embarrassing after a little while, since a decided preference to be on guard with me by certain other men was solely mercenary. Still the rabbits and pigeons were a menace to the war effort, and if there were no Germans to tickle with the shotgun the game provided good practice. Even when we were equipped with rifles, and uniformed, I still carried the shotgun around, or at least some of my "gun-bearers" did the carrying. Those were great days really, and indeed very pleasant to re-live in agile memory.

The shotgun I used mainly was an old Harrington & Richardson (Worcester, Mass., USA) single barrel 12 gauge which I bought for 25/– in the following manner:

A friend of mine was in a village public-house after a morning shoot slaking a thirst which had been engendered by a few miles of tough going over plough. One of the yokels seeing his gun asked him if he was interested in buying a good single-barreled shotgun, a 12 bore. He went home and brought it along. He wanted 50/– for it, but my friend offered him 20/–. After much bickering my friend pointed to a pigeon which had just settled in a large tree facing the public-house front door, and said:—"You see that pigeon. Well, I'll take a crack at it and if I get it I'll give you the pigeon and 25/–. O.K.?" The local agreed. My friend inserted a cartridge, took careful aim and fired. The pigeon slumped from the tree, the yokel gathered it in and 25/–, and my friend got the gun. He passed it on to me later that day for the same price he had paid. I have it still, and can quite honestly say that it is the best twenty-five shillings worth I have ever had; I would not sell it for ten times that amount. I have secured clean kills with that gun at ranges at which I should not have thought it possible to make hits. The range at which my friend hit the pigeon was nearly fifty yards and he confessed that he was very surprised when the bird dropped like a stone. I have bagged a number of high flying duck with it, and would not thank anyone for a Churchill in its place. I look forward to much more game falling to its trusty 32" barrel.

Once we got a good quantity of .22 ammunition we indulged in a considerable amount of small bore indoor shooting, but I am afraid that this type of shooting is not my meat. I am not blaming the rifles, although some of them were of no use at all. One rifle which I did use at that time, and shot much better with it than any other .22 I have ever used, was an old Lee-Metford which had been tubed for .22. It was a splendid shooting job and at 25 yards, which was usually the limit of our small bore shooting, it was capable of putting up some extremely close groups.

[235]

Each platoon had one Browning automatic rifle, and nearly everyone shot well with this weapon. Due to its weight this rifle was entrusted to the care of our platoon giant, a butcher weighing 244 lbs. and standing 74" high. He was a capable performer with his personal weapon, and it always amused me when he went through all the normal rifle drills with it.

It was interesting to see how many men experimented with shotgun cartridges in order to increase the range and killing power of their weapons. Improvised shotgun projectiles of all kinds made their appearance, and many were positively dangerous. We who knew something about the job stressed that it was dangerous to try increasing the range of a shotgun by cutting a cartridge through the middle. It was pointed out that the only possible result of this was to shoot a projectile of greater diameter than the actual bore of the gun, since the outside diameter of a 12 bore cartridge case is greater than the actual diameter of the bore of the barrel, and the inevitable effect of such a practice is to produce pressures which are highly dangerous. It was stressed that this method should never be tried in any circumstance, but I am afraid that in many instances our counsel fell on conveniently deaf ears.

Very tentatively we suggested to some of the more bloodthirsty volunteers that they might pour melted wax into the shot charge after loading, but warned them that with this procedure there is a very definite danger of bulging the barrel at the choke. Apropos of this melted wax idea, one morning one of the volunteers demonstrated to some of his followers the dynamic effect possible from such a projectile as that formed by melted wax and the shot, choosing as his target an old barn door which hung slackly on rusty hinges. Now the door was in pretty bad condition, and knowing from previous experience the capabilities of such projectiles I expected the door to be in a mess after being hit. But even I did not bargain for what actually happened. The firer took up his stance about 20 yards from the barn, put the gun to his shoulder, took aim at the centre of the door and pulled the trigger. Most of the watchers were standing close to him and probably involuntarily blinked at the noise of the explosion of the charge. They must therefore have been greatly surprised when, after the blink, they opened their eyes wide to find that the door had vanished! On the impact of the solid projectile the door simply disintegrated, and all that was left was a brown mist hovering over a heap of brownish rubble and splinters, and the rusty hinges! The door must have been in a far worse condition than was apparent from looking at it, but nevertheless it was a most spectacular demonstration, and everyone went away very impressed with the terrific power of such a projectile fired from a 12 bore gun.

To the would-be improvisers of shotgun projectiles my advice was that they should take a 16 bore cartridge and cut it in half through the felt wad and load the half containing the shot into a 12 bore cartridge instead of the usual shot charge. The pressure developed by such a projectile would be normal, but I warned them that even with this idea there was a risk of bulging a barrel at the choke in the case of a heavily choked weapon, since although the diameter of the 16 bore cartridge is less than that of a 12 bore barrel it is not always less than that of a very fully choked muzzle; therefore they were advised to see whether the 16 bore cartridge could be inserted into the 12 bore muzzle before using such a projectile.

At this time quite a number of "lethal" bullets made their appearance for use in shotguns, and I never could look at these without a grimace of distaste. Assuredly I should not have liked to be on the receiving end of such projectiles at close range. It took quite a time to persuade some men that such bullets were perfectly safe to use in shotguns, and especially that they could be used in any barrel from a full-choke to a true cylinder without any fear of damaging the choke. The pressures developed by cartridges loaded with "lethal" bullets are lower than those loaded with shot, and after some hard work we finally persuaded the extreme novices in the world of firearms that such cartridges were safe. And then, of course, we had to point out that there is no really high degree of accuracy with such cartridges. Personally I have found that the combination of an ordinary shotgun and "lethal" bullets is very effective up to 30 or 40 yards, and I think most men who have shot with such a combination will agree with my range, and contention.

❖   ❖   ❖   ❖

There can be no doubt that the Home Guard was a marvellous organisation, and that it did a tremendous amount of good. I am sure that it prolonged the life of many men, taking them away from a life of total sedentary and lack of healthy interest. Thousands of men discovered the delights of shooting for the first time, and it is good to see the number of current rifle clubs which owe their origin to Home Guard days. And there is no doubt that any young fellow going into the Armed Forces from the Home Guard had a great advantage over the recruit who had not been in the Citizens Army.

Personally I enjoyed every minute of my brief time in the Home Guard—the comradeship, the long night watches, the route marches, the exercises and the infrequent excursions to the range. And I laughed a good deal—there were many humorous incidents. One of our jobs was to provide men for an observation post which was on top of the high tower of an old church. The tower was so small that it was extremely difficult for more than one man to be standing up there at a time, so the customary practice was for one man to stand leaning over the parapet whilst the other sat on the cold stone floor with his feet dangling in the murky space of the belfry well. It was an hazardous climb up to the tower, on wooden and steel ladders which passed between the great bells, and across narrow wooden planks which looked most unsafe; a final leap had to be taken from a short steel ladder in order to grasp the edges of the trap door and hoist oneself up on to the tower. It was a most unpopular venue of duty and when it was finally struck off the duty list there were many sighs of hearty relief.

My colleague on my first night's duty there was a very fat insurance agent who was extremely nervous. It took me a long time to persuade him to move from the final ladder to the trap-door rail, and then considerable physical exertion to pull him up through the door; during this last operation I managed to clutch hold of his braces so tightly that both buttons came off the back of his trousers. He took a first "look-see" from the parapet, and started to shiver immediately. It was certainly eerie up there and he gave a startled yelp as an owl passed very near the tower. A little later he said that he could see movement down below amongst the grave stones, and altogether he felt very sorry for himself. Just after midnight, and that church clock certainly made a noise when it chimed, he interrupted a one-sided conversation on shooting by saying that he wondered how his wife was getting along, and that he hoped the sirens would not go, since his wife had never been left alone previously; immediately he had passed this remark brought on no doubt by that fact that we could hear the low distant hum of Jerry planes, the air raid sirens sounded, and with a loud bleat he commenced running round the very restricted confines of the tower, and did not stop until he was out of breath. I expected him to fly over the parapet at any second.

To one who was used to firearms it was always amusing to see how a lot of the Volunteers handled weapons; many of them were really scared. We had quite a number of accidental "let-offs" and it was usual in these instances for the firer to be much more shaken than his comrades. One night we were mounting a guard at the local electricity works, and had been given the order to "charge magazines." The NCO in charge, a veteran of the World War I, came round to inspect the charged magazines, and as he passed each man the latter drove home the bolt over the top round in the magazine, pressed the trigger and applied the safety catch. One over-zealous individual apparently drove one up the spout and away she went—the look on the next man's face, and that of the NCO, was worth a guinea a box.

One night on duty at a golf clubhouse, which had a flat roof and was situated in an ideal observation site, I was the NCO in charge, and was watching one of the men loading his M 17 and as the bolt went forward I saw that he had taken a cartridge into the breech. I told him what had happened but he denied it, saying that he was always extraordinarily careful and that he would bet me five shillings that there was no cartridge in the breech. I got up from my chair and leapt across to him, but I was too late, since with the remark "I'll prove it" he raised the muzzle of the rifle ceilingwards and pulled the trigger. The noise was deafening, and a loud howl coming from the roof made me think, for a terrible moment, that he had hit one of the guard. But it turned out to be just a howl of fright, the bullet having sailed up into the night sky and missing him by about a couple of inches. A terrific shower of plaster came down from the ceiling and the culprit's face was covered with a white film, which added lustre to his already ghostly pallor. The entry hole of the bullet was very small indeed, but up on the roof, which was thin asphalt, an area about 12" in circumference had been torn up.

One further similar incident is worthy of note; we had gone into a neighbouring city shortly after a terrific blitz in order to carry out anti-looting patrols. I took a party out and for a couple of hours patrolled the still smoking streets, keeping a sharp look-out for anyone lurking in, or close-by, damaged shops. At the conclusion of the patrol we returned to a regular Army barracks where we were to bed down on the floor for the remainder of the night. Getting the patrol into line I gave the order "Unload." There was a furious rattling of bolts, and sharp metallic rings as the rounds hit the concrete floor. Then came the report. One man had miscounted and the bullet passed through the high ceiling into the next floor greatly disturbing a couple of military policemen who were asleep on the floor. The bullet had passed between them. They were a little annoyed, and I am sure that the culprit, by this time ashen-faced, with shock sweat pearled on his forehead, was most heartily glad that he was in the Home Guard rather than the Army proper! I am quite ready to believe that every time he passed a military policeman from that night onwards he trembled.

So many of these incidents happened that an order was issued that the NCO in charge of each guard should be a last-war veteran, and that he should personally load and unload all rifles of the guard when going on, and coming off, duty. Naturally, we who had been riflemen for years were greatly incensed at such an order, and our natural reaction was that if we were not to be trusted to load and unload a rifle it was high time that we packed the whole thing in; but in the cause of discipline we stifled our annoyance and went on our first guard after the promulgation of the order prepared to be treated like the smallest of small boys. The NCO i/c the guard, a sergeant sporting the 1914 ribbon, was not a popular member of the company, and an order such as that just issued was definitely to his liking. All the time he was loading the rifles, watched with a smouldering heat by at least two of us, he was prating about the care of handling weapons and that it was quite right that only old soldiers should be entrusted with the job and so forth; we were soon heartily sick of his prattle. The night passed off without incident, and then at stand-

down, at six o'clock, he was fussing around taking our
rifles from us and jerking the bolts backwards and forwards
in the approved manner, again impressing upon us his
responsibility. The guardroom was only a small place, with
three-tier bunks for the off-duty chaps on either side of the
wall. The NCO was unloading the last rifle when there was
a terrific crack, and the next split second through a shower
of brick dust there hurtled a bullet snarling through the
air like a most angry wasp. There was a terrific dive for the
bunks! The NCO sat on the floor with a dazed look on his
face. We saw that he was very close to tears so did not
taunt him. But he never lived that episode down; and on
our next guard duty we were again allowed to load and
unload our rifles!

*   *   *   *

Rifle Ranges

The ranges I have fired on during the War years have been
legion. Some have been good, some bad and others indifferent. But there has been one thing which has been constant throughout, and that is the weather. It was almost
invariably bad, or damned bad. During my early service
days I did a fair amount of firing on ranges in South Wales,
and in many ways these were excellent, but since they were
within a stone's throw of the sea the sand was a nuisance,
especially with the LMGs. But it was to a certain extent a
"natural" range, the sandhills forming natural firing points,
etc., and was therefore of far more value for service training
than the more orthodox types of range.

Of the latter type by far the best I ever fired on was a
range in Northumberland. The warden, an ex-service man,
was quite young and a marvellous fellow, and everything
about the range was perfectly kept and maintained. A very
fine shot himself, he had been a county champion, he was
as keen as mustard on the greatest of all sports and anyone
whom he knew to be an enthusiastic rifleman could ask for

anything and be sure of getting it if it were at all possible to procure it. I became very friendly with him and he frequently loaned me his competition rifle, an S.M.L.E. fitted with a Parker-Hale aperture sight, which was truly a delight to use. At any range, the bulls came with an almost uncanny monotony. My unit did a great deal of firing on this range, and after a time all the men became really keen, and the general standard of shooting improved tremendously. Unfortunately we had just reached this enthusiastic stage when we received orders to move, and never again were we privileged to use such a range, or find so much time and opportunity to shoot.

Some time later, when in the south of England, the CO said that we simply must find a range somewhere which gave a decent length shoot. We found one after being told about it by a neighbouring unit, and searching for it for some hours despite the fact that we had the map reference! There were no firing points, but the two-target butts were modelled on the real thing, and had they been maintained they would have been very good indeed. We found that we could get a seven hundred yards shoot on this range, but the men I took there, and myself, were never able to do justice to our shooting since we had to keep a most wary eye on the large number of skittish young bulls which frequented the range area, and many times on our way up to the butts we moved with far more haste than decorum because of the most evidenced intention of those bulls.

Early in 1944 the CO ordained that every man in the Squadron should fire the War Course. We were in the north of England, and the only range available in that lonely spot was one of six targets, four of which were serviceable. It was situated in a heather-clad valley and had been in operation for sixty years, so the range warden, an octogenarian whose limbs creaked in perfect unison with the ancient target frames, proudly informed me. The first time we collected the range warden we were in a 3 ton lorry and it took the combined efforts of my sergeant and myself to hoist him into the cab. The next day, a bath-chair not being available, we used a Jeep.

The range warden did not think much of such rifles as the S.M.L.E., the P 14 and the No. 4. The Martini-Henry was the last weapon he had fired. My remark that he probably shot well with a Brown Bess passed completely over his silver-haired head; he probably thought that I was talking about his Grace's deer-stalking pony, for he never tired of talking of his Grace the Duke of —— on whose estate the range was situated. The only other topic of his conversation was the many crimes of the Home Guard.

The range orders were lengthy and included an order that red flags should be hoisted at points ABC and XYZ before any firing took place. The warden announced quite proudly that there were no flags, and that no flags had been flown since World War I.

For seven long, weary and sore-throating days the valley was enlivened by sleet and snow and rain and my monotonous chant of the formal range fire-point orders. On the last day it was the turn of the Headquarters people, the batmen, the cooks and the M.T. wallahs, to fire. I expected an exasperating time, and I got it. The first practice was 100 yards grouping. I commenced my speech:—"On the command 'Load' you will go down and load with six rounds in the magazine and one in the breech. On the command 'Fire' you will fire the first two rounds into the butts on the right-hand side of your target—I repeat, on the right-hand side of your target. This is just to warm up your rifle and ensure that there will be no loss of elevation with the five shots you are placing on your target for your group. Remember the first two shots must *not* appear on your targets. I don't want any target with seven shots on it. The white aiming mark is placed on the centre of the target for your guidance in this grouping practice—so use it. Take the same point of aim each time. I repeat, take the same point of aim each time." I paused. One of the detail turned and said "Would you mind repeating that, sir?" I did, with red face and rising heat. I gave the order "Load" and all four men swooped down on the firing point like a set of rugger players. The orderly room runner cleaved a furrow eighteen inches by two inches in the mud. I deemed it advisable to inspect the barrels before they loaded. Three of them were choked with mud. I began again, and repeated the orders. They fired. After five minutes' agonized waiting, the firing point telephone rang—yes, it actually worked sometimes! —and the irate voice of my sergeant in the butts wanted to know what the blankety-blank those perishers were playing at—there were seven shots on No. 1 target, four on No. 2, nine on No. 3 and none at all on No. 4!!

The shooting in respirators was tragic, culminating in one man detailed for No. 1 target aiming at No. 2 target and being signalled a wash-out from No. 3! At the 300 yards application practice I paid particular attention to the CO's batman, whose paunch adequately prevented him from adopting anything like a good position. With an agonized look on his pudgy face he twisted and squirmed uncomfortably, pointed his rifle towards his neighbour and bleated, "Please, sir, this rifle won't fire." I told him to push forward the safety catch! He grunted, placed his thumb on the safety catch and I watched, totally devoid of speech, whilst his fat forefinger curled round the trigger. The rifle fired, the bullet hit the ground about ten yards in front of the firing point, and the batman let out a terrific howl as the butt came into contact with his chin. As he tenderly rubbed his chin he gazed at me in a most hurt manner. Ruefully he continued to fire. The second shot hit about thirty feet above the target. His third shot hit the slightly raised 100 yards firing point. I mentioned these "strikes" to him. His fourth shot sent up a shower of earth just below his neighbour's target. His fifth shot hit the top of the butt a shade nearer his own target. "You were low again" I told him. And then the white disc appeared over the bull! The batman, his fat face beaming triumphantly, looked up towards me. When I asked if his favourite billiard's shot was the "in-off" he replied with a contemptuous sniff. By the good grace of fortune we had no accidents, but a serried mass of waving barrels reduced me to a nervous wreck. I was still weak at the knees when I returned to camp in the late afternoon. The CO beamingly asked me, "How did it go—did they shape all right?" I might have been disrespectful, but I just smiled, sadly!

❀ ❀ ❀ ❀

DAYS OF DAYS

I have never laid claim to be a really good, let alone a brilliant, shot. But looking back on the last six years there have been days when I have thoroughly enjoyed myself on the range; and on those days I built up a reputation within my own unit which frequently caused me some perturbation when endeavouring to live up to it. In the earliest days of my service life I did fairly well with a P 14 with which rifles my unit at that time was armed. As a recognition token of this apparent skill I was issued one of the six S.M.L.E. rifles which the unit armoury housed. Why the officer in charge thought that the Lee-Enfields should be given to the chaps who had shot well with the P 14s I never understood. I like the Lee-Enfield and think it a jolly fine rifle, the best when rapid fire is needed, but for accuracy the average S.M.L.E. was some way behind the P 14. Anyhow, after a short time I was given a discharger cup, for the housing and projection of 36 grenades, to fit the S.M.L.E. and thus became a rifle-grenadier in addition to a rifleman. This was a job which I heartily disliked, and I had the misfortune to drop my first grenade slap-bang into the specified target on the first field firing exercise after becoming a "grenadier." It was a sheer accident; I had just closed my eyes as I pushed down on the trigger, but no one

GERMAN KNEELING POSITION

A very poor position, according to American ideas and practices.

Shooting from a tree, as taught by the German manual. Note that rifle rests in crotch of tree while left hand supports the butt of the rifle.

"The big telescope afforded a terrific advantage to the British sniper." (The observer in above sketch is using the telescope case as a head rest.)

believed me, and I remained a marked man for the grenade and discharger cup until I reached the elevated rank of junior NCO.

At OCTU we were issued with S.M.L.E.s and told that these rifles were no use as regards shooting! This surprising statement was amply borne out when we went on to the ranges for the first of our very limited visits. My first three shots at 100 yards were wash-outs, and according to the signal, very low and much to the left. My target was an end one, and aiming well to the right of the butts and high my fourth shot was signalled as an outer low. For my fifth and last shot with 600 yards on the sights I took an aim half-way up the flagpole which was standing on the extreme righthand edge of the butts, and lo and behold, up came the disc to signal a bull. On the next practice I did a little better; at least, all the shots hit the target! I would have been very discouraged had we not been forewarned about the prowess of these rifles, and the facts that no one else did much better, and plenty were worse, and that we were told that in view of using such rifles no notice would be taken of the scores obtained! This, to me, appeared queer training for embryo weapon training officers! The LMGs were no better, and far more shots hit the earth in front of the butts than went on to the targets.

Once having been commissioned and joined a unit, where I was soon made weapon training officer, and being told by my CO, who was very keen on shooting and a splendid shot himself, that I could have all my own way as regards training methods, I proceeded to enjoy myself. The men, knowing of my enthusiasm for firearms and shooting, were always keen that I should fire alongside them, and they always did their damndest to beat me. Fortunately for my prestige this rarely happened, not because of my superlative shooting ability but rather because they were frequently terrible in *their* shooting. I may be wrong but I have always maintained that one of the greatest shooting attributes is consistency, and I much preferred to have a rifleman who, though perhaps incapable of really brilliant shooting on one day, or certain days, was always to be relied upon to put up a decent score. I was fortunate enough to have such a rifleman in my unit. If he never had a brilliant day he never had a bad one, and I could always rely upon him to put up the best score in the Squadron shooting eight. At this time the unit was equipped with the P 14, and the majority of these rifles were capable of first class performance. At the request of the CO, I kept back one of these rifles when we changed over to the No. 4, and that was the rifle which accompanied me when we went over the water on D Day.

Throughout the time that I was weapon training officer I never missed a range day, and consequently I must have fired thousands of rounds through hundreds of rifles. Testing a man's rifle is always a tricky business for the firing point officer, and if a man was shooting badly and asked me to test his rifle I always wondered what was going to happen! Invariably, to get the feel of the weapon, I fired a couple of rounds into the butts to accustom myself to the trigger, etc., and then banged home a shot on the target proper. And since I am essentially human it was always a source of great satisfaction when the white disc appeared. Sometimes, of course, it was not a bull which was signalled, and then I used to fire five rounds to see exactly what was wrong. In the case of the P 14 rifles it was very rarely that the rifle was at fault.

A rather curious feature of my shooting was that I frequently shot better when I was not feeling too well, and sometimes when I felt like jumping over a five barred gate my shots would stray where they shouldn't. During those glorious training days I did manage to put up the best score in the Squadron on the full war course, and one morning, with a chap's rifle I had never handled before, I scored eight hits in eight shots on a three seconds exposure snap target; this may sound very commonplace but the range was 300 yards, and the shots fired in a squally wind and driving rain, conditions which made it extremely difficult to determine whether the target was exposed or not!

One day, during practice on a 30 yards range, two of the men asked one of my colleagues if he would test their rifles. Both had been shooting very badly and blamed their rifles. In order to impress, my colleague said "Oh yes, Mr. Shore and myself will just knock a hole in a couple of pennies if you will put them up at 30 yards." The two pennies were produced with alacrity and fixed on top of the target frames and we settled down on the firing point, myself cursing the other chap for being such a boastful fool, and surrounded by about thirty eager men all hopeful that we should miss by a mile. We fired at the same instant and both pennies disappeared. I think that both of us, as we sauntered pseudo-nonchalantly up the range, were of the opinion that the disappearance of the coins was the result of the target frames being hit. But to our great joy both pennies were well and truly "pranged." That spot of shooting greatly impressed the men; they knew that we had never handled those rifles before, and from that day our reputations were made, and since the other officer left the unit shortly afterwards I was left alone for nearly three years with a reputation up to which to live. On occasion it took a good deal of "flannelling" to get around apparent failure! The odds against our hitting those pennies must have been terrific, but such things do happen—sometimes.

I am the first to admit that I have been lucky with my shooting on many occasions, and I can recall a number of times when I have been fortunate enough to do something decent when a few of the men have been around. In Holland I had sent out to me some Hun head targets and at any odd moment it was my custom to take a few of the chaps on to an old German 100 metres range. I regret to say that the average standard attained was absolutely rotten, and one morning out of eight men shooting only one of them hit the

Hun head target. I admit that some of these men, and their rifles, had been kicked around more than a little, and that it was a nasty morning which made the targets difficult to pick out even at that range, but they certainly should have been capable of doing much better. One of them asked if I thought *I* could hit those "wee" targets as he called them, and proffered his rifle. From past experience in England I knew this fellow's rifle had been a particularly good specimen, and I took it from him with confidence. I fired five rounds at the target, and was gratified to find that all five shots were within the centre scoring ring and that four of them could have been covered by a $1\frac{1}{2}''$ circle. The men were suitably impressed.

I used to be both amused and annoyed by their attitude towards shooting in gas masks. They would laboriously don their respirators, perhaps fire one shot and then, in muffled tones, would come the cry of "I can't see; everything's blurred." And then shots would be flying all over the place unless one ordered them to unload. Because they couldn't see the bull they could not see anything. It took a long time to impress upon them with words, and demonstrations, that even with misted eyepieces it was simple enough to score inners if not bulls, provided one fired *at the centre of the large target* which *could* be seen through even badly blurred eyepieces.

Early in 1944 nearly all the unit were given leave, and during the time they were away the CO said that it was imperative that, in view of things to come, all the rifles should be re-tested, and any found wanting should be discarded. The only decent rifleman remaining at Headquarters was the very consistent shot I have mentioned earlier, so I roped him in and in three days we tested thoroughly about 130 No. 4 rifles. It was quite a big job, but I suffered no shoulder soreness at the end of it. We finished up on the last afternoon firing at sixpences with the rifles we had selected as being the best of the lot. It is curious how much satisfaction one gets from defacing the coin of the realm!

Very few of the men in my unit had ever fired a rifle before entering the service. One or two who had been keen users of air rifles showed immediate promise. If I discovered that a man had used a Webley air rifle I knew that he should have some knowledge of the shooting game since I have used such a weapon myself for years. In the days before the war I kept a Webley .22 air rifle down at the office and spent many happy lunch hours banging away at barrel vent pegs set up on nails; these make excellent targets for all types of .22 shooting for when hit they fly sky high and disintegrate, behaviour which is encouraging and satisfying to the shooter. In the office itself when the Powers that Be were absent I used to set up long sticks of red sealing wax, of which the office had what turned out to be *not* an unlimited supply, in a shallow bottle placed on top of a steel cabinet and fire at them with the Webley. It was very satisfying to see the sticks break up, to hear the patter of the falling pieces and to see a cloud of red dust descending. The spent pellets lodged in the wall, fortunately in a very dark corner of the office. I have often wondered what the decorator thought when he came across the pellet strewn wall some months later—I was away playing a sterner game! At the time of the sealing-wax smashing I was 31 years young —are not all ardent riflemen and shooters boys at heart? Agreed?

One more lucky shot which sent my stock soaring occurred in Holland in the winter of 1944–1945. I had been visiting one of my posts and had just left when I saw a large hare loping over the field to my left heading for the path along which I was walking. I loosened my holster and drawing my S. & W. .38 fired just as the hare leaped on to the track. It was its last leap. The shot having been spotted by the chaps at the post, the NCO came dashing out, and was profuse in congratulation, but more profuse in thanks when I presented him with the beast. In the fullness of my

[251]

thanks to the gods of shooting who ordained that I should be so blessed of them, I could do no other!

Once it became generally known that one was most interested in firearms, or that one's knowledge of weapons was something more than the authorities had laid down an officer should know, it was surprising the number of queries which came one's way. And the more questions one was asked the more one stood aghast at the deplorable lack of knowledge of firearms, and all matters apertaining to firearms, exhibited by the majority of service officers and men. When stationed in southern England in the autumn of 1943 the CO received a complaint from a very incensed farmer that some of our chaps had been shooting at, and killing, a number of his sheep, no doubt with, from one point of view, the laudable intention of supplementing service rations by a choice bit of roast mutton. The CO promised to look into the matter and sent for me, telling me that here was a job after my own heart! Well, to start with, I had to first find the farmer who had lodged the complaint; in his white heat of temper he had gone off without leaving his address, and since there were numerous farms in the neighbourhood it was like looking for the proverbial needle in a haystack. During the course of my search I received many other complaints about gates and hedges and such like, but since the farmer race must always have its grumble I took little notice, and in one case actually had a complaint myself since I politely asked one farmer if he would kindly remove the corpse of a sheep from a ditch close to one of my sections since it was not the most pleasant perfume in that district of stenches. When I finally found the farmer I wanted, it was to be shown the cartridge cases which had been found about the area from which the sheep had been K.O'd. As soon as I saw the 9mm cases I could say emphatically that no man in our unit had been the culprit since we had not one single round of that particular brand of ammunition. Later, further complaints came in about sheep being killed by rifle shots, without any "case" evidence; this was a much wider field and I should not have been surprised if some of our more ardent spirits were not involved. If so they must have shot much better than their prowess of the range suggested, since I have frequently found that the hair-brained specimens are poor performers with all weapons.

❀ ❀ ❀ ❀

Near Shaves and Two Hits

Apart from the narrow escapes in Europe I had one or two near squeaks in England before going over; I remember one day field firing on a range in Norfolk. My chaps were supposed to be giving covering fire to a platoon going forward, and to this end I had taken up a position on the extreme right of the range with my 12 LMGs. The other platoon was going up the range from a start point about 400 yards to my left, and as we crawled forward and into position overlooking the spot at which the snap targets representing the enemy would appear in due course, I saw that the attacking force had moved off. As usual on this type of field firing range there were a number of surprise targets—a fatigue man seeing the attackers were approaching would pull a lever which hoisted a number of targets to view.

On this particular day the fatigue man was probably asleep or so enjoying a smoke that he forgot about his job, and did not see the platoon until it was almost past him on his right. He acted and up went the targets. By all the rules of the game the attackers should not have engaged the targets since a moment's thought would have told them that to fire at that angle would result in the bullets falling on the covering fire party. Anyhow they did open up, and the result was that I, and my machine gunners, emulated rabbits in our attempts to get under cover from the fire which fell like rain. The first intimation I had of the shower of lead was when a thistle which was only about three inches in front of my nose was suddenly lopped off and fell to the ground. Fortunately no one was hit, and there is no doubt that it was good experience. My chaps were very boastful about it the next day, but my remarks to that platoon commander are not printable.

Some weeks later we were again on field firing practice, but the venue on this occasion was a very small make-shift range, used by the local Home Guard. The CO was very keen on the idea of the men becoming accustomed to advancing with covering fire, so every afternoon for a week I took up a party of men to this small range, put up a few targets, and then leaving my sergeant to bring the men forward on my given signal I went out to a flank with an LMG and proceeded to give covering fire as each party advanced. I kept up the fire until the men were about five yards away and then they went in with the bayonet. They certainly gained a good deal of experience from this sort of stuff, and after a time they became used to bullets tearing up the earth and sand about five yards in front of them. One afternoon I gave the sergeant the LMG, told him to do the covering fire, and I took the men up the range. I had become a little weary of the fellows tearing into the targets and hoisting them aloft on their bayonets, so with each party that I took forward I impressed upon them the necessity of missing the targets with the bayonet on the "charge." I may as well have spoken to myself since, I suppose, with the excitement of the firing or with relief at the cessation of the LMG fire, all the men seemed to forget my injunction and the invariable result was a tossing of the targets like hay on a fork. As the men advanced behind the sand being torn up by the LMG fire they fired from the hip and there were times when I expected someone would shoot off a toe or two. When the last section of men had gone through I gave the order "Unload" and checked that the order had been obeyed. Usually all the men had fired their rounds at the target and everything was O.K. But one member of this last section "eased springs," closed his bolt swung straight round and with the rifle pointing at my stomach he pulled the trigger. Yes—there was one in the breech, and it missed my guts by the narrowest of margins. I rated him severely, and I think he was the most frightened of the two of us— then. It was about a couple of minutes later when the nearness of the shave came fully home to me—I was going on leave next day—and then I perspired freely.

I figured in a small way in a very curious incident on an airfield in South Wales early in 1942. There was a twin Lewis ack ack post a few yards away from a hut which housed the crew on duty on the gunsite. The same hut was also occupied by a patrol. On this particular morning I was NCO in charge of the patrol which was off duty, and, owing to the weather, the gun crew was also standing down. It was bitterly cold and most of us were crouched around the bunk house type of stove in the centre of the hut. Suddenly there was a long burst of machine gun fire and a shattering of wood. We hit the deck pretty smartly as the bullets sped over our heads and disappeared through the opposite wall of the wooden hut. The firing stopped and we dashed outside. There was no sign of anyone in the gunpit. We examined the guns; the barrels were warm and both guns were cocked. Taking the two magazines as being filled to capacity when placed on the guns, some forty odd rounds had "gone away." No satisfactory explanation of why the guns suddenly fired, and stopped, was ever forthcoming. One thing was certain—no human being had touched them.

Once or twice on the Continent I had near squeaks from our own chaps who appeared to take great delight in practising shooting with their own, and captured enemy, weapons at any odd time in any place without a single thought that such indiscriminate practice might spell finis to the poor unfortunate devil who got in their way. But fortunately I was never hit. So to date, touch wood, the only accidents in which I have been the principal figure, that is, the receiver, have been by shotgun. The first occurred on the last day of the shooting season in 1941. There were three guns out and we were tramping in single file along a glade in a small wood when I decided that nature must take its course and stepped behind a small bush which was only about a yard from the path. I had just completed nature's dictates when I heard a shot, and next instant a rabbit fell at my feet and I was very painfully conscious of a searing sensation in both feet. At the shock nature took a hand again!

I soon knew the full story. The leading gun had put up a rabbit and without thought he had swung and fired. He got the rabbit all right, but me as well! He was using a 20 bore. Quite a well-known shot he was very distraught at the accident, the first one he had been responsible for during many years' shooting experience. At the time I was wearing gum boots, and three pairs of socks, including one hefty pair of sea-boot stockings, but there were eight pellets in the right foot and seven in the left, one or two of which had penetrated down as far as the ankle bone. With the aid of matches and a pen-knife these were all dug out and, though damned painful, my feet managed to carry me throughout the afternoon's sport. Once home and the feet bathed I found it really difficult to walk for a couple of days. The marks of the pellets can still be seen around my ankles. I shudder to think what might have happened had it been a pheasant which got up and not a rabbit!

The other incident occurred about a year before the one narrated above. I was out shooting with an inexperienced friend one afternoon; he was just behind me when a flock of tame pigeons came into view, and not recognising them as domestic birds he flung up his gun and fired. The noise past my right ear was shattering as indeed it might be since a couple of the pellets had caught my ear. Had he been another yard or so behind me, or standing slightly to the left of his actual position, I should have been material for the undertaker. Even now some seven years afterwards I can still sweat when I think of that "incident."

An amusing incident in which I played the part of the firer and which might easily have had fatal consequences occurred one evening in March 1945 in Holland. Seeking a place in which to shoot and test rifles with comparative safety to everyone around I got some of my chaps in an off period to build a stop butt. This did not take long and the result was that we had quite a decent little 30 yards range. Naturally I wasn't content with this and with a little ingenuity on the part of the Unit armourer I managed to get a hundred yards firing point if such it can be called for it consisted of an old German bed mounted on metal poles which were embedded in a ditch, the ditch being coincident with 100 yards from the butts. It was a wide ditch too and since the land on the far side was "verboten" territory and the nearside was a wide road which was frequently used, it had to be the ditch or nowhere. And since the ditch at that time of the year was full everyone will appreciate that it took the art of an acrobat to get on to the bed, and once there it was by no means comfortable. Anyhow it sufficed to give me some practice. Half way down the range and slightly to the right there was a straw rick upon which some Dutchmen had been working during the day. Taking my favorite No. 4 at about 17.30 hours I went down to this range, fixed up a couple of head targets, clambered on the bed in the ditch and prepared to enjoy myself. The light was going fast. As I came up from the stop butt I had had a good look round to make sure that no one was about. I settled down as comfortably as possible, took careful aim and as my finger made final contraction on the trigger I became aware of a Dutchman crossing the range after appearing from the back of the rick. He uttered a terrific shriek, jumped about two feet in the air and fell down in some four or five inches of water, there were many pools around the rick, writhing convulsively. My saner judgement told me immediately that I could not have hit him since no one smacked with a .303 will act like an acrobat, but I put the rifle down, rolled off the bed into the ditch and splashing my way to the side, clambered out. When I reached the Dutchman I helped him to his feet; he was shaking and groaning terribly. I satisfied myself that he was suffering only from fright and then commenced to curse him as volubly as I could. Towards the end of the cursing, when my breath was running out, I placed my hands on my hips, the right hand close to my pistol holster. The Dutchman seeing this movement, and apparently thinking that I was intent upon finishing him off, again leaped into the air, turned and ran like a deer. Since there were quite a number of ditches and dykes intersecting the fields in that area it does not take much imagination to visualise that his departure was really interesting. By this time it was too late to re-commence shooting so after inspecting the target to make sure that I had connected with the one shot fired I collected the rifle and went back to my HQ. I have often wondered what tale that Dutchman told when he arrived home that night.

✿   ✿   ✿   ✿

HUNTING
AS SNIPER TRAINING

PRIOR to the end of the war in Europe there had been very little opportunity of indulging in any sporting shooting, but in one area in Holland in the winter of 1944–1945 there were many hares and quite a few coveys of partridges. These partridge were very wild and small, and it was quite difficult to get within range of them. But when one did manage to bag them they provided excellent eating and were a most welcome change from the normal, humdrum service diet.

I was amazed both here and in certain parts of Germany at the almost entire absence of bird life. Even the dingiest town in England has its crowds of friendly, inquisitive sparrows, but in large areas of Holland the only birds to be seen, and then only seldom, were the magpie and the crow. Even the heavily wooded areas showed no signs of wood-pigeon.

In Germany, generally, we got plenty of sport . . . wild boar, roebuck, duck, hares and rabbits and an occasional capercaille and wood-pigeon. In the Training Centre area the scope was widened by the inclusion of red and fallow deer. On occasion, hunting in Germany just before and just after the war ended was a precarious affair.

Terrible execution of game took place by American, British and Canadian troops, and, of course, by the thousands of DPs (Displaced Persons) who became armed, as the victorious Allied troops swept over the country, and a positive menace not only to game but to us. Many of these DPs were Russians and Poles, and a large number of them had worked voluntarily for their German masters, had fawned upon them and to a certain extent had a fairly decent time. Usually of the lowest mentality, they turned on the Germans like wolves when we were sweeping through Germany, and their many crimes would fill volumes. Personally I always felt like shooting such curs whenever I saw them, and I was by no means alone in that sentiment. Certainly I had a greater respect for the SS; they, at least, fought to the end well, if savagely, and one knew exactly where one stood with them.

Many Allied soldiers killed deer just for the sake of killing, and to a peace-time hunter and rifleman such wholesale slaughter was abhorrent. In the Sennelager area on one occasion over thirty head of deer, mostly hinds, were left dead after a "hunting" party armed with LMGs (and judging by the size of the wounds .5 LMGs had been used!) in AFVs had been around. It would not have been so bad had the meat been taken for consumption, rations at the time were not plentiful, but the carcasses had been left to rot. At Fassberg on one morning in May I saw the bodies of five roe does hanging in a Canadian armoury; these had been brought in to supplement the food supply but even so it was pretty dastardly, especially when one saw the four fawns these does had been carrying. There was no question of these people enquiring as to such a thing as the "closed" season. Actually I picked up a copy of an old "Closed season for game register"; found that roebuck came in on the 16th, June in that area and had the good fortune to get a nice little buck on that evening—a clean killing shot with one round of .303 from a No. 4 service rifle at a range of about 130 yards. Both entry and exit holes in the neck were small and neat.

One evening in May I was approached by a party of men asking for the loan of five Bren guns. When I asked them why they wanted the LMGs they said "To go hunting deer." I felt like clapping the whole lot under close arrest. Naturally they did not get them from us, but someone must have obliged, since a couple of evenings later when I was out with my platoon sergeant and a corporal we were skirting a marsh upon which there were a number of duck when a couple of Brens opened up from the opposite bank. We three dived for cover pretty rapidly as the bullets were ricocheting off the water and judging from the whines were coming into our area in divers ways—head-on, side-ways-on, etc. Occasionally full bursts went straight over our heads. We were pinned down in a particularly evil smelling drain for about ten minutes. I blew my whistle; we shouted in unison; and I fired a couple of shotgun cartridges but all to no avail. The shower of lead still came over. Finally the corporal, one of my best shots, crawled away and reaching a fairly safe position from which he could see the Bren gunners he fired a couple of rounds over their heads. That silenced them very quickly and they ran away. We tried to catch them but failed, and although I made enquiry of the units in the area I was not successful in finding the people responsible.

A very similar thing happened later on three occasions, but we knew the remedy, the efficiency of which was proved each time. There is no doubt that when one went hunting or nature watching at that time one ran a bigger risk of being hit than in many sectors during the war months. I knew of cases where men, who had never fired a machine carbine before, went out into the forests and just blazed away at anything they saw, and at any movement. They could not shoot, but that did not make any difference to them. One evening going down a glade I felt the angry whistle of a bullet go past my head. I dived off the path and made my way cautiously in the direction from which the bullet had come; there I found a couple of fellows using a Mauser rifle, firing at a bottle set up in the middle of the path!

One interesting shot was at a very large hare one evening when the light was failing. This hare I had spotted through binoculars; it was about four hundred yards away, and the ground rising immediately behind afforded a safe rifle shot. I noticed that there was a ridge about 150 yards from the hare, and a corporal and myself crawled there, cautiously peered over the top to find the animal still standing in the original spot. I borrowed the NCO's rifle, he told me that it was firing high, took as good an aim as possible in the bad light below the hare and fired. I saw, or thought I saw, a cloud of dust rise and through it the hare jump and fall. The corporal using my binoculars confirmed this; we went along and picked up the hare which was certainly very dead, shot in the neck. The bullet had struck the ground well in front of the target but had ricocheted absolutely straight some inches above the ground judging from the wound in the hare. We paced the distance from the point at which the bullet had struck the ground to the target and found it to be thirty paces. This, I think, is a point in favour of the argument put forward by the six o'clock aim devotees—that with such an aim a low shot is a potential killer by ricochet.

My platoon sergeant being a butcher in civilian life was the obvious choice for "game-skinner," and he very soon became heartily sick of the job. At that time our service rations were niggardly, and the meat sent up to our cook was always rotten and unfit to eat, so that it was imperative that I should go out and bag something for the pot. One night when the sergeant had two roebuck, three hares and half a dozen rabbits to attend to he was on the verge of mutiny!

MOVEMENT—AS TAUGHT AT THE SNIPING SCHOOL

When crawling on the stomach, or the elbow and knees, the best method of carrying the rifle was to grasp the sling with right hand close to forward swivel, muzzle to front, and allow the rifle to lie along the forearm, as shown in sketch above.

SNIPER PAIR IN TRAINING

one shooting, one observing with telescope . . . *around* cover.

Note the tremendous difference the sniper smock and camouflage veil make in a man's "merging into the ground," compared with the battle-dressed and bareheaded observer. It is especially interesting to note how the khaki of the "sniper's" trousers stand boldly out against the ground—the smock and veil of dark matt shades tone into the ground much more than the khaki trousers.

When down at the Training Centre it was the custom of the Sniping wing instructors to hunt frequently in the surrounding forests. This was indeed the most perfect way of keeping in trim for the instructional job, since once it was no longer possible to hunt and kill the Hun what could be better than to go out after game. We used our sniper rifles, and the results obtained showed that they were not too bad for the job. Naturally we should have preferred a lighter, more handy weapon—a Mannlicher-Schoenauer .256 with 'scope sight would have been the ideal—but such rifles were not available. In addition I used to take my Winchester carbine along, and here, and more especially later, this carbine stood up well to the job of hunting small deer.

Our usual practice was to go out after the completion of the day's work, and once having arrived at the hunting ground leave the truck on the outskirts of the forest, with strict instructions to the driver to garner wood and have a good fire awaiting us on our return, with the water boiling for the inevitable tea. The party, usually consisting of myself, three Lovat Scout NCOs and a German Jager, would go into the forests, and after splitting into two sections, each section knowing the working areas of both (in thick country this precaution is essential), we observed, stalked and shot until dark. We then made our way back to the truck with or without game as Dame Fortune decreed. We squatted round the leaping fire, ate sandwiches, drank tea, smoked and talked. I, for one, shall never forget those halcyon nights. After polishing off the contents of my pocket flask we retreated a little from the fire, laid down our groundsheets, adjusted the single blanket and went to sleep, under the stars, very happy. Usually, one of the Lovats, a deer-stalker by profession, and a very fine fellow who I am proud to consider my friend, stayed awake throughout the small hours, sat huddled close to the fire, continuously smoking his pipe and peering into the leaping flames. Sometimes lying back in the shadows, really too happy to sleep, I watched him sitting there, a smile lurking around the corners of the strong mouth which held the pipe stem so tightly. He had the aristocratic mien of the Redskin. Hunting for "D" was Life. I am sure that he was very content on those starry nights in Westphalia.

We were usually out of the blanket and about by 4 A.M., ready for the bacon sandwiches and tea. If we had been fortunate on the previous evening we had stag's liver, and once one has been so blessed of the gods as to have stag's liver fried in the open in the early morning he can never again taste anything more delicious. And then we were again ready for the chase. Occasionally we used the hides, or shooting platforms, set up by the Germans, but we all preferred to walk, find and stalk our quarry. We carried on until about 7.30 A.M. and then scooted back to the truck and hared away for the school, arriving just in time for another cup of tea and a wash and shave before the first parade.

Had it been possible I am quite sure that such trips would have been a daily occurrence. Our bag was never a big one, but hunting enjoyment is never assessed on the kill alone, and had we never shot anything I do not think that the enjoyment to some of us would have been minimised to any appreciable extent.

One point worthy of comment is the nature of the wound caused by using .303 ammunition. It must be generally agreed that the British service cartridge of .303 calibre (bullet weight: 174-gr; powder weight: 37.5 grs; chamber pressure 39,000 lbs. per sq. inch; muzzle velocity: 2,440 f.p.s.; muzzle energy: 2,350 foot pounds) is too large and too powerful for the shooting of medium-sized game such as fallow and red deer. Yet in the numerous specimens killed by this cartridge, and the wound was always closely examined, I came across only one in which the size of the wound had resulted in most of the meat being spoiled. In my opinion it was merely a case of hitting the beast in the right place. If one obtained a true shoulder hit the entrance hole was very small, in most cases hardly discernible and the exit hole was not of much greater proportions. (Using the cartridge "untreated" of course!) The one bad wound referred to above was the result of a belly hit; here again the bullet entry was not large but the exit was not a hole but a great tear. Using the Winchester carbine with the standard service cartridge wounds were very small, and even when the point of the bullet was cut away leaving a flat nosed lead bullet, or with further modification a hollow nosed bullet, the wound entry and exit holes were quite small.

I have mentioned the German shooting towers. Throughout the forest areas of Germany one found these structures. Often they were about 25 feet high, built of small logs, with the means of access a log ladder up one side. Those which had obviously been erected many years were very precarious structures and great care had to be exercised when climbing up into them. Usually they were exceedingly well camouflaged by virtue of their position, close in to a belt of high trees, and age, and commanded open clearings where it was the custom of deer and pig to graze and root. Although using them occasionally, we all felt that such shooting was hardly in the nature of sporting shooting. I admit that shooting from such points calls for the exercise of considerable patience and fortitude in bad weather. Perched high in such an eyrie in the coldness of dawn, with icy condensation drops torturing the neck, and remaining motionless with every sense alert is no joke, but it lacks the fundamental thrill of the normal chase.

Shooting from these towers, or "looky-lookies" as a young German Jager called them, is rather a tricky business. Manoeuvrability of the rifle is difficult, and since the range from the bottom of the towers to the target is in many cases limited to about 100 yards and the box is 25 feet, or higher, hitting the target is not so easy as it would appear. When at Fassberg I carried out some experimental shooting from such a tower situated on one side, and *in*, a tree, using tin cans for targets, and found that successful hitting necessitated a good deal of alteration in elevation. This experience of tree-shooting, albeit on what one might term a "comfortable" platform, confirmed my often expressed, and always firmly held, opinion that a sniper up a tree was no *sniper!* We used the towers mainly for observation and, on occasion where there was a good field of view, we found them very useful. The Germans considered them extremely valuable adjuncts to pig shooting; they are certainly safe! . . . except when the wood has rotted!

Such shooting platforms, towers, hides—term them what you will—afforded a good illustration for a point brought out in one of my lectures to students at the Training Centre. This lecture dealt with the history and development of the British service rifle, and contained references to the birth and exploitation of the rifled barrel. Any student of firearms history knows that for some considerable time, feeling of the British Army authorities was against the introduction of the rifle to the exclusion of the smooth bore musket. This antipathy was general in military circles, and rifling was mainly confined to sporting weapons where accuracy and range were of greater importance than speed in loading. Consequently the rifle developed in those countries where game shooting was more popular and practised than in England. Nowhere was this development more rapid than in the forests of the Central European continent. The German has always seemed more fond of shooting his game sitting than of working for it; that this trait which led to the development of the rifle, and rifling, was still manifest in the "sporting"German of pre-World War II is shown by the preponderance of the "looky-lookies" or shooting platforms.

During my shooting career both as a civilian and serviceman I have met men possessed of wonderful vision. The Lovat Scout NCOs were extremely good at observation, but each of them acknowledged that in the German forester who frequently accompanied our shooting expeditions they had met their master. This particular fellow was positively uncanny in picking out deer. On one vilely wet morning four of us were making our way along a path thinking how wet we should be in another four hours, when suddenly the German stopped and pointed with a cautious finger at a tree about 200 yards away. "Roebuck" he said. Not one of the Lovats or myself could see it. I was standing about three yards behind the Scouts and suddenly detected a very slight movement against the brown slash of the tree where the dark bark had been hacked away. With glasses I could see that the movement was of a small buck whose fawn colouring was a perfect match for his background. From their angle of vision the Lovats still could not see the buck, and expressed their doubts as to the beast being there. It obliged them by leaping away. Later we were to experience further examples of this German's powers of observation. "D" with a wealth of stalking and observation experience behind him always maintained that this Jager possessed the keenest vision of any man he had ever met.

During one of our hunting jaunts there occurred a curious incident which merits narration. A party of six had gone out in the early afternoon, and on arrival at the usual rendezvous we split up into two groups and set out. My party headed for the high ground, and tramped about four miles without picking up the trail of anything worth shooting. We did stumble across a spot which looked as though a herd of about a hundred pigs had been rooting and digging, but discounted the idea of spending the night there since it was difficult of access and the only shooting platform in the area was in a bad shape; many rungs of the ladder were missing and an attempt to mount the thing resulted in ominous creakings and a break of further rotten rungs. During the tramp we heard a number of shots from the area which was being covered by the other party, and passed comment that they must be having good sport.

A couple of hours later we returned to the truck for tea, and found that we were the first arrivals. About ten minutes later two of the Lovats came in struggling under the burden of a very fine fallow stag which had fallen to the rifle of "D." It was certainly a good specimen and "D" was like a dog with a couple of tails, a lot of bones and many pleasant smells. The remaining member of his party was missing and when I asked about him I was told that he had occupied the extreme right sector of the party's area, and although they had heard some shots they had not seen anything of their companion. Since the sergeant in question was quite capable of looking after himself no one was worried. There was one point about which I questioned "D" though and that was whether he considered all the shots he had heard to be rifle shots. It had struck me that one or two reports I had heard when on the high ground were either pistol or carbine shots. "D" agreed that the reports he had heard were not all rifle shots, but said that he thought other hunters were about.

About three-quarters of an hour later the missing sergeant was seen coming down the glade; he was limping badly. We went out to help him in and found that he had shot himself in the leg with his .38 pistol! He was looking pretty white about the gills and small wonder, since he had tramped, unaided, about a mile and a half from the scene of the accident.

The explanation of the shooting was quite simple. He had seen a good specimen of roebuck and had fired, hitting the beast which dropped instantly. He make his way towards it but when about ten yards away it bounded to its feet and was away in the brushwood before he had time to bring his rifle into his shoulder. After looking around for some time he came to the conclusion that he had lost it, and wandered off to pastures new. He went on for some time without seeing anything and was on his way back when he again saw the wounded buck. He edged closer and fired and the beast dropped as though poleaxed. When he got within a yard or two of the buck he saw that it was still alive. Drawing his pistol from its holster he bent down to administer the coup de grâce through the head. As his finger closed round the trigger the beast gave a convulsive movement of the head, caught the sergeant's hand, the pistol fired and the bullet entered his leg just below the knee. He finished the beast off, and then having staunched the blood pouring from the wound, he bound up the leg and set off on the long trek back to the rendez-vous.

We packed him off to the Centre immediately, my colleague going with him to ensure that he received prompt attention. When he left he was still under the impression that the bullet was somewhere in the leg . . . and asked that I probe for it with a pen-knife! He was wearing gum boots, and since any movement hurt him a good deal it was thought wisest to send him to hospital without touching the boot. On arrival at the hospital it was found that the bullet had passed out of the leg just below the ankle. Both entry and exit wounds were small and clean cut, and the sergeant was out of hospital within two days, and riding a motor-cycle on the third day! He considered himself a handgun expert, and had a very fine trigger pull on the pistol—a Smith and Wesson .38; this, no doubt, was mainly responsible for the accident. He was certainly a good pistol shot, but an accident of that nature takes some living down!

One form of so-called "sport" which was popular on airfields by many officers who should have known better was to shoot rabbits and hares during the hours of darkness from Jeeps. The poor creatures were blinded in the headlights of the cars, shooed off to start running and then blazed away at by one or two or three guns. Knowing intimately some of the men who carried out such "sport" I realised that many of the rabbits would be shot sitting when the poor devils were blinded and bewildered. One evening I was engaged in a heated altercation in the Mess with the exponents of such a game, who became very indignant when I ranted against such butchery. I was informed by one officer that it took a good shot to collect such a bag as they who had been out on that particular night, and that if I went with them I should change my tune about the whole matter. From this it was but a step to accuse me of not wishing to show up my shooting prowess; this was just the remark I wanted this particular chap to say, since it gave me the opportunity of remarking quietly, but not so quietly as to enable a number of other officers hearing me, that I had £50 doing nothing with which to back myself against him in target and sporting shooting with all types of weapons and under any conditions. Having something of a reputation as a rifle shot, deserved or not is beside the point, I need hardly say that my challenge was not accepted.

Talk on hunting in Germany would not be complete without some mention of the BAOR Boar Hunt which took place in the woods and hills surrounding the Ruhr in November 1945. The object of this exercise, which Corps orders described as "Operation Butcher," was to create a reserve of meat for German civilians in what was expected to be a very hard winter. In effect it was a military operation covering the systematic slaughter of red deer, fallow deer, wild pig, hares, partridges, pheasants, woodcock, snipe, wild geese and wild duck. One account of this farcical operation, from official sources, is as follows:—

"We were 110 troops and officers plus a few German State foresters dressed picturesquely in their green knickerbocker uniforms with Tyrolean hats mounted with shaving brushes. Results:—one buck which really did buck. Rounded up in a horseshoe drive of excited amateur beaters, it charged back on its tracks and knocked down an astonished Tommy. The German Forstmeisters reckon that the Corps district, which covers territory of hundreds of square miles, ought to produce 1200 tons of meat and game in the coming winter. But they deplore the British Army methods of the chase; 110 men padding inexpertly among the forest twigs are no match for the quick-eared boar and deer, even with wireless sets to keep communication. A bugle sounding 'advance' ringing through the forest is too much for them. The Chief Forstmeister suggests smaller units of the chase and British Battalion commanders are inclined to agree. A deer and a fox and a jay was the total bag of one unit on their first hunt. But orders come from Brigade level and until negotiations can take place guns are almost literally at a deadlock. 'Operation Butcher' was about to end, but additional drives will be necessary throughout the winter. Meanwhile the bugle sounds 'advance' and at the end of each drive sounds 'cease fire' and 'stand fast' and a Bren gun carrier fitted with a stretcher stands ready at the forest fringe ready to remove any casualties. Best results so far have been obtained by a unit which bagged six stags in one day. But this is still not keeping pace with the operation order which says, 'The game must be driven into corrals.' One Division tried out five snipers posted in trees."

Comment on such a report, such an operation and the methods adopted appears unnecessary. The methods have a musical comedy fantasia, and are in perfect keeping with the non-effective usage of snipers in many Battalions and higher formations during the war . . . and again we find "snipers in trees." It would appear that even the Bren gun merchants I contacted at Fassberg and Westphalia could have taught the Director General of "Operation Butcher" a thing or two. An important point about such an operation was the ridicule which must have been heaped upon it, and upon those responsible for its execution, by the German foresters—masters of their individual craft. I would only add that I am sure that with half-a-dozen Lovat Scout NCOs I could have accounted for more head of game in a week than the figure which was the total bag of the early part of "Operation Butcher."

My last two days' hunting in Germany took place on the 12th and 13th January 1946. This was at the end of the sniper instructor course I had been running for NCOs of my Regiment at Schleswig and Sylt. I had applied to the Military Government people for permission to hunt deer for a couple of days near to the end of the course, and I came back from the island of Sylt when I heard that such permission had been granted. The permit carried the injunction that, owing to the shortage of bucks, old does to the limit of four should be shot—"Special care should be taken to pick out does since at this time of the year the bucks are without horns" so ran the letter covering the permit.

The hunting area was about two hours' run from Schleswig and necessitated crossing the River Eide, a narrow but fast flowing river, on a very primitive ford float. The roads to the hunting ground were very bad indeed and one wondered why the TS did not part company with the rifles. The first day the hunting party comprised myself and three NCOs. We left the truck about a mile from the killing area. Proceedings started with my 16 bore accounting for a rabbit which had the temerity to cross the party's path. Many deer were seen in the open, more than twenty being counted in one herd. But the ground was *not* "good

stalking ground being open heather covered heath" vide
the permit letter, but mainly consisted of dyke-boundaried
fields of very short grass and many swamps and pools,
the most uncomfortable stalking ground imaginable.

The students worked well, their observation being
particularly good. Personally I made the best stalk of my
life and one of the most enjoyable, despite being damnably
wet as the result of doing part of it in a dyke with water
seeping over the top of my gum boots, resulting in the
reaching of a position, by dint of stomach crawling for
the last thirty yards, unobserved, fifteen yards away from
nine deer. I naturally did not shoot but greatly bemoaned
the fact that I had left my camera in the truck. One interesting fact emerging from this day's hunting was that there
were far more bucks than does in the area. I came to the
conclusion that the Powers that Be wanted to ensure that
their office walls would be adorned by a good collection
of horns and bleached skulls next year.

One of the students using a sniper rifle secured a good
specimen, and another using my Winchester carbine got
a nice little roe. Both were clean, one round kills, in the
shoulder. The other student had one shot with the sniper
rifle prior to the above kills, but missed. He informed me
that not being sure of the sex of the beast he had selected
and stalked, he waited until it urinated!

The weather on the first day was fairly good. But snow
fell during the night, and when we set off again next morning the roads were in a dangerous condition. It was
intensely cold too. That day we stalked until three o'clock
in the afternoon under extreme conditions; certainly the
worst I have ever experienced. Snow and high wind at
times resulted in visibility being nil. The snow froze
immediately it alighted on one's clothing, and on the way
back to the parked truck we trudged along encased in a
mantle of ice. No shooting took place on that day although
a number of deer were seen.

HISTORY OF BRITISH
SNIPING & SHARPSHOOTING

1755—1935

NO RECORD, irrespective of brevity, of the history of British sniping and sharpshooting would be complete without mention of the King's Royal Rifle Corps—the old 60th.

The futility of setting slow-moving, heavily equipped troops against enemies who were accustomed to fight in dense forests and pathless country was clearly shown when, in the North American warfare of 1755, General Braddock's troops were routed on the banks of the Ohio river by a combined French and Indian force. Accordingly the British Government raised from the American settlers a force whose arms, dress and mobility would equal those of the enemy.

That mobile body whose birthday is given as Christmas Day 1755 was named the 62nd, the title being altered in 1756 to 60th, Royal Americans.

The 60th, snipers and sharpshooters from their inception, throughout the Peninsular War "crawled like snakes" and used the back position. It was distinguished by its quickness of action and in making the most of all favourable circumstances. "The 60th Riflemen showed great tact in taking advantage of the ground, and dexterity in the use of their arms," wrote Colonel Charles Leslie of the 5th

Battalion. He goes on to write that General Fane had seen a Rifleman shoot one or two French officers who were exposing themselves in front of their men, and in his excitement the General exclaimed: "Well done, my fine fellow! I'll give you half a doubloon for every other man you bring down." The prospect of about half-a-guinea was enough inducement for the Rifleman to load again, a slow process, and to fire and hit another officer. He then looked at the General and said, "By God, I vill make my vortune!" There is a sequel to this story. An officer named Landmann, seeing himself covered by a French marksman, ordered a Rifleman to shoot the enemy. The Rifleman deliberately ignored the order, and instead of the marksman he brought down a French officer. Landmann, who had been missed by the shot fired at him, angrily demanded to know why the officer and not the marksman had been shot. The cool answer of the Rifleman was, "It was more plunder."

The fear and admiration which the Riflemen, and their shooting prowess, roused in the breasts of the French were made known by Marshal Soult, Commander in Chief of the French Army in Spain, in a letter to the French Minister of War in Paris dated the 1st, September 1813. Soult stated that the loss of prominent and superior officers was so disproportionate to that of the rank and file that he had gone to some pains to discover the reason for so extraordinary a circumstance. The Marshal wrote:—

"There is in the English Army a Battalion of the 60th, consisting of ten companies—the Regiment is composed of six Battalions, the other five being in America or the West Indies. This Battalion is never concentrated, but has a company attached to each Infantry Division. *It is armed with a short rifle; the men are selected for their marksmanship;* they perform the duties of scouts, and in action are expressly ordered to pick off officers, especially Field or General officers. Thus it has been observed that whenever a superior officer goes to the front during an action, either for the purposes of observation or to lead and encourage his men, he is usually hit. This mode of making war and of injuring the enemy is very detrimental to us; our casualties in officers are so great that after a couple of actions the whole number are usually disabled. I saw, yesterday, battalions whose officers had been disabled in the ratio of one officer to eight men! I also saw battalions which were reduced to two or three officers, although less than one sixth of their men had been disabled."

One of the Marshal's staff officers declared that " 'Les Riflemen' killed all our officers between July 25th and August 31st, viz: 500 officers and 8 Generals."

Small wonder that the French did not consider the Riflemen entitled to quarter *"for the reason that their fire was aimed, a practice considered unfair."* (My italics.) It is good to note that although this opinion may have been held by the French, they certainly did, in actual fact, give the Riflemen quarter in their customary chivalrous manner.

Although there was effective use made of the sniper during the Indian Mutiny, it is generally recognised that sniping in the grand manner first came into prominence during the Boer War when the Boers, many of them expert marksmen, caused great damage amongst the British troops, particularly the officers. There is no record of the Boers using telescope sights. But a Boer marksman on his own ground, trained to the use of the rifle from boyhood, versed, by his hunting experience, in judging distance, use of cover and possessing eyesight second to none, was capable of much execution. The story has often been told of the advice given to many young British soldiers going out to the Boer War for the first time—"Keep well clear of officers and white rocks." The officers were easy to distinguish by their equipment, and the white rocks provided the wily Boers with most excellent sighting-in or ranging marks.

But it was left to World War I to put sniping absolutely on the map as being of high military significance. Britain did not take the lead, the Germans were the first to introduce skilled sniping, and the Duke of Ratibor's Jagers recruited from the German foresters and equipped with rifles fitted with telescope sights caused many casualties amongst British officers, NCOs and men before any steps were taken to stop the massacre. They certainly dominated that area which lay between the German and British lines. For some time after the inception of German sniping it was not thought that the heavy casualties were caused by aimed fire, but by stray bullets. It was only when it was pointed out that these "stray" bullets appeared to have a penchant for striking the unfortunate victim in the head or heart that the full significance of sniping dawned on authority. Information obtained from German prisoners brought much to light about the activities of the German snipers, and, under the magnificent lead of Hesketh Prichard countersniping was started; the amount of the debt owed to Major Hesketh Prichard, D.S.O., M.C., is incalculable.

Prichard (his book "Sniping in France" dealt with sniping and the Sniping School he ran in France in World War I; incidentally, Major Underhill whose sterling work in World War II is frequently mentioned in these pages was an instructor at Prichard's school) was a widely travelled hunter; Argentine, Chile, Newfoundland and Labrador were amongst his happy hunting grounds and during trips in these areas his only rifle was a .256 Mannlicher, a deadly accurate little weapon. Prichard and his intrepid band of original snipers used a number of sporting rifles and Major Underhill has told me that a .256 Mannlicher did grand service prior to the Huns using bullet-proof plates in 1916-1917, adding—"then we had to get greater actual hitting power such as .350 and .450 elephant guns to burst their loophole plates when their posts were located. But there was no reason why the lighter rifle, with AP ammunition, should *not* have done the job. AP was not perfected until about the end of 1916." I would have given a really good price for a telescope sighted .256 Mannlicher before I went into Europe in June 1944 and I am quite sure that such a rifle would have done everything one asked of it. If a .256 is a killer of moose and caribou—and even elephant—it would certainly be good enough for any unwary Hun. I know that to kill big game with a .256 necessitates the bullet going into the right place, but surely that is a sniper's job.

In 1916 came the establishment in the British Army of the Battalion Intelligence section; this consisted of eight snipers, eight scouts and eight observers under the command of the Battalion Intelligence officer, with a Scout officer as second in command.

In trench warfare, sniper and observer worked in pairs as a team, and it is significant that the same combination operated well in World War II. By early 1917 there can be no doubt that the British and Canadian snipers in France had completely dominated their Hun counterparts. And it was noticeable that men on our side again became human and walked upright, and their morale had increased a thousand-fold. Prisoners gave some very interesting figures of casualties in the Bosche lines, one stating that in a period of three months his company had lost twenty-six men shot through the head by British snipers. Other random figures given were ten men killed in a fourteen day tour in the line; seven men killed out of one company in five days.

The Canadians took to the sniping game like the proverbial duck to water, and their total tally was an enormous one. It is estimated that during the year 1916 British and Allied snipers accounted for nearly three battalions of the enemy. Static warfare, of course, lent itself to sniping extremely well, and it was possible to build really good and strong sniper hides, and to determine ranges with a fine accuracy. One ex-ghillie claimed a bag of ten Bavarians in one evening from a hide on the Bapaume road.

But, of course, sniping is definitely a sport which can be

". . . these white robed and cowled snipers kept the Norwegian villages under constant watch . . ."

BRITISH SNIPING ACCESSORY

Showing author wearing a black "night cowl," which proved to be a most useful little gadget for night work—dusk and dawn.

One of the bitter complaints which the British troops had against the Boers, during the Boer War, was the fact that you couldn't see the blighters on account of their whiskers, especially the older ones who wore a full-dress suit of hair.

played in any type of warfare, and in the closing stages of World War I when action became mobile the snipers were of great use in mopping up fanatical German rearguards. Many German machine guns and gunners were left behind to hold up the Allied advance as much as possible, and these men undoubtedly fought a great fight. A large number of these machine gun posts were sniper protected, and our snipers had first to deal with their German equivalent and then proceed to the main task of liquidating the machine gunners and their weapons. It is significant that the Hun used the same tactics on many occasions during the latest campaign in North West Europe. Frequently he had one or more snipers, or sharpshooters, in concealed positions wide of the machine guns, or forward of the guns in such a position that they were below the field of fire of the LMG's. More than one unthinking British sniper intent solely on getting the machine gunners paid the penalty for his lack of thought and knowledge of the wiles of the Teuton. One had to be very observant to pick out these protective men; they were well concealed, and their fire was masked by that of the machine guns.

To anyone, rifle-minded, who travelled in Germany before World War II it was quite evident that the Huns had for some time taken their rifle training seriously up to a certain point; they had certainly not allowed their acknowledged great interest in fire-power to entirely swamp and engulf an appreciation of the rifle as the basic infantry weapon. There was about a good deal of shooting consciousness, and a friend of mine who lived there told me that he had never before seen so much pre-occupation with telescope sighted rifles. Proverbially slow on the uptake, and by no means a suspicious people, I suppose that most of us thought that this great interest in shooting and telescopic sights was just another manifestation of the militarist mind of the German, or of the ruling ideology; and, of course, the German pre-occupation with anything in the nature of lenses or optical instruments was very well-known. However once the war was under way we were soon to find out that the Hun started sniping where he left off in World War I.

The Lovat Scouts, the Regimental crest of which appears on the title-page by the kind permission of the Senior Officers of the Regiment, were founded in 1900 for service in the Boer War by the late Lord Lovat, father of the present Brigadier Lord Lovat DSO, MC.

The Scouts were Highlanders skilled in the arts of stalking and shooting and very soon made their presence felt in South Africa where, with their uncanny prowess in observation and the use of the stalking telescope, they became known as the "Eyes of the Army." And they beat the Boers at their own game of sniping and sharpshooting.

In World War I there were two formations of the Scouts in the field—in Gallipoli and Salonika, and France. The composition of the Regiment was on the original lines, the officers drawn from the districts around Beauly, Inverness-shire, bringing with them the men from their estates and properties. And their role was the same too—specialists in observation, stalking and shooting.

In World War II the Lovat Scouts served a trying vigil in the Faroe Islands, and then after mountain training in Wales they went to Canada for some months training under extreme conditions of snow and ice in preparation for battle. When the Regiment went to Italy equipped with the lightest types of mountain tackle they were probably the most highly trained men in military history.

At the time when an Indian Division was fighting southeast of Florence, the Scouts were put under this command for long distance patrolling and reconnaissance.

During one such operation the Scouts captured Prato-magno Ridge which enabled the whole battle to move forward and Florence to be taken.

In both World Wars officers and NCOs from this unique

Regiment were attached to Sniping Schools, and there is no doubt that these specialists performed an incalculable service. In my experience I found the idea prevalent that if one's instructor was a Lovat Scout everything was just as it should be—the fame of the Scouts as observers, stalkers and snipers was widespread.

It gives me the greatest of pleasure to recall that in 1945 I was so intimately associated with gentlemen (officers and other ranks) of this individual and very fine Regiment. And I am very proud to be granted the signal honour of reproducing the Regimental crest on the title-page of this book.

BRITISH SNIPERS IN
WORLD WAR II

Back in 1937 it was mooted in certain British Army
circles that there should be a large number of snipers, or
at least sharpshooters, in each Battalion, but the ideas,
although good and packed with common-sense came to
nothing, and the start of World War II found us without a
sniping school and without snipers. I understand that there
was soon a small sniping school set up in Scotland, primarily to teach ghillies, prime stalkers, to use the telescopic sight and to learn the art of instructing, and a little
later there was a small school in France before Dunkirk.
When plaintive cries for snipers came from France in the
initial months of the war, a sniping school was started at
Bisley in early 1940; the War Office's appeal to Bisley for
help met with an immediate response, and for a time things
went well, and the large majority of the students were jolly
good fellows and as keen as mustard. Some of them, however, could not shoot and the riot act had to be read to
commanding officers and a threat made that everyone sent
to the school would have a shooting test before each course
and anyone who could not make a three inch group at 100
yards with the sniper rifles would be sent back to their

units. Then came Dunkirk, heavy air bombardment of this country, and with the Hythe School being bombed out and removed to Bisley there was a certain amount of friction, and eventually the Sniping school closed down; it was reported that it was almost impossible to secure telescope sights. And for a time Sniping sank back once again into Oblivion. At first the title of the sniping school at Bisley was the "N.R.A. Snipers Wing."

I have spoken to many men who were in France from September 1939 until the time of Dunkirk and to date have not met anyone who could tell me that he saw any sniper rifles in that campaign. According to various Army pamphlets, etc., the official sniper's rifle of the British Army was the P 18—the P 14 fitted with the P 18 sight, but I cannot gather any information as to the whereabouts of these rifles. Perhaps they were in Battalions' stores, and maybe no one knew how to use them! I have seen it recorded that one of the Army's finest shots could not find a single, solitary British telescope sighted rifle in the Middle East in the summer of 1941. In 1942 things were looking up, and an establishment of eight snipers per Battalion had been approved, and something had been done, or at least started, towards equipping those snipers with a good rifle fitted with telescopic sight.

After Dunkirk, sniping was thought to be completely out and the sole cry was for more dive bombers, tanks, anti-tank guns, artillery and fire-power generally. And so, although snipers equipped with the P 14 rifle and 1918 pattern 'scope continued to exist on paper, there was no sniper training carried out at all. After Tunisia and Sicily, however, the position was totally changed, and one of the dominant cries was "Sniping." Sniping became a War Office priority, and every assistance was given from the High Places.

One of the objects was to produce instructors in every Battalion in the formation which was to become universally known during the European campaign as 21 Army Group, in order that a trained body of snipers was in each unit before D Day. And this was achieved mainly due to the efforts of two men previously mentioned, Majors Wills and Underhill, although the latter characteristically gives all the credit to Major Wills.

The first school under the new scheme of things was at Llanberis in North Wales, and no less likely spot could have been selected in the British Isles, from September 1943 to March 1944. This region is the wettest in the whole of Great Britain and the work was carried out in almost insurmountable weather difficulties.

One of the most important features of the training at the school was the two day courses held for Battalion Commanders; these courses brought out a point which was outstanding for the rest of the war. The CO's came to the school for the course shortly after partaking of their Christmas dinners, and being somewhat naturally peeved they were prepared to scoff, but stayed to applaud. With very few exceptions they knew nothing about sniping when they arrived, but when they left they were as excited as children who had discovered a new game, a most exciting, invigorating game. Their eyes were opened completely to the possibilities of this great sport of sniping; they became converts and disciples going away to spread the gospel. The man who thought of this innovation—the making aware of sniping to Battalion Commanders—was a genius. These courses were of far more intrinsic worth than a hundred courses for snipers and instructors; because if the Commanding Officer of a formation is disinterested there cannot exist in that unit any sniping in its true sense. But if the OC is keen on the game then sniping thrives; so do the snipers and there are many scalps on the sniping totem. It is essential that a lead be obtained from the top.

In Italy, except for isolated units, sniping never occupied the pride of place as it did in N.W. Europe. And this was mainly due to the fact that despite the strenuous efforts of a sniping officer, who knew his job thoroughly and was sent out there, the sniping school never occupied the niche that was carved for it in Normandy and Holland; obstructionism at its worst was encountered.

From information gained from various sources it would appear that similar OC courses in the American Army would have paid very handsome dividends. I am told that in certain units in which the OC was not interested in riflemen there was little or no sharpshooting carried out; whereas when the OC was a rifle fanatic the picture was reversed, and that particular unit not only used their snipers and riflemen as they should be used, but they suffered far less casualties as a result of a strict sniping routine, practice and plan. And the enemy were dominated by a few men and not by hundreds.

A sniping wing which trained students for the Central Mediterranean Forces ran an excellent little course, and spent the last week of it chasing gazelle near Bethlehem, good training and magnificent fun. But they were, in the words of a sniping authority, but babes in the wood, lacking in equipment—they had no telescopes at all—and that which they possessed was in poor condition. An OC course was suggested to them and later carried out, as successfully as that at Llanberis.

At a Mountain warfare school in Lebanon there was an ideal site for a sniping school, but there was not a separate sniping wing, the sniper training being included in the normal course. One of the most keen interests of this school was the camouflage side of sniping in the mountains.

There was a sniping wing at Mediterranean Training Centre and they had just started up when a sniping expert paid them a visit. But sniping was a very small peg in a large hole. At all other centres of instruction everyone was very enthusiastic when put into the picture about sniping, but here things were different and every stumbling block was placed in the way of someone wanting to get things done. The men at the head of the school thought they knew a lot about sniping, and in reality knew very little, and as is usual with this type of individual they were resentful of suggestions. And whereas at Llanberis the sniping wing had a free hand in dealing with the Powers that Be at this place everything had to go through the normal stagnating channels, and there was no free hand at all.

It is clearly apparent that to do its utmost good a sniping wing should be entirely on its own, and mobile, as was the B.L.A. Sniping School in N.W. Europe in 1944–1945, not far behind the line and in touch with the forward area units all the time. After Cassino, the school about which I am writing was 300 miles or more behind the line and was completely out of touch. And all the efforts to get the staff sergeants up to the line for a shot or two were useless. The only possible way for the officer concerned to get up to the forward areas was to go there on leave! Every unit in the line was crying out for assistance and advice, and some of the sniping instructors were sobbing out their hearts to respond to the plaintive cries and yet a relatively minor officer type, of a species occasionally found in all Armies which goes out of its way to obstruct rather than help, stood obdurately in the way. It is ironical to think that these obstructionists were often decorated for their services! The instructors knew that they could help far more by two or three days spent with each unit in, or near, the line, giving direct and personal help, rather than by teaching a number of rather indifferent and bomb happy junior NCOs 300 miles behind the line on courses. The few visits paid to the line by the officer instructor proved such a statement. The average sniper in Battalion was a lost sheep, and one could have helped him a great deal, and when that help was possible on those too-brief trips not only were the snipers themselves greatly appreciative but so were their Company commanders and COs. It was the mistaken thought of the Training school commandant referred to above that anyone paying a visit and offering advice to line units was not welcomed, and being the type he was, nothing, of course, could change that opinion. The fact was that if one knew the stuff one was treated as a god from the Blue. Small wonder then that a certain ardent sniping officer looks rather bitterly back to that time in Italy in 1944, and with regret because "one knew that one could do so much to help get sniping going, and yet one had not an earthly chance of doing so."

The sniping school party which eventually became the 21 Army Group Sniping School landed in Normandy on the 17th, August 1944 and after a recce of the Caen and Falaise area started building a range N.E. of Courselles a day or two later. By dint of much hard work and strenuous scrounging (some unconscious (?) wag addressed a letter to the Commandant at "Swiping School") a range—4-target with markers gallery, complete with 4' targets, head and head and shoulders targets, built up and enclosed firing points, and 'phone lines back to 500 yards—was soon completed. Obstructions such as bracken which obscured the field of view were very effectively dealt with by a few practice shots with a flame thrower. By the end of August the first course for instructors was in progress. Towards the end of September the school, which had been wanted badly by the Canadians and who had given it splendid support until the war moved too fast for their arrangements, was en route for pastures new.

On October 1st, the school reported to the Scottish Division which was extremely keen to have it, and on the next day moved with the Division into the Nijmegan salient. After a recce for a range site the school finally came to rest at the little village of Zon, only about five or six miles behind the line. Within a week everything, including a range, was ready and a course assembled. The students were given a short address by Major General T. G. Rennie,

CB:DSO:MBE, Commanding the 51st Highland Division, in which he stressed the importance of sniping. A day or two earlier General Rennie had told the Commandant of the school "You have already done a magnificent job of work." On the 24th, November 1944 the school was finally recognised by the news being received that it was to get Army Group status. That was SUCCESS—and the superlative recognition of Sniping.

British Sniper's Equipment

At sniping school there was a table showing the necessary items of equipment for the sniper, and where such equipment should be carried. This schedule was not always rigidly followed—some individuals liked to hunt as lightly equipped as possible. The table contained the following:—

No. 4 Rifle. TS. Carried.

Denison Smock. This garment, windproof and waterproof, was designed for the airborne troops (it had more pockets than a poacher's jacket) and being capacious, roomy (forming no hard outline) camouflaged and incapable of "rucking" (a tail-like portion of the cloth passed between the wearer's legs and press-studded into the front section) it was just *the* thing for snipers. It was very interesting to note how attached a sniper became to his Denison smock; this smock might have become the symbol of airborne troops and snipers but it was possible to find "store bashers" wearing them in the winter of 1944–1945, and even officers stationed in gay, peaceful Brussels donned the raiment!

Face Veil. The face veil(s)—many snipers had two—camouflaged-patterned in brown and green were extremely useful, not only for covering the head and face and breaking outline, but also for use when constructing small hides, or draping over hedge bottoms. The veil, in use, can be seen in the photographs of the British sniper.

Scout Regiment Telescope. Had three sets of lenses and was of the three draw type, with a ray shade which pulled out forward and adequately prevented the sun shining on the object glass, and a small shutter on the eyepiece. It was easily stripped and cleaned. Magnification was about 20 diameters and was capable of picking up clearly small objects at long range, and penetrating shadows. One telescope was allotted to each sniper team, and was usually carried by the second man in that team . . . according to the schedule, over the left shoulder.

Binoculars. As will be readily understood there was no standard pattern of binoculars used in sniping. Personally I had an excellent pair and when at the sniping school in March 1945 everyone was eager to use them. Binoculars were usually carried by the sniper in the team, slung around the neck, and when he picked out anything he deemed suspicious the usual procedure was for him to put the telescope man on the spot to gain confirmation. An alternative carrying position was in the top left pocket of the smock, minus, of course, the case.

Compass. The compass issued was the normal prismatic type. All snipers were trained in the use of this instrument. It was invaluable for observation report work (as was the watch, also an issue to snipers, synchronised before going out) and getting to a preselected spot in the dark. Carried in the hip pocket of trousers. Watch was carried in top left battle dress pocket.

Additional items which the school suggested as being necessary were:—

Two *#36 Grenades*, carried in the lower pockets of the smock. These grenades, in my opinion, had a two-way psychological value; they could be very comforting when one came across German pockets unexpectedly; on the other hand many men always distrusted 36 grenades and crawling with a couple in the smock pockets gave rise to a high nervous tension in some men since there was always the thought that one should be continually feeling at the little devils to make sure that the safety pins were O.K. Men who were subject to this nerve reaction always had my sympathy for during my early service days 36 grenades and myself were superbly fraternal. They seemed to follow me everywhere, and I shall never forget taking part in a rather rough and hurly-burly battle exercise with five of the grenades clanging and dancing in a small pack slung at my belt. I was given quite a wide berth by my fellows.

After the war at the Training Centre it was interesting to note the reactions of NCOs (senior NCOs for the most part) some of them veterans of El Alamein, Sicily and N.W. Europe, when they were scheduled to throw 36s on the grenade range. Quite a number were visibly relieved when they left the throwing bays unscathed! This same reaction was shown by many after successfully firing the PIAT, the infantry anti-tank weapon which became known as the V.C.'s weapon. During the War many instructors became so used to the 36 grenade that familiarity bred contempt and they committed the heinous sin of not playing the safety game. As a demonstration of the "safeness" of the grenade they would pull the safety pin out, lay the grenade down on the ground, count two (the fuse setting was four seconds) take it up and throw. Some of these instructors paid with their lives for this contempt. In the earlier years of the war 36 grenades were fired from discharger cups, attached to rifles, by use of ballistite cartridges. With practice it was possible to fire these grenades with accuracy up to about 200 yards.

50 Rounds .303 Ball. (A bandolier of ball ammunition used in the zeroing of the rifle.) Slung over right shoulder.

Water Bottle. Slung over right shoulder.

5 Rounds Tracer Ammunition. (This might have been useful for indicative purposes, but I have not heard of tracer ever being used by British snipers.) Carried in right trouser pocket.

5 Rounds Armour Piercing Ammunition. This ammunition

was useful for shooting up machine guns, etc. One round of AP through a built-in machine gun post would be a terrifying "wasp," and a hit by an AP bullet on the gun itself would be, and was, devastating. Carried in left trouser pocket.

One Emergency Ration. Carried in top right pocket of smock.

At the sniping school they had tubes of green and brown camouflage cream for smearing over the face and hands. When dry this gave a very effective matt finish. It will be readily understood that such things were not likely to be met up with in the Battalion sniping sections, but a wise, and no hair-brained foolish specimen was worthy of the title, sniper, never went out with a pristine brilliancy about his face and hands; there was always the mediums of dirt, mud and the black from the bottom of the cook's dixies! I always favored the wearing of roughly made gloves of sandbag hessian; these provided adequate cover for the hands, could be made so that complete freedom was given to the trigger finger and could be thrown away when of no further use.

The matter of camouflage was largely left to the individual; after all one can only go into the question from the "principles of" point of view. The most important point on this question to me has always appeared to be "Put yourself in the place of the enemy; when taking up a position look at it from the point of view of the enemy, or your quarry." We gave the sniper his flat-toned smock, his veils and the basic principles of camouflage. The rest was up to him.

SNIPER TRAINING SCHEDULE

The training given by the school was comprehensive as can be seen from the following rough precis-syllabus:—

General: Organisation; Equipment; Tactical handling of snipers.

Observation: General; Telescope; Binoculars; Location of fire.

Fieldcraft: Concealment; Camouflage; Movement; Stalking.

Shooting: General; Sources of error; Zeroing; the Sniper Rifle; Dusk firing; Holding; Elevation Table; Aiming off—Wind and Movement; Recognition of targets; Judging distance; Field firing exercises.

ORGANIZATION

The establishment of a Battalion sniping section was:— One sergeant, one corporal, two lance corporals and four privates. Although no specialised sniping officer existed on Battalion war establishment it was considered most essential that an officer having a thorough knowledge of the game should supervise the snipers' selection, training and handling in battle; and it was emphasised that the success of the team depended on the enthusiasm, judgement and skill of this officer. And it was an essential that a 100% reserve of snipers be trained.

The snipers' task was to kill individual enemy with single shots—very quickly aimed shots if necessary—and they were warned of the danger of firing a rapid succession of shots except in self-defence. The war-time standard of shooting was ability to hit with regularity a man's head up to 200 yards and a man's trunk up to 400 yards. These were minimum standards. Selectivity of targets was stressed, and training given in recognition of enemy badges of rank.

In mobile warfare, it was pointed out that the sniper could stalk and shoot up isolated enemy posts and under favourable circumstances could infiltrate through enemy positions and give great assistance prior to an attack by shooting enemy weapon crews from the rear. (It is my opinion that this infiltration scheme was far too often neglected. Snipers should have been frequently used in this role and taken into consideration in the fire-plan of an attack.) Another use of the sniper in mobile warfare was a counter-sniping role against the snipers who might be left behind by a retreating enemy.

Under static conditions the snipers' task was the complete domination of that ground between their lines and that of the enemy. The limited number of snipers available rendered it impossible for them to be used at all times of the day. It was emphasised that the best times for operations were dusk and dawn, or during moonlight; particularly was this operative when our fire superiority had forced the enemy underground during daylight hours and where his patrols were particularly active by night.

Observation

Mental alertness was stressed, and an attempt made to endow all students with a hunter's observation and reasoning faculties. They were taught to use binoculars in the right manner, and it was emphasised that in his telescope a sniper possessed a "weapon" of the greatest importance. Training was given in night observation.

Location of Fire

I always considered that one of the most important parts of the school's training was that which dealt with the locating of enemy fire. This is a most difficult job, but provided that certain principles are understood a good deal of information can be derived from the sounds of the fire itself. The noise, "the crack," which a bullet makes when forcing its way through the air is quite separate from the report made by the weapon which fires it. Therefore if the bullet is fired from a modern rifle or LMG towards the observer, the first noise heard is a sharp crack made by the bullet as it passes; later, and less distinctly, comes the duller "thump" of the explosion. When the range is short the time lag between the crack and the thump is very slight, but with the increasing range the interval becomes longer, until at a stage of about 1,000 yards when the bullet having slowed down a good deal, the time lag starts decreasing. Below this range it is eminently possible to judge the approximate range of the firer by the time variation of crack and thump; the latter, of course, gives the clue to the firer's position. Once training has been given in this matter, the sniper could judge the range and direction of the firer, and having determined the area watch for muzzle smoke, blast, or movement, with the naked eye, or use his binoculars or the telescope with its ability to penetrate shadow.

Training in concealment and camouflage was good, and the demonstrations on this subject were excellent. A man will always learn more from *seeing* than telling, and demonstrations are always popular, especially if they include some humour.

Dummy Heads

In the first World War much successful use was made of dummy heads to draw the fire and thus determine the position of enemy snipers. These heads were very cleverly made of papier mâché and moulded from plaster casts, and were coloured by well-known artists. When many of the students at the sniping school in Holland in 1944/5 saw such dummy heads they expressed the opinion that they were of no use in a mobile war. Certainly we could not visualise a sniper team struggling along burdened with such impedimenta. But that, on occasion, such "drawers of fire" were used in World War II in Europe is proved by the following story. "Willy" one of the heads that the sniping school people brought out from England was borrowed by a unit which had been troubled by a German sniper who proved very difficult to locate. The head did its work successfully; when exposed for some time the German had six shots at it without a hit, but this is not so disgraceful as would appear on the surface, since when he was pin-pointed by the smoke

[294]

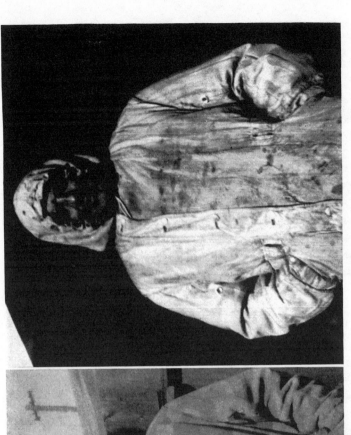

German Sniper Clothing

Left: German camouflage jacket worn normally; the camouflage is in a blotched pattern of brown and green.
Right: Same jacket worn reversed; for use in snow.

DUMMY HEAD IN POSITION

At a range of 400–600 yards this target would call for considerable "finding"; many enemy snipers would waste ammunition shooting at such a dummy head and at the same time give their own position away.

DUMMY HEADS

Dummy heads were used a great deal in World War I, and although their appearance at our Sniping School occasioned some derisive comment (they were dubbed "old fashioned") there are factual accounts of their successful use in World War II.

from the several shots it was found that he was operating at a range of between 500–600 yards. It is interesting to record that he was not treated in perhaps the orthodox sporting manner but in a very effective way by the medium of two AFVs going out to well and truly "brass him up."

✳   ✳   ✳   ✳

Stalking

A good deal of time was devoted to stalking, occasionally with the added interest of field firing at the conclusion of the stalk. Great attention was paid to silent movement and keeping direction, a difficult job in mist or darkness, and accurate use of the compass was stressed. Some training in the reading of air photographs was given.

Shooting

All the shooting instruction was good, but in my opinion there was a too close affinity with normal range work. Sniping ranges and targets could have been more *natural;* it was largely *range* shooting rather than *sniping* shooting, and there was not enough of the field firing practices which were more closely akin to sniping shooting.

Shooting from hides and buildings was practised. One of the most spectacular demonstrations in which all the students took part was the dusk or night firing. The whole course would be assembled on the firing point and a figure target set up about 100 yards away. When it was too dark to see the target sufficiently through iron sights to take an aim, all the students in details of six upwards got down and using TS rifles fired five rounds each at the target. The hits were nearly always "possible" of the large number of rounds fired. The use of the telescope sight under conditions when it was not possible to get an aim with normal sights was certainly driven home to everyone by this demonstration. A further point stressed was that it was the contrast between the target and its background rather than the state of the light which governed its visibility; for instance, a target on a sky-line can be aimed at in almost complete darkness.

The courses for snipers were of seven days duration; those for instructors ran for fourteen to sixteen days.

The Commandant of the school laid down that if the student had:—Guts, physical fitness and a keen desire to qualify for the sniper's job the school could teach him to shoot, observe and stalk, but that if he were already a good shot so much the better—he was excellent material. That there was such admirable material is shown by the following account of one sergeant pupil of the Gordon Highlanders who had attended the school's second course on the Continent and who was a fine shot. The CO of the school mentioning this NCO in his course diary early in September wrote:—

"He has been faultless in the first three days' shooting, dropping only one point. Watch him. If he has the temperament for sniping he will surely get Huns." This sergeant in the demonstration "Accuracy versus Volume" which was always a feature of school training, where a sniper armed with TS rifle was in competition with a Bren firing at twelve (six each) plates, the targets falling when hit, downed the six plates in six shots in just over half a minute; in that time the LMG was pointless. In October, 1944 this NCO bagged four Huns in one outing, which is a most excellent day's work in any company.

Another ex-pupil of the school, who had been made NCO in charge of his Battalion sniping section, reported in early October that his section had been credited with 24 kills. On the morning of October 14th, this sergeant went out with a corporal, another former student, Hun hunting and for some time they enjoyed themselves hugely, killing three Jerries. Shortly after the third Hun had paid the penalty for his unawareness a hidden Spandau opened up and the corporal was shot through the head. He was not killed instantly, but from the first there was little hope. He was brought in, and everything possible was done for him but he died on the following morning. This casualty brought the total of students, on the last course at the school in Normandy, killed to three, but against this the course had at least sixteen Huns to its credit.

Efforts had been made to have the Battalions keep "Game" books and by the middle of October reports of sniping activities were coming in to the school; these were, of course, "recent" records and certainly not complete from the opening of the campaign in Europe. Many of the Battalions in the 51st Division were making excellent use of their snipers, and one sniper section had accounted for twenty Germans since entering the salient. At the end of October many interesting claims were made by students at the school in respect of their particular units, including one of 101 kills with a junior NCO sniper top scorer with 22 scalps to his credit. Another Battalion of the same Regiment was reported to have bagged 28, and the sergeant who volunteered this information had himself accounted for four.

At the beginning of November the 51st Highland Division said that units in the Division were using the current moon to put into practice the night shooting as taught and demonstrated at the sniping school, and that as a result the Camerons got four Germans on one night. It was further reported that all the Powers that Were in the Division could now see the full possibilities of snipers dominating No Man's Land and thus making it possible for the bulk of the troops to be pulled back to comparative comfort of barns, etc., by day.

The following is an extract from a letter dated 19th, November 1944 written by Major-General T. G. Rennie to Major Underhill, OBE, Commandant of the sniping school:—

". . . The students have come back from all your courses

keen and enthusiastic, and their COs are delighted with the results they obtain in action.

"We now have some 60 snipers in the Division and they are invaluable. The 7th Armoured Division snipers taught by you have had a good bag in the recent battle. Thank you for all you have done for us."

Any man would be highly delighted at the receipt of such a sincere, glowing testimony to his work! Major General Rennie, one of Nature's gentlemen, was killed crossing the Rhine in the initial assault with his Division. So well liked was this senior officer that when the news of his death was received at the sniping school, and I was there at the time, there was more than one moist eye. And it was certainly heart-shaking to see the grief written so plainly on the faces of one or two hard-bitten and dour Scots of the glorious 51st.

Whenever possible the last three or four days of each instructor's course was taken up by a tour of the forward areas—a "Practise what you Preach" exercise. The following is a brief report of one such tour:—

Each party was shown the covered roads to the place from which it would operate as a firm base for its hunting, or patrol, trips. In this particular area the only plan to follow was to push well out into No Man's Land in search of game. The task was defined as:—Watch for signs of the enemy. Engage all targets within 400 yards, as the intention is to dominate the area.

Results from the shooting point of view were disappointing, no effective shots being fired. Recce results were quite valuable, and proved beyond doubt that the Germans had withdrawn from close contact and that they were very thin on the ground. From watching fire directed at others it was possible to determine that Spandau posts and OPs and mortar posts existed in the Battalion area. The resultant attack in this area proved the worth of the tour's observation, and must have resulted in the saving of time and life.

Regarding this tour the school commandant thought that all training methods of the school were fully justified but also came to the conclusion that benefit would result from pushing Fieldcraft—more particularly the ability to push out long distances and lie up, especially just prior to an attack by our own troops. If fire-plan could allow for snipers remaining out many lives would be saved as Spandaus, tank traps, and mortar posts could be dealt with from behind immediately they "came up" and advertised their positions on the lifting of our barrage. Careful prior selection of positions would be essential. "I am more than ever convinced that the two great essentials for a sniper are:—(a) A burning desire to at all times locate and kill the Hun and (b) Guts enough to accomplish the desire. It is surprising how many there are who do not want the job of sniping."

A few incidents from this tour:—One of the instructors and an officer student were crawling along a ditch in the enemy sector, and within fifty yards of a tank trap when a German type police dog pointed them. After some sweating, apprehensive moments full-blooded, low voiced cuss words caused it to depart. When several hundred yards in front and crawling back towards our lines the CO of the school saw ahead a farm worker. As he drew alongside the man the latter looked down at the CO in the ditch in the same manner one looks at small boys playing a Red Indian game, his expression clearly saying "Carry on with your game of soldiers. I must get on with the serious business of life." And he returned to his task of topping and tailing mangolds between the lines. The CO no longer thought that he was "one hell of a fellow." Again, and in exactly the same circumstances, the CO looked up from his ditch to see a Nun in her neat, though austere, black and white habit calmly walking through No Man's Land carrying a baby of about twelve months old; she was taking it to hospital for treatment. "Any tendency to swollen-headedness on my part departed and I immediately found humility."

The task was to ascertain if certain houses in the area were held in strength by the Bosche. It was night, with no moon but fairly starlit. First came a tiptoe walk, then a very careful ditch crawl to a point several hundred yards in front of our line, close to a notorious cross-roads. Arriving at the end of the dyke the team found a piece of chicken wire with a hole in the centre big enough for a man to crawl through and showing signs that it had been a regular route for some time. Having got through the wire a very cautious and wary couple looked over a small bank to see quite clearly in the bluish starlight the tops of two German steel helmets about four yards away. The problem set was:—to turn back was to place themselves at a disadvantage; it was "evens"—two to two; to lob a grenade might bring trouble in the shape of the garrison, if any. Having decided to go in, the intrepid couple found that the two helmets adorned not square heads but two wooden crosses! The two unlucky Bosche had been KO'd by snipers of the Battalion on whose front the school was working.

Two sniping parties had cleared two houses each—it was necessary to examine every house in No Man's Land every time one passed by—when they heard queer noises emanating from the back of another house. Cautious investigation revealed a starving sow and a famished foal unable to get out to find food and water. Predominant thoughts were mines and booby traps but eventually natural humane instincts prevailed and doors were wrenched open, the unlucky animals dashed out and proceeded to eat and drink everything in sight. On this jaunt, evidence such as fowls, *not* new-laid eggs, sucking pigs and tame rabbits, and cows very dead as the result of not being milked showed quite clearly that the village in front of our section of the line was not occupied in strength.

The battle which followed this tour of duty in the line substantiated the conclusions drawn from the observations made during the tour, and the Battalion on whose front the sniping school people worked took all its objectives with but two killed and four wounded.

In February 1945 an instructors' course toured the forward areas and gained valuable experience. One of the school instructors who played a big part in the success of the tour has given me this record:—

". . . we proposed to spend the last three days of the course in the usual 'Practise what you Preach' exercise, with the Canadians who were holding part of the line opposite to the Reichswald Forest. The Hun was showing himself a good deal in that area and was sending out a number of patrols, strong patrols, at night. The moon was on the wane, and there was quite a good carpet of snow on the ground; both these factors filled us with the hope that we could do much damage in the early hours of the morning. It is easy to see a man inside 150 yards when there's a moon and snow about, as you know. We constantly emphasised the value of the 'scope sight on such nights but it was seldom exploited, if realised, by operational units. We went up to the forward areas in transports but when we arrived at Nijmegan we found that plans had to be altered since the Canadian's CO did not altogether care for the idea. However we obtained permission from the Officer Commanding the 49th Division which was holding the bridge-head across the River Waal at Nijmegan to attach ourselves there, and they were certainly glad to see us. One half of the course went to the right hand side of the sector, under two of the School instructors; the other half, myself included, went to the left of the sector.

"When we arrived at our destination which was a small village, we formulated our plan and split up into small parties, and joined up with the various platoons who were standing-to in their respective positions. This part of the bridge-head was held by the Recce Battalion, and held very thinly too. The Bosche sent out patrols frequently so we

were all very hopeful that things would happen—to the
Jerries! I had with me two officers, one of whom was afterwards killed at the Rhine crossing. The sergeant in charge
of the platoon to which we were attached was very glad to
see us, and took pains to show us the general lay-out. They
were in a very big house which commanded a good view of
the road which went east. There were sentries out and they
had been instructed to notify us immediately anything
came their way. The sniping party loaded up, attached
telescope sights, and made themselves as comfortable as
possible in one of the many rooms of the house.

"Round about 03.30 hours the telephone rang and a Hun
patrol was reported at the stand-to position on our left,
where another school party was in position. (This section
got the Hun patrol leader!) At 04.30 hours someone shook
me by the shoulder—I was fast asleep—and shouted
"They're here." When we arrived upstairs I was given a
pair of binoculars by a Bren gunner and shown the patrol.
There were about 12 Huns, and they appeared to be about
100 yards away, but since judging any distance at night is a
difficult task, and distances always appear to be overesti-
mated, they were, in reality, only some fifty or sixty yards
away. One of them carried what appeared to me to be a 3″
mortar, but this turned out to be a Panzerfaust. When I
thought that everyone was in position I took the best
chance I could get and he fell in the snow very slowly
never to come up again.

"The rest of the patrol got to ground, some of them went
in behind trees and one or two of the foolish ones just lay
in the open. I took another one, he that carried the Bazooka, and after I had taken the second pressure he seemed
to burst into flames. I do not know yet what exactly happened but I rather fancy that the bullet which went
through his face and came out at the back of his neck struck
and set alight a sort of home-made incendiary bomb which
maybe he carried to set fire to an AFV. I do not think a

Bazooka bomb would take fire in such a way as did actually happen. Meantime there were a few shots fired by the rest of the chaps and after firing two shots from the same position I thought that I ought to move a little, but since every window by this time was occupied I just kept my head down. The Bosche were shouting to each other and apparently in a state of panic. We should have taken advantage of this but we did not realise exactly what was happening until too late.

"I took a cautious look through the corner of the window and saw two of the Jerries turning over one of the casualties in the snow. I could have shot them very easily, and many a time I have been vexed that I did not but at the time I thought they were attending to one of their wounded, so I left them alone. But one of them picked up the Panzerfaust and fired at the house. The projectile went through the wall a few feet above my head and rattled both myself and the rest of the boys considerably. In a few seconds after getting over this rather unexpected blast I took another look and saw the patrol running away. I kept the pointer of the TS on the leading edge of one of the Hun's chest and squeezed. He was hit all right; he gripped convulsively at his chest and then fell. He struggled to his feet and moved off to fall into a ditch on the opposite side of the road. This German must have been taken away by the remainder of the patrol since he was not found when the round-up took place later. After the Huns had vanished we stood-to for an hour just in case they returned. Everyone knows that the German will try to do everything in order to carry out a set task, no matter how difficult. But in this particular case the trying was not very earnest."

One or two lessons were learned as the result of this exploit. The first was never to fire from a house if suitable positions could be found outside. A patrol being fired upon from the vicinity of a house it naturally follows that *they* will fire into the house. Whereas if the sniping positions were outside, better, and longer, targets would be presented to the snipers, with the obvious safeguard of not being so good a target themselves. Some knowledge was gained about snow camouflage. This Hun patrol all wore snow suits which appeared to be the result of improvisation—rather surprising this—and they were not as good as our own. But even though they were clothed in white they all stood out against the snow background, and the Lovat Scout who tells the story, says "I can still visualise that patrol. They seemed to me to be dressed in yellow clothing." There is no doubt that it is most difficult to get a white which will blend and harmonise perfectly with snow, particularly in moonlight. In my own experience a moving, and to a less extent a stationary, figure clad in a snow suit against a snow background in bright moonlight appeared to be limned in yellow-blue. Unless one is lying in a static position snow suits are a mixed blessing; imagine passing a dark object or tree!

The same Lovat had another little "breeze" with Jerry some time later. It was a long range shot, something over 500 yards, and although the result was not certified, Jerry almost immediately made that particular sector very unhealthy with machine gun fire, and next day plastered the place pretty well with mortars. That one rifle bullet certainly wakened him up, and gave him something about which to think; and knowledge of German procedure leads one to believe that the shot certainly went home!

From information obtained from many sources early in 1945 it was clearly apparent that we had definitely got the upper hand of the Germans in sniping. And it was interesting to read that Colonel Von Stolzmann, chief of a Department in the German High Command, in a broadcast to German front line troops, called for more trained snipers and better marksmen.

The school's definition of Sniping could not be bettered. It was "The art of drilling round holes into square heads!"

MISCELLANY

Standards of Service Shooting • Further Examples of
Lack of Firearms Consciousness and Knowledge
Calibre-Stopping Power—and Wounds

THE standards of British service shooting were deplorable.
During the last few years I have had a large number of men
go through my hands on miniature, classification, field
firing and sniping ranges and whether right or wrong I do
claim to be qualified to speak on the subject. Personally I
think there can be but one explanation—instructors and
instruction. Instructors have been hidebound to pamphlets;
instruction has been archaic. To a large number of so-called
instructors, the rifle has just been a "thing," not a vivid,
live weapon of precision which will give of its best only if
properly treated—and respected. In short, many NCOs
brought the old-fashioned NCO-ish mind to musketry
training.

I have experienced men who were visibly terrified every
time they came to the firing point, due solely to the fact
that when they first handled a rifle some "instructor" impressed upon them the terrible dangers of such a weapon.
Surely one of the very first tasks of an instructor is to ex-

plain how safe a rifle is by pointing out the details of the mechanism. Once a man has the idea of such mechanism he realizes that the only dangerous part of the rifle is the muzzle end, and that is the point farthest away from him. After the end of the war in Europe I still met men who expected to lose an eye because of the bolt flying back every time they fired. And these men certainly flinched! And it was no uncommon thing to come across examples of bawling and shouting on firing points resulting in nervous types become shivering masses of terrified humanity. Some "instructors" used their imagination in the wrong direction.

Above everything else, the instructor should be an enthusiast. If he sees, and hears, an enthusiastic instructor even the most belligerent of "fed-up" types will grudgingly at first and later, willingly, give his attention to the job in hand. In this connection it is only necessary to compare the enthusiastic atmosphere prevalent at a sniping school with that found at a normal school of instruction. I think that it is essential at the outset of his rifle training to show the recruit that rifle shooting is a sport. In the past there has been far too much undue interference with position; if one coaches a natural sportsman one does not, if wise, unduly interfere with his stance and style and mould him into an orthodox pattern. If one does, the result is most frequently chaotic.

It is necessary to instil into men a sense of pride in being able to hit that which is aimed at; no man *desires* to be a bad shot. Basically the interest is there—it merely requires fanning to flame by the contagious enthusiasm of a true instructor—since at some time or other every boy ardently desires an airgun, or a catapult, and after obtaining it becomes very proficient with it (without being taught in pamphlet sequence) much to the disgust of the neighbours' cats. And how frequently has the officer in charge of a firing point to check men for talking? The men released from the tension of firing, their tongues begin to waggle; but the

[306]

talk is almost always the same: "How many bulls—or hits? Three? Oh, I got four!" And so on.

During the past few years there have been many cases of NCOs being used for shooting coaches who did not know the meaning of the word. Frequently they have been very poor shots; it is essential that any coach should have reached a certain standard in shooting. Another point occurs to me here; I am confident that an officer who has not got "the common touch" can never succeed as a rifle instructor, and there are many officers yet to be found who cannot speak freely with men. And if the men feel awkward in an officer's presence (and that feeling is always the fault of the officer) the "atmosphere" spells complete negation to any instructional ability he may possess.

During war-time, much range work was looked upon as a kind of half-holiday or organized games parade, where a man would lie uncomfortably on the firing point being badgered by NCOs and officers (the latter often cursing the fates that ordained that he should have bully beef sandwiches for lunch whereas his brethren are dining much more sumptuously in the mess) and then lie (if sunny) or stand (if wet) smoking in the rear awaiting—impatiently —for the end of the practices. Incidentally I often wondered why it was thought that any type of ammunition was good enough for range work—such as old ammo taken from machine gun belts—and rifle practice, irrespective of whether it was English or American ball, incendiary, armour-piercing or tracer? More than once I have picked up chargers of .303 ammunition during range practice and found them composed of a mixture of American ball, English ball, tracer, incendiary and armour-piercing. Much more stress must be laid on the vital importance of using good, uniform ammunition.

The standards of lecturing were poor, and too many instructors were "note-bound." *Interest* lectures dealing broadly with firearms are important and break the monotony of a course in which mechanism and "mutuals" play a part. I found that lectures dealing with such subjects as "History of the British Service Rifle" were received with enthusiasm, but I always endeavoured to lecture without notes and tried to bring matters home to men sometimes by the use of, maybe, crude metaphor—such a system pays and arouses interest. Allow the men to see that a lecturer is a red-hot enthusiast, and that his knowledge does not spring solely from the pamphlet or academic file, and they pay strict attention to that which is said.

A bayonet fetish was prevalent in many quarters; it was most frequently stressed by fire-eating instructors who had never seen any sort of action. I have always asked what can the bayonet blade do that a bullet cannot? All *riflemen* are appreciative of the fact that a rifle is, or should be, a, or *the*, weapon of precision, and therefore the fixing of a bayonet for firing is sacrilege. (I have before me a copy of a well-known journal which includes an illustrated article on sniping. The three illustrations show snipers firing from behind cover complete with telescope-sighted rifles—and bayonet fixed! It is both ridiculous and ludicrous.) The No. 4 rifle was zeroed at the ordnance factories without bayonet and yet it was laid down that units must zero with the bayonet fixed—and once I was informed that foresights were not available for the zeroing of rifles! *I* encouraged bayonet fighting for three reasons: (a) it is damned good exercise; (b) is liked—normally—as a form of training causing laughter; and (c) it affords magnificent opportunities for "handling" a rifle. I have always encouraged drill tricks ("freak" slope arms, etc.,) because if a man can do these things he is well on the way to becoming a true weapon handler. It is the same with pistol instruction. I found that if I could give an exhibition of "cowboy" revolver tactics, spinning on the fingers, fanning, synchronized shooting with a pistol in each hand, and throwing and catching the weapons, I gained the attention of pupils, and if men armed with such weapons are encouraged to follow such an example they begin to take a pride in their skill, and in time they can really handle their weapons.

There were centres of instruction where there was no suggestion of firing a couple of rounds into the butts before commencing the practice proper. My rule was always that small targets should be placed in the butts in order that these two first shots should be "aimed!" I found numerous cases of so-called instructors getting down to test a man's rifle and immediately commence firing at the target proper. It is always wise to fire a couple of rounds into the butts to get the "feel" of the rifle. Nothing can be more disastrous than to take a man's rifle to show him that *he* is at fault and then shoot badly onself!

✻　　✻　　✻　　✻

"A man may know all the text books by heart and be able to repeat them forward and backward, may be an expert rifleman and all that, but it is only in actual combat that he can find himself."

I make no apology for again quoting this passage from McBride's "A Rifleman Went to War"; no one can deny its truth and significance. Its logic should be taken to heart by those who direct Army training, and it should be perfectly clear that it is essential that *instructors* should have actually been in theatres of war, and therefore possess *true* knowledge. Such instructors must have the respect, albeit grudgingly by some hard-bitten cases, of students; they may not be able to repeat a pamphlet parrot-like, but if they bring true knowledge, enthusiasm and a genuine love of a rifle to their task a golden future for Army riflemen is assured.

There is no doubt that both in England and America the civilian shooter did a great service by coming forward and helping, directly and indirectly, to train the recruits in rifle shooting and weapon handling. I would be the last chap in the world to decry their efforts or to detract from their good faith, intelligence, skill and the results they obtained. But I do want to point out that in some cases the trainees came away from such tuition without a clear, true picture of service shooting. A number of such instructors trained men on World War I methods, and did not take into consideration the fact that World War II conditions might be a little different. And in certain instances the men who turned out full of vim and vigour to train soldiers in the early stages of this last war had done just the same job in the 1914–1918 war. In short, they had never seen active service at all, and they had no conception of what battle shooting or combat firing was like; now I maintain that such individuals can do far more harm than good.

Surely it is good common-sense to argue that the men who train the riflemen of the future should have had personal experience in modern war. The young recruit will look up to an instructor who has himself been through the mill, and whose knowledge comes from first-hand experience of war, and not from pamphlets, text books, or totally civilian experience. I well remember three staff instructors coming out to Germany some months after the war in Europe had ended. All were warrant officers of the old school, and all entitled to wear on their breasts the ribbon of the Defence Medal. They had no campaign ribbons and since they were to instruct men, the majority of whom were veterans of the desert, of Anzio and Normandy, it does not leave much to the imagination to know the type of reception they received. At their job of pushing down an unwilling throat pamphlet sequence of weapon knowledge they were good, but, to start with, they had not "got" their classes; their knowledge of weapons was "peacetime" gained by familiarity with them in the quiet training grounds of England. Their little field schemes were perfect—on paper and without an enemy. Their shooting on normal ranges at known distances was excellent. But on

New Type of British Target

This type was definitely an improvement on the normal stereotype targets, but in the author's opinion it did not go far enough. No two dimensional target is of full value in sniping shooting training.

A 3-DIMENSIONAL SNIPER TARGET

This is one of the life-size dummys, used at Sylt for sniper training. In addition to being used as targets to shoot at, these dummys were used exclusively to teach Observation; being embellished with various badges of rank and different uniforms. They were used in all the various positions; crawling, prone, sitting and standing and were hauled around to simulate moving targets by means of wires.

service one seldom shoots at known ranges and with a perfectly peaceful, poised mind—and one is a target oneself.

It is easy to lay down the exact manner in which a Bren gun must be carried down a peaceful English country lane, or across a luscious meadow; but it is a vastly different thing humping it across shell-pocked ground, with cracking lead about, or crawling under wire when to be caught in the barbs is the least thing to worry about. These men knew their weapons, but they did not know their jobs, since it is essential that to train soldiers in the use of weapons the instructor must have done the job in earnest—not ten or twenty years ago, but in the latest possible avenue of experience.

One had only to visit some of the training camps in England and to study the instructors there to realise that their teaching could not have been the best possible. Instructors usually fell into two groups; we had the young instructors who were often ex-school teachers and had got their job because of their facility of speech and because they were able to assimilate knowledge themselves better than the next man. And many such men stayed in England throughout the war, turning out pupils by the thousand, pupils who had rudimentary knowledge of the weapons they used, but who wasted thousands of rounds of ammunition on service before they became really trained, and during the time they were picking up the hundred and one tips of active service shooting and use of weapons which could have been taught to them by their instructors in England had those instructors done the job themselves first.

The second class of instructor consisted of men of more advanced years with the ribbons of the first World War on their breasts, with minds which had never kept pace with modern war developments, and whose memories of active service had been roseate tinged with the passage of time. They were definitely out of contact, but I think they were of more use than the other type. There must have been many men in the British Army of 1939 who could have brought to bear their then modern experience on the Frontier, Palestine, etc., in the training of the thousands of men pouring into the services.

In 1941 I had the good fortune to be trained by two NCOs of a famous Regiment both of whom had some recent experience, and one in particular, a quiet taciturn sergeant who never opened his mouth without uttering sound, sage counsel. He had experience on the Frontier, in the Palestine trouble, he was at Dunkirk and he had been in Norway. But such an instructor was an exception.

Surely it stands out a mile that when a war is in progress some of the staff of the training establishments should be sent out to the Front, and do their tour in the line, and then when they come back—and if they do not it is either a matter of bad luck or perhaps proof that they did not know that which they were preaching!—they can put over their stuff, modified or adapted to meet the requirements of the current war as shown by their own experience, conscious of their own *right* to train men, and happy in the knowledge that by virtue of that experience they have the attention of their students who are certainly quick to ascertain whether their instructor has done some of the things about which he speaks and has put into practice that which he preaches.

The spectacle of an instructor Warrant Officer fresh from England, after the war, putting sniping school instructors, many of whom had spent months in the line, through a demonstration of Section in attack on an enemy pill-box one Sunday morning was most amusing, and rather pitiable. Later when things became hotted up a little and tempers were showing signs of fraying I had to step in and endeavour to soothe the school instructors with whom my sympathies naturally lay and at the same time as diplomatically as possible explain to the WO that that which he was seeking to demonstrate was all very well in cold print in a nice clean pamphlet but that it would not work, and did not work, in actual battle in World War II and that it would certainly not be acceptable to the students on the Monday morning, many of whom had seen much more war than any of us, and that there was every justification for the sniping instructors to become incensed at having to take part in such a farcical charade. A mind moulded by nearly twenty years of stunted archaic instruction was difficult to persuade, but this particular warrant officer was in many ways a decent fellow, despite his nickname of Belsen Bill, and it was good to see that during his few weeks in Germany he, and his ideas, mellowed and modified a good deal by his contact with men who had handled weapons perhaps not according to Bisley and Hythe rules and regulations but who had secured results.

Long sojourn in military instruction schools does not appear to breed tact and diplomacy, and one of the warrant officers who came out to us rather upset some of his active service colleagues by moaning about leave; he was due for leave, he said, and wished that he could have it . . . he had not been out from England more than a fortnight. It was then early September 1945, and I discovered that he had already had seventy days leave in 1945 !! I was amused one day to hear the same fellow talking to some students of a Scottish Regiment and shooting a terrific line about the Hun 'plane which had swooped over their school and dropped a bomb; I was forcibly reminded of the story told of two allied soldiers who went into a cinema in London to see the film "Desert Victory." When they came out one of them was bomb happy and the other put up another medal ribbon!

That was one of the most important things about the sniping school—Major Underhill had always plugged the idea that it was useless to teach sniping, in war-time, miles and miles behind the line. If the school is "close up" the instructors can have a go in the line; the students can be taken into the forward areas and practise that which they have been taught—for the sniper students—and that which they should preach—for the instructor students. And, apart from these considerations, of paramount importance, though they be, there is the sterling factor that such a sniping establishment can render yeoman service in keeping the battalions' sniping rifles in good shape. With a sniping school only a mile or two in the rear of the line there was absolutely no excuse for any unit complaining that their snipers were not on top of their job, or that the sniping rifles were not in perfect condition. A half-day spent at the school would determine two things: the quality of the rifle and whether the man was qualified for the job.

In periodic tours of the line it was possible to determine whether the man one thought would be a good sniper actually was A 1. A man could do well at the school, have the knowledge, the stalking ability, prowess in observation and shoot well. His bearing could suggest guts and cheer-fulness—and yet lie. *His manner in the forward areas was the crucial test*, and if he passed that then his report could be as comprehensive as possible. There were, of course, many things by which one could judge a man's calibre at the school . . . his bearing as the result of a painful accident or something of that nature; such things could be taken into account in the final assessment as to whether the man would make the grade or not. This is just another illustra-tion which goes some way to prove that in the war-time sniping school, as it was run in Normandy and Holland in 1944 and 1945 by Major Wills and Major Underhill, there was the best possible example of a war-time military training establishment. Such a statement cannot possibly over-value the services of the two officers named.

✤   ✤   ✤   ✤

The lack of firearms consciousness and knowledge which was so manifest in the Free Forces of the occupied countries of Europe and in our own forces is evidenced also in the newspaper reports published in this country dealing with murders and suicides by shooting. I remember seeing a report in one daily paper to the effect that a soldier in occupied Germany had been shot and killed in a brawl by a companion who was armed with a 32mm pistol. After such a startling disclosure we regarded it only as a matter of time before they reported that some royal personage had been given the "present arms" by a body of men armed with 40mm Bofors guns.

Occasionally we also get shooting or rifle stories which may be rated good literature by the non-knowledgeable public but which is dismissed as utter tripe by the rifleman reader. I recall reading a sniping story which dealt with a Russian girl sniper "Anya Karinova" whose barrel was garnished by a *bough* tied to it, whilst her rifle bore 157 notches; alongside each notch were one or two letters "KV for Kiev" and so on. By virtue of so much wood carving the weapon must have been considerably lighter in weight than when it left the factory. "Anya" is engaged in a sniper duel—of some *ten* shots—with a German who is "an eagle amongst eagles" and "calmer, more patient and more dangerous than she had ever hunted before." He is indeed so good a hunter and sniper that he is " 'dissatisfied' with the white wall behind him which stood out in relief giving a compact background for the Russian's aim." And, incidentally, his sniper rifle appears to have binoculars mounted on it. Eventually the Russian sniper is hit and wounded, and the German sniper killed—as he deserved. And, we suppose, the 158th notch duly appears on the almost indecently naked rifle.

The lack of a true appreciation of firearms of many of the Resistance people in all the countries we liberated was matched only by the ignorance and foolhardiness of the youngsters, and some Servicemen, who played about with German ammunition in the most dangerous manner. On more that one occasion I found my own men cheerfully stripping touchy German fuses to "see how they worked"; just as in their youth, not far distant, they took great delight in taking watches to pieces. One day in Belgium I noticed a couple of young boys having a very good time playing with some S.A.A. which was lying on the road close to a wrecked German flak wagon. They had taken a couple of bricks, were placing 7.9mm ammo between the bricks with the base of the case upwards and banging away at the primer cap with a rusty nail and a large stone. In halting French I warned them of the danger, and they too obediently went away. They returned immediately I had vanished from sight, and an hour later my sergeant sent them down to the dressing station in his section truck; a bullet had passed clean through the left foot of one of the boys, and lodged in the right foot of the other!

It was in Brussels that one of my sergeants shot himself with a Sten gun; in a crowded tramcar of all places, and anyone who had experience of Brussels tramcars in the early days after the liberation will not need telling that that vehicle *was* packed to capacity. Accompanied by another NCO the sergeant had gone down into the city; both, according to orders, were carrying their personal weapons. During the trip the sergeant decided he would have a cigarette and taking the Sten from his shoulder he placed it butt first on to the floor of the tramcar preparatory to reaching for his cigarette case. As soon as the butt touched ground there was a sharp report and the sergeant felt a searing pain run through his right arm and right side, but did not realise for a moment what had happened. I went to see him in hospital the following day, and later the same day I was saddled with the summary investigation of the accident—a most thankless job since I liked the particular NCO immensely and realised that no matter what I could do there could only be one finding for such a case—that of negligence. It was a good job the magazine was not on the Sten otherwise there might have been wholesale killing. As it was the bullet had entered the sergeant's hand close to the wrist, ploughed a way through the forearm, made its exit at the elbow, entered his body just above the right hip, and the second exit was at his back; the third exit, apparently, was through the car window! I shuddered to think of what that investigation would have meant had there been some Belgian casualties! I made as thorough a scrutiny of the case as possible, and did find that the type of ammunition of the spent cartridge case which the other NCO had fortunately recovered was prone to slightly protruding caps, which may have had some slight, I repeat, slight, bearing on the accidental discharge. But, of course, the fault lay in the sergeant not examining the breech of the carbine before he left the unit. He had cleaned the carbine earlier in the day, and afterwards hung it on the wall in the shed his section were occupying with the magazine in the magazine housing, and there can be little doubt that he had placed the magazine in position before letting the breech block go forward under control, with the result that a round had been fed into the breech.

During the war there were numerous cases of Sten guns accidentally firing as a result of the carbine either falling on to the floor, or the men placing the weapon on the ground butt first. When the solid breech block was forward it needed only the slightest jar for it to jerk to the rear and then, on returning forward, the striker, solid in the face of the block, would hit the cap with enough force, particularly if the cartridges used had a rather delicate primer metal, to set things going! My sergeant was doubly fortunate; he recovered very quickly (when I wrote to his wife and told her of the accident, and not to worry, she replied to the effect that her husband's recovery would be very speedy if there were male nurses in attendance!) and got away with a "reprimand" when charged. And about a week later he went into dock again—with boils!

An interesting example of lack of firearms knowledge by a so-called specialist is shown in the following:—Just before the war in Europe ended I picked up quite a good double-barreled 16 bore shotgun, which had a rifle barrel slung beneath the web. It was in quite fair condition, a hammer gun but light in weight and beautifully balanced. I had some very good sport with it later. Just behind the locking lever on the upper side of the small there was a push-forward catch very similar to the normal safety catch fitment. When the raised tip was pushed forward the word "Fugel" was uncovered.

Naturally, having such a gun it was imperative to find just how everything worked, and so it was that I discovered that when the lever was pushed forward the firing pin of the right barrel was held in the withdrawn position, and would not operate when the right trigger was pulled; it therefore served as a safety catch for that barrel. On the other hand the firing pin of the rifle barrel was operated. So, in a nutshell, the position was that if one wanted to use the rifle section of the gun one pushed forward the catch and pulled the right trigger and away went the bullet. Ammunition for this rifle barrel (9.3mm—very long case) was very scarce indeed. One day I was speaking to an officer who had just come over from England to do disarmament work. He told me that he was an expert in small arms, and had spent a very interesting time with German shotguns and sporting rifles. I asked him if he had a 3-barrel gun similar to mine, and he said "Yes." Here, I thought, is a good opportunity of obtaining some ammunition, and I jumped in with that request. He had a couple of boxes of such ammunition, but had not used any since "the trigger for the rifle barrel is missing!!" This "expert on small arms" did not know that the rifle barrel firing pin was operated by the catch set on top of the small. I was amused, and disgusted, but showed him how the gun operated. My disgust increased when he point blankly refused to let me have even half-a-dozen rounds of his precious ammunition! I could have kicked myself for telling him how that rifle barrel firing pin was operated! This slide could be a damned nuisance, and on more than one occasion I missed perfect shots at duck because of the catch being inadvertently slipped forward; thus when my finger closed around the right trigger to let go at a perfect target just nothing happened. And usually the shock of nothing happening was so great that by the time I had pulled the left trigger the target presented was by no means as good, and more often than not I missed—badly.

Many officers in the British Army knew nothing about snipers and sniping; they had not the sense to realise the killing potential of their snipers, and consequently, in these circumstances, the men who were armed with the special rifles and were supposed to be snipers were not even trained riflemen. One day I had a telephone call from a Major who wanted to borrow a couple of sniper rifles since he, and a captain colleague, were going out that night to shoot deer in an adjacent forest. He said that he thought a telescope sighted rifle would be just the thing. I reluctantly said that he could borrow the rifles provided they were returned on the following morning; I asked him when he wanted to zero them. He seemed quite surprised at this, and wanted to know if they were not shooting all right. I said that the rifles were in perfect shape but naturally if he were going hunting he should zero the rifle into himself as it were, and get the "feel" of the weapon. This apparently was something of an innovation to him, but finally he said that he would come along for the rifles, and then proceed to the range with the Lovat Scout sergeant I would detail to go along with them.

They came, picked up the rifles a little gingerly, and went—to the range. And this is what happened. When the party reached the range they moved down to the 100 yards firing point whilst the sergeant fixed up a couple of targets. The Major told the Lovat that he did not really think very much about sniper rifles since his company snipers had never had less than an 8″ group with their rifles. Such sacrilegious talk was nearly too much for the sergeant. Anyhow the Major settled down, and seated himself on the forward edge of the firing point. The sergeant saw him lift the rifle to his shoulder and peer through the 'scope sight and naturally thought that he was just having a "look-see," so he gave his attention to the Captain who was squirming uncomfortably on his stomach holding the rifle as he might have held a Bren . . . left hand, back of hand upwards, around the small of the butt, right hand clinging grimly to the bottom of the magazine, and the forepart of the rifle resting on a large grass sod torn from the neighbouring bank! Just as he was bending down to patiently correct the Captain there was a loud report from the Major's direction, and the sergeant turned round to find that officer had fired, almost toppled backwards as a result, and was rather ruefully tonguing his jaw. To the sergeant's respectful "What are doing, sir?" the answer was a curt "Zeroing." The sergeant was very patient and by the end of the afternoon both officers had actually obtained five inch groups. They were exceedingly pleased with themselves. And they hunted that night.

The next morning I sent another sergeant along to pick up the rifles. As he was leaving the Mess with the rifles he overheard the Major telling some brother officers that after all he was right about those damned sniper rifles "they were no good." He had had some excellent opportunities the night before, really good heads, but despite the fact that he had "twirled the knobs all over the place" he had not hit a thing. The sergeant reported this to me when he brought the rifles in; and out of curiosity I glanced at the elevation and deflection drums . . . the readings were 1000 on the elevation drum and eight minutes of angle left on the deflection drum.

Early in 1945 I was away from my unit for a day or two and when I returned I was informed that the Colonel had been round to one of my sections and had discovered something really terrible, so bad indeed that he wanted to see me immediately I returned. When I asked the cause of the trouble I was told that the Colonel had asked to see one of my chap's rifles and had been amazed and shocked to find that the trigger had only one pressure! Having found something about which to complain he set off to look for more rifles in the same condition and found them . . . about four in all, but none of the other three belonging to my men. I went along to see the Colonel and I quite enjoyed myself. After ranting and raving about the matter he asked me what had I to say? I had plenty, and had the greatest of pleasure in informing him that I was well aware of the fact that "A's" rifle had but one pressure, that it had been in the armoury for attention, that I had personally seen to it, without success, that "A" had become quite used to the rifle having only one pressure, that he was the best shot I had, was capable of putting five shots into a two inch group at 100 yards with the rifle at almost any time, and that he was an excellent sniper. Warming to the subject I asked him what was detrimental with a rifle having only one pressure provided that the man was accustomed to it, and was he aware that many authorities held the opinion that subject to a man becoming used to such a fine trigger setting he would probably shoot much better with a single pressure trigger than a two pressure since there was no tendency to dwell on aim and so on.

The Colonel was rather taken aback, but, of course, took refuge in the usual rigmarole of what if the Brigadier came round and found such a rifle—what would *he* say? And to such talk what could I say? A week or two later when at sniping school it was good to hear the Chief Instructor confirming my beliefs in a lecture on shooting.

When I again rejoined my unit I broached the subject once more with the Colonel but was soon pointedly made to feel aware that further discussion on the matter was superfluous.

The almost total lack of fundamental knowledge of firearms and shooting found in many servicemen from the private to high ranking officers had to be experienced to be believed. Naturally there were a number of regular officers who were fanatically keen on shooting, but it was certainly a red-letter day when such a person was encountered. If proof be needed of this assertion one has only to recall the misuse, or total disuse, of snipers in some battalions of the British Army.

I maintain that during World War II far too much emphasis was laid on superiority, or volume, of fire—firepower or lead-spattering, have it as you will—by the authorities. To many, the individual rifleman did not count at all, and it was small wonder that the feeling spread amongst the men that the rifle was out-of-date. Everyone clamoured for a weapon which would send out masses of bullets at an alarming rate. I personally experienced one case of an officer, shortly before D Day, declaring that he would see to it that his weapon was a Bren or something of that nature. And I am sorry to say that he really meant it. Had he remained with us he would have gone across on the Great Day. For the good of the unit he was posted away from it some time before the Event. Only the minority cherished the rifle as it should be venerated. And if sniping schools did nothing else they did at least fill every student with a true appreciation of his rifle as a weapon of precision and of accurate firepower with practice, which gave him pre-eminence amongst fighting men. A man who could really use his rifle was more deadly than the average man with an LMG, as I have seen, and demonstrated, many times.

Taken all round my experience showed that the average

soldier was not vitally interested in his personal weapon whether it was a rifle, machine carbine or pistol. I think there is inherent in many Englishmen a fear of firearms, and this fear is intensified by many NCO instructors who have no fundamental knowledge of instructing. The majority of men seemed to take more interest in machine guns, but whether this was from a personal protection point of view or not is difficult to assess. In the main I found the average man's handling of weapons atrocious; he was awkward and bungling, and it was terribly difficult to get into men's minds a true appeciation of the rifle. Because, I suppose, my own burning enthusiasm was so noticeable I succeeded to a certain extent with some of my own men, but I was never satisfied. I once got the orderly room people to do a stencil of the U.S. Marines' Rifle Creed and circularised a copy to every rifleman in the unit, a scheme which met with the full approval of the CO. But it was apparent that only a few men took it to heart.

✻   ✻   ✻   ✻

Calibre

Calibre and stopping power was a subject upon which there was always a conflict of opinion. In this country I think the majority of men who can claim to speak about firearms matters with some justification hold the view that a big bullet travelling comparatively slowly is *the* stopper. Right or wrong I personally claim that the high velocity smaller calibre shell is the most effective.

Velocities of 2,000 feet per second and over result in hydraulic bursting effect, which is the term used to cover the effect resultant at strike which causes instantaneous high pressure at the point of impact being immediately transmitted to the fluid of the body, or the fluidity of the tissue, in all directions. This in turn causes the phenomenon known as shock, which, in some cases, is the direct cause of death. There can be no doubt that a hit, or wound, which will be mortal in some individuals will certainly not result in death to others, and therefore the question of stopping power is not one upon which it is wise to be dogmatic.

I have no personal experience of being struck by a bullet, my wounds and injuries being confined to shotgun wounds, a nasty gash due to Teutonic ingenuity and a shrapnel slash, so I am not in a position to describe the sensation of being hit by a bullet. But quite a number of bullet wounded men have told me of their sensations, and I remember one fellow who had been hit in the shoulder by a Jap sniper (so-called, the range could not have been more than 50 yards and my informant was fully in view) telling me that he experienced a burning numbness, but that he was instantly aware of the cause and immediately his mental state was one of great fear of death. In the case of a man hit in the head by a German sniper in Belgium there was really no sensation except that of receiving a stunning blow, a purplish cloud before the eyes and then blackness, Oblivion.

We are told by medical men that the sensation caused will largely depend upon whether a bone has been injured, upon the size and weight of the projectile and its speed. Small projectiles travelling with moderate velocity through soft tissues only may give rise merely to a tickling sensation, or, if faster and heavier, may seem like the prod of the end of a stick. But if the momentum of the projectile is great the recipient may be chiefly impressed with the force of the blow. The length of time during which pain will be absent after an injury will depend somewhat on its severity. With minor wounds insensitivity might last only a few minutes, or hours in the cases of graver wounds. An immediate consequence of a major wound is that the individual usually falls down; this collapse is the result of a general loss of muscular tone caused by shock, and is not necessarily accompanied by faintness, nor is it due to faintness. Men lightly wounded by rifle or machine gun bullets have, without exception, told me that they felt severe pain immediately, but were not knocked down, nor did they faint. On the other hand severely wounded men have said that they were not conscious of pain, but felt the ground coming up to them as they dropped. One man who had done a good deal of boxing in civilian life and who was severely wounded in the lung said that his experience was matched only by a bout in the ring some years before when he received a smashing blow beneath the heart and went down on the canvas with a thud. He felt no pain at all, nor did he lose consciousness.

Capacity to resist shock and pain is a function of the nervous system and varies in the individual, and therefore the Human Factor enters a good deal in to the question of Stopping Power. And in my opinion this factor is elastic enough to embrace the individual animal, and therefore it is quite understandable to have varying results on animals of the same species using the same calibre, and velocity, of bullet and hitting in the identical spot; nearly all hunters have experienced such happenings. To those who maintain that heavy calibre is not consistent with stopping power the following stories will be meat and drink. A Sikh constable fired six shots with his Webley .455 (lead bullets) at an armed criminal he was pursuing, registering five hits. The criminal continued to run; and so did the constable, and finally overtaking his quarry he stopped him by the simple expedient of battering in his head with the butt end of the Webley. Subsequent examination showed that only one bullet had stopped in the body, this was barely deformed, and the other four had passed cleanly through. A similar incident occurred when a police sergeant discovered an armed Chinese robbing the till of a shop. The Chinaman opened fire with an automatic pistol at about six yards range, firing several shots before the pistol jammed; none of his shots went home and meanwhile the sergeant had returned the fire swiftly and more effectively as regards hitting, with a .45 Colt automatic, commencing at about ten feet and firing his last and sixth shot at about three feet as he closed in on his opponent. Later it was found that all six shots had been hits; four had struck fleshy parts of the body and passed through; one bullet remained in the shoulder, and the other had lodged close to the heart. Yet, in spite of all this, the Chink was still standing, and had to be knocked unconscious by the butt of the Colt as he was climbing over the counter in an endeavour to get away. In this instance the heavy jacketed bullets did not waste their substance on mere penetration, one of them inflicting an almost fatal wound, but yet they did not stop the man in his tracks. Against these incidents I have heard of authentic cases of men dropping instantly when hit by bullets from a .380 Colt; in one instance such a bullet lodged near the spine, but after a couple of seconds the man got up again and endeavoured to make off.

One of the most feared weapons, or bullets, during World War II was the Mauser machine pistol, with its high velocity 7.63mm cartridge. I understand that there is an authentic case of a man being struck in the arm by such a cartridge and the damage sustained being so terrific, the flesh and tissue pulping and threading, that despite prompt medical and hospital attention, amputation of the arm was found necessary.

✻   ✻   ✻   ✻

BRITISH SNIPING RANGE

Upper view is the firing points and lower view is the butts of a British sniping range constructed on a German field firing range in the summer of 1945. The main object was to get away from normal firing point construction and practice, yet not entirely interfere with the natural topography.

The above photographs were taken on the island of Sylt, and they give a rough idea of the type of range and training ground available for sniper training. The sand, often painfully driven against one's face by a constant swirl of high wind was a continual nuisance, then there was a great deal of swirling mist. But these drawbacks paled into insignificance against the overwhelming advantage of being able to shoot in all directions.

Upper view shows use of the Scout Regiment Telescope. A steady rest is imperative when using this bulky and powerful instrument.

Lower view shows a demonstration of the Hawkins position. This position can only be used on favourable ground; on most of the training island this position was impossible owing to folds in the ground. Note how the wearing of gloves prevents hand glare; compare this with bare hands shown in other illustrations.

HOW A SNIPER WAS MADE

The sniper-to-be was supposed to report to the school complete with sniper rifle, Denison smock and binoculars. Many students arrived not so equipped but the school authorities were usually able to make the necessary provision. A moderately high standard of consistent shooting ability was expected, yet again there were times when such prowess was not within the capabilities of some of the students, but considering the short duration of the course wonders were worked in certain individual's shooting ability.

It was a generally accepted fact that once one was introduced into the school one soon came under its spell—and a great enthusiasm for "the Game" was born. The opening talk, to which no one could listen without being inoculated with a "relish-bug" for the job in hand—the students were told that the sniper was a man amongst men; the salt of the earth—was followed by a demonstration showing the capacity of the No. 4 Sniper rifle; it was essential that all the students fully realised that the rifle with which they were armed was capable of deadly, accurate work.

[327]

The first practical work was the zeroing of the students'
rifles using iron sights—the normal, tangent aperture backsight; it naturally followed that if the man could group
with iron sights he was going to shoot finer with his
telescope sight. Instruction was then given on the TS and
later the student zeroed in his rifle with the 'scope sight
fitted. After this, instruction was given in aiming
off for wind and movement. The first principles (theoretically, demonstratively and practically) of movement were
given, and finally the first long hard-working day came to
an end with a lecture on Fieldcraft . . . the use of natural
cover, when stationary and during movement, permitting
the free use of weapons.

The man of average intelligence quickly saw that fieldcraft was mainly the exercise of common-sense, hunter's
sense:—the avoidance of breaking skylines; looking around
cover, not over it; keeping in shadow, mindful that the
position of shadow can change; the merging into one's
background; the avoidance of isolated or conspicuous
cover and all unnecessary movement. He realised the value
of camouflage, the necessity of having some contrast in
colour and tone so that a disruptive effect was obtained.
He was shown that practical camouflage methods he could
take towards personal concealment included the head
and face covered with a camouflage veil; the hands, smeared
with camouflage cream, mud or dirt, or gloves; the body,
by wearing the Denison smock which could be improved
for some purposes of concealment by tufts of hessian
garnish stitched on to it; some protection for the rifle
could be obtained by either painting it or wrapping garnish
around it; the body of his telescope could be covered by
a face veil or an old khaki sock with the foot cut out; the
binoculars obscured by a strip of camouflage hessian tied
around the front of the bracket.

Emphasis was laid on the fact that he should train himself to be able to "pierce" enemy attempts at concealment;

[328]

this had a double purpose—he became more careful with his own forms of camouflage. Later demonstrations and exercises in concealment and camouflage heightened his perception and constructive faculty.

In MOVEMENT he was practised in the arts of stalking—of walking silently, where balance is essential and assisted by having the knees slightly bent and arms hanging loosely, a position from which one can get down to cover very quickly; of crawling on hands and knees, on elbows and knees and on the stomach—all with rifle, which must not reveal or impede movement, be available for instant use, and therefore not caked with mud or dirt. (When crawling on the stomach, or the elbows and knees, the best method of carrying the rifle was to hold the sling with the clenched hand near the forward swivel, muzzle to the front and the rifle resting along the forearm).

Into STALKING came the application of many of the canons of Fieldcraft. Stalking cannot be taught in a few days; it can be learned only by experience; so the student was given some general principles and told that experience would do the rest. And the principles included Reconnaissance of ground (e.g.: exact location of enemy to be stalked must be memorised with reference to pronounced landmarks or objects—likewise the sniper's own selected final position; route; points of observation during stalk, etc.); Retaining direction—use of compass, maps and air photographs; Night work with its necessity of silent movement, and avoidance of "skylining."

It was pointed out to the would-be sniper that during certain phases of War, such as static periods and in defence, he should if possible, build a hide, or hides, since highly efficient work can be done from them; a well-built hide affords cover from inclement weather and in it there is possible a certain amount of movement without any fear of possible detection. Such hides could, and did, vary considerably in type and structure dependent on the terrain and the amount of material available and on the individual sniper's, or sniper team's, ingenuity. Camouflage, undue movement in and around the hide, and light shining through loopholes from a poorly constructed rear were all important points stressed in this matter of hides.

From the actual shooting point of view the sniper was warned of three things:—the danger of firing from a hide at dusk and dawn when the muzzle flash might give him away (better to have selected positions just away from the hide); on frosty mornings and damp days smoke shows clearly and therefore when the snipers are in the hide and shooting under such conditions they must keep the rifle muzzle well back from the loophole; the ground outside the loophole should be damped if there is any danger of dust rising from the muzzle blast when the shot is fired.

A point emphasised in connection with the construction of hides was that when a man first built hides he invariably made them too small—with no headroom. Likely locations were given as under hedgerows, in ruined buildings, rubbish heaps; a slit trench with improvised head covering was a popular form. A primary consideration, of course, was the field of fire. The art of deception was necessary, and it was important that alternative hides be constructed and the sniper's occupation of them to be irregular with no conformation to an "inhabiting" schedule.

Under certain conditions shell-pocked buildings provided excellent posts for sniping. It was customary to build some form of rest well back from the loopholes in the walls, windows, shutters or roof, and in this way the sniper was within inner shadow and most difficult to spot.

As a rule the student greatly enjoyed the stalking practices; it was hard work but the competitive spirit, especially the individual stalks, engendered enthusiasm.

Some time was spent in teaching the student the essentials of shooting; he had to know the sources or error in the man—holding, flinching, faulty trigger release, faulty aiming, incorrect breathing and so on; in the weapon—neglect, oily barrel, dirty chamber, nickelling, loose screws; and in the ammunition—oily, dirty, wet, chamber heated, and using different brands which gave varying elevations.

It was emphasised that apart from being a really accurate shot he must be capable of hitting fleeting targets. It was suggested that in view of this occasional necessity for a rapid shot the sniper should have his rifle with the sights adjusted to 300 yards. In conjunction with the Mk. VII cartridge this would ensure a hit on a man's trunk at any range up to 400 yards with little if any necessity to aim up or down. In zeroing it was emphasised that the least possible lateral or vertical error should be left on the sniper's rifle.

Application and snap practices back to 400/500 yards were fired frequently during the short course, but the most popular form of shooting was the field firing at comparatively short ranges at head targets well camouflaged and difficult to pick out, which appeared for very short periods. The general opinion was that much more of this type of shooting could have been indulged in with profit all round.

In the space of two or three days the student became fully conversant with the telescope sight and in ninety-nine cases out of the hundred he was impatient to set the pointer in the centre of a Bosche's head; this fervour was inflamed by the hot-blooded oratory of the Chief Instructor who, during lectures, was the perfect example of sniping fanaticism. (The Chief Instructor maintained that under the conditions which constantly present themselves in an attack, two snipers who knew their job thoroughly could do more damage with 20 rounds of small arms ammunition than 10,000 rounds fired through machine guns.)

Our sniper in the embryo fired at dusk and was duly impressed with the possibilities of the sniper rifle adding scalps to his totem when it was too dark to shoot with normal iron sights. He was warned of the suicidal potential of a dusk sniper who fired more than a couple of shots from the same position. Use of the sling was taught (and it was surprising to find that many men had no idea that the sling could be such an asset to shooting steadiness) and much prominence was given to the Hawkins position.

Students frequently asked questions about tree shooting, but it was pointed out that trees are never good sniping positions; although they may make good observation points on many occasions. Detrimental points to tree shooting are—unsteadiness; leaves give no clear vision for shooting (and if the tree is not in full leaf there is a lack of concealment) and there is a good deal of movement resultant of muzzle blast, and furthermore there is the difficulty of firing down-hill. (Incidentally there was little elaboration of this important point during my student-term at the school. Such a defect was remedied when I ran my one man Sniping School some time later.)

One very useful tip given to the student was that of "lining up" or "dry zeroing" his rifle when it was impossible, or not healthy, to check up by firing in the forward areas. The procedure was simple; an aiming mark was selected about 100 yards away; the bolt was removed from the *fixed* rifle and the aiming mark centred in the bore, then the telescope adjusted accordingly. The resultant error was small enough to be ignored at normal sniping ranges.

The student was taught the ethics of OBSERVATION— to "see" and to "see intelligently." It was pointed out that the average townsman's vision has become partly atrophied by his non-natural use of his sight, and that sight is both a mental and physical state. A man trained in observation notices anything unusual; he recognises the importance of small, apparently insignificant things. Nothing even slightly unusual is disregarded by the true sniper scout. From a mass of individual reports, maybe seemingly trivial, much "golden" important information may be sifted, and the Intelligence people may be able to build up a full and vital composite picture. (Later when I lectured on this subject of "seeing" I pointed out that many men had an "X-ray" vision when they saw a voluptuously curved, scantily dressed female! This was sight with imagination—a combination which could be very useful for the scout.)

The student was told that knowledge of wild life was invaluable on occasion. Many positions have been given away by the antics of startled, or suspicious, birds and animals.

Observation exercises with the telescope and binoculars were repeated frequently, and the importance of correct distance judging stressed very highly. Map reading, air photograph study were gone into as thoroughly as time would allow; and a period or two given to the study of enemy identifications, badges of rank, collar insignia, etc. Obviously it was essential that the sniper should be capable of selecting the most important targets.

At the end of a few fleeting, happy days the war-trained sniper left for his unit. He was no longer a disciple of the "fire power" cult nor an adherent to the close-range gangster weapons class, but was possessed of a supreme faith in the ability of the rifle to give maximum results on worth-while targets. He may not have been quite the product he should have been—the Time factor was against the emergence of a fully trained man—but with his newly found knowledge and skill allied to guts and an enthusiasm for his job he was a man to be feared, and quite capable of putting to sleep both wary and unwary Huns. And the records show that in many cases he was not only just capable but adept—and he did kill Bosche!

ONE MAN SNIPING SCHOOL

IN DECEMBER 1945 and January 1946 I ran a one man
Sniping School in Schleswig and Sylt. The students were
NCOs from my Regiment, embryo instructors in the Great
Game. Although it meant the postponement, for some
weeks, of my return to civilian life, a procedure which
earned for me the sobriquet of "bloody fool" from unknowledgeable and misunderstanding brother (?) officers,
I welcomed this long sought opportunity of putting into
practice certain warmly held theories on sniper training.

There were many obstacles in the path, of course. It
is difficult for one officer to run such a course single-handed,
irrespective of the number of students, and it occasioned
very long hours of work. But I must admit that the extremely keen interest shown by all the NCO students
more than repaid me for the work done. At the time there
were no sniper rifles available in the Regiment, so I had
to take a trip down to the Training Centre about 300
miles away in an endeavour to borrow TS rifles, telescopes
and other items of sniper equipment. The journey down
was not without incident; after about 120 miles the car
in which I was travelling hit a tree, with the result that

I sustained badly bruised knees and a cut forehead. But we eventually arrived at the Centre in a borrowed truck after an hectic ride over ice bound roads in the dark. I received a very warm welcome from my old colleagues and senior officers, and when I left for the return journey thirty six hours later I had everything I wanted to start up the course, except the targets which were made and painted by myself and the students when I got back to Schleswig.

The following notes on the course may be of interest to all riflemen.

Hunting. From the first moment of the course the strictest possible emphasis was laid on the fact that sniping was the art of the hunter adapted to war. At the risk of boring them the students were never allowed to forget that salient, supremely important, point. This concentration on the "Hunting art" was not confined to observation, stalking and shooting but to "Reading the Signs" of which more later.

Common-sense. Throughout the training special emphasis was laid on the use of *practical* common-sense in all things, and the students were persuaded to think for themselves. I have found that many instructors will not give any man credit for the possession of common-sense.

Observation. As much practice as possible was given in observation. From the initial range practices all students used binoculars and telescope during *all* shooting.

During the real sniper training at Sylt emphasis was laid (a) on the fact that it was no fault to "think" one sees something—the means of confirmation was handy in the forms of binoculars and telescope; (b) that the hunter is "inquisitive"; (c) that it is not enough to "see" an enemy, but one must know "who he is" and "what he is," and (d) that there are such things as tracks, dependent on the nature of the ground, and that such must be looked for, and interpreted.

[335]

Point of Aim. Believing in the "6 o'clock" aim as being *the* sensible point of aim for service shooting we used that point of aim throughout the course; with a TS it is practically impossible to take a correct central aim on a dark object, there being no guide when the pointer is imposed on a dark mass. And one should see the spot to be hit.

Three-Dimensional Targets. If this course did nothing else it at least proved the enormous value of the three-dimensional targets used; these took the form of *life-size dummies*, clad in battle-dress. The "flesh and tissue" consisted of a mixture of straw and crumpled paper which gave them an apparent "life-density." Actually the dummies were so life-like that, at Christmas time, a slightly inebriated gentleman who walked into the storeroom in which they were housed was not only immediately sobered, but almost fainted with fright. These targets were used exclusively in the sniper team schemes of "Observation, Stalk and Kill," and they certainly presented the nearest possible approach to the real thing. It is my sincerely held opinion that once one is assured that the men being trained can shoot, as the result of grouping practices and one or two application shoots back to 400 yards or so, a test of the man's vision and his rifle, it is essential that the sniper-trainee shoots exclusively on life-size three-dimensional targets. One shot fired, and a "kill" registered at the conclusion of a sniper team "observation, stalk and kill" exercise is of far more value than 100 shots fired at old fashioned application targets, or silhouette targets. Any stunt, moving, crawling, even and uneven step, etc., can be done with such dummies. An example of the ludicrousness of the normal type of Hun Head target, or head and shoulders target, mounted on three-ply wood, used in field firing exercises was shown in a demonstration I staged at Sylt. The sniper team observed the target and stalked it, but the only possible place of coming up to a killing position was on the left side of the target, and therefore the target presented was the thickness of the three-ply wood at about 150 yards! Do let us have realism in training!

Such life-size dummies lend themselves to observation exercises; they can be embellished with badges of rank, etc. During the course one of the exercises included the observation, stalking and "killing" of two dummies, one of which bore officer badges of rank. The pips could be seen through the telescope in rather poor visibility at over 500 yards, and the test was "which target would the sniper take first once he had got into position for the killing?" Another interesting stunt was the "crawling" dummy. The dummy was made to crawl by signal wire around the shoulders, being pulled across ground affording fair cover by one of the students safely hidden behind a sand bunker. The movement was extremely natural and afforded excellent practice.

Being very adaptable, by kicking, the dummies were placed in all positions, crawling on the hands and knees, lying prone, firing around cover, sitting, standing (fixed by a stake in the ground) and with side exposures. All positions gave excellent shooting practice. The war-time sniping school standard of three hits out of four at a trunk and head target at 400 yards is, I maintain, not good enough for the sniper. In any case how often will such a target present itself in actual fact? The sniper must be trained to hit "men" who adopt natural war positions, therefore once again the value of the dummy target shines most brightly. I had been shown the new type of "crawl-wall" figure target. Although definitely showing a genuine attempt to get away from the archaic types of target I maintained that it did not go far enough. All targets used for sniping training, after the elementary stages, should be of life-size, whether consisting of head, trunk or complete body. Roughly I should say that the figure on what I have termed the "crawl-wall" target was half life-size, which theoretically means that if these targets are used at 300 yards range the snipers are hitting a life-size figure at 600 yards. I am all in favour of training snipers to hit and kill at ranges up to 800 yards, and maybe beyond, but they must be *at* those ranges, and all the targets should be life-size. I have trained men who shot brilliantly on the miniature ranges on the 25/200 targets but *at* 200 yards they could not score 50% of the possible . . . and it was not the fault of the rifle. Similarly a man may hit a half-size figure, or human representation, at 300 yards and be incapable of hitting anything at 600 yards.

Experience has shown that it is far more difficult to hit a certain spot on a human figure, at any range from 100 to 400 yards, than it is to contact with the same size spot on a target. The *natural* posture of man, such as lying down on a slope, results in a far more difficult target being presented, and the students on the course were amazed at the difference in elevation, or point of aim, necessary to contact with a given spot, such as a *vital* area, when the "human" target was "lying" on a slope. Such vitally important practice and experience can be gained only by using life-like dummy targets.

I repeat that the value of a single shot fired at such targets from the first available "killing" spot, irrespective of range within effective limits, after "observation and stalk" is of far more intrinsic worth than 100 shots fired at any artificial, two-dimensional target, whether it be on a four feet square target or in silhouette. In the stalk and kill one has the tiring and nerve effects of the stalk; the movement of getting into position, a *natural* position, for the shot; and the judging of the distance to the target; and the *team* is exercised, not the individual alone, since the second man must use the telescope to determine the effect of the sniper shot.

On the question of "marking" the shots on such targets —marking the hit is a damned good test for the observer!

The hits can be delineated with varying coloured chalk so that each man knows exactly where he hit on his examination of the "body" at the conclusion of the practice. I had the NCO who marked the shots signalling the hits and position by using coloured flags, the same colour chalk and flag for the individual firer. Another system of recording could be that adopted by LMG ground to air practices at drogue—the tips of the bullets being dipped in varying coloured paint.

One innovation introduced with the aid of the dummy targets was "vital spot shooting." I have gathered the impression that an idea most prevalent is that it does not matter, even at short ranges, where the enemy is hit from navel to the top of the head. I told the students that, again in keeping with the "hunter" idea, that it was at least more humane to kill the enemy instantly, and that this, at comparatively short ranges, should be eminently possible. The practice introduced was this:—three inconspicuously chalked areas were placed on the carcass of a sitting dummy—target was at approximately 100 yards; after the preliminary shooting practices *all* ranges were approximate in keeping with service conditions where there are no exact range firing points!—(a) eyes and forehead (b) heart and (c) solar plexus region of the stomach, and three single shots fired at the "area" specified, just given as "head," "heart" and "upper stomach." The results were very interesting, since none of the students registered in the chalked "heart" area, all shots being too much to the left. It was felt that this was very valuable practice.

At the risk of being classified as an insufferable bore I repeat that I consider it absolutely essential that life-size dummy targets should be used exclusively for the training of snipers once the preliminary shooting practices of zeroing and application of zero at all effective ranges have been carried out.

Aids to Better Shooting. Experience confirmed that the majority of men dwell far too long on aim and consequently do not get their shots away quickly enough. Two of the students shot much better when their aiming and pull-off was speeded-up. (In pursuance of the "hunter simile policy" it was pointed out that the Eskimo walrus hunters are probably the fastest aimers in the world, and darned good shots; if they merely wound the walrus, which dives when hit, they must get away a second shot at once.)

All movements should be free and smooth, and there should be no concrete tension of the muscles of the arms and hands.

Many men fire with the butt too low in the shoulder; the sights should come to the eye, not the eye to the sights.

Throughout the course EXPERIENCE was a dominant theme; only by experience of shooting under service conditions, at unorthodox ranges and life-like targets in all positions and postures, will a sniper know his rifle intimately.

No matter how apparently remote from sniping, talks and discussions on shooting and rifles are of great value in training snipers. The more knowledge a man possesses the more interested he becomes. In particular knowledge gained from such talks is invaluable to the instructor-to-be since he is, at all times, likely to be asked difficult questions by some barrack-room lawyer type of individual in his squad. During my period at the Training Centre one student asked me a couple of questions immediately after a lecture; (a) what was the difference between a pistol and a revolver? and (b) what is a carbine? Having had a little previous experience in such types of questions I rattled off my answers in almost a pamphlet style much to the delight of the other students. Their, to me, exaggerated amusement and delight became much more understandable when I learned later that my answers did not tally with the replies given rather haltingly by a Sergeant Major who had been asked the same questions!

General. As many weapons as possible were fired. This catholicity of practice breeds interest and enthusiasm. Small, roughly cut pieces of brown paper were pasted on application targets and used as "bulls" during the very limited periods of normal range firing. Only hits on the brown paper counted; this type of shooting mark provides much more interest, and difficulty, than normal bull-plugging.

At many schools of instruction there is far too much emphasis laid on the "aggregate score results of shooting" and this may be one of the reasons for the continuance of use of stereotype targets.

Care must be observed when sniping in a damp atmosphere; e.g. early morning, when the smoke from a discharged rifle hangs about and may easily disclose a concealed position. Care too should be taken to ensure that the muzzle of the rifle is not immediately over a patch of sand or loose dry soil which can be disturbed by muzzle blast. If this is unavoidable the sniper on taking up his position can water the ground, by urinating on it. A sniper should always watch for possible overhead obstructions to his line of fire, and therefore he must visualise the curved flight of the bullet.

If a man is trained in "vital area" shooting on dummy targets he is much more prone to hit the enemy even if his shots wander an inch or two from the mark. There are many times when a man hit in the non-vital spot comes up again; in fact, there are times when he does not go down. Sniping is hunting, therefore the shot *should* be a killer at short ranges. Surely when hunting one does not aim at the "biggest area available."

Watch a man's checking of his breathing. Many men exhale, or inhale completely. In hundreds of cases this defeats the object of restraining the breath, since both

[341]

methods may cause trembling and strain. All that is necessary is to *check* the normal breathing for the split second during the taking of the final pressure, and many men do this perfectly unconsciously.

If the men are firing with iron sights in poor light whiten their foresights; better results will follow immediately. Why the Army has never adopted a white ivory foresight is completely beyond the comprehension of many sporting shots. Such a sight could be easily blacked over when required; for shooting in bad light a white foresight is of inestimable value.

Shooting through a telescope sight with one eye closed is tiring; if one can get men to shoot with both eyes open so much the better. Young men coming up for shooting instruction who have done little or no shooting previously are excellent raw material for the moulding of the "two eye" stance.

Many men cannot close one eye without the other being affected in some slight degree. To give such men a black patch to cover the "unwanted" eye is to save them, and the instructor, endless trouble.

Wind. Hunters, and snipers, often worry unnecessarily over the effect of wind on their aiming. With a muzzle velocity of over 2,000 f.p.s. a bullet will virtually ignore say a ten mile an hour wind for about 200 yards. Even rather a strong breeze, unless it is blowing at direct right angles to the bullet's course, will not have a great effect on the medium range shot. It is amusing to see some men who are bitten with this wind-bug as a result of windage tables, endeavouring to test the wind's strength; they apparently expect an animal, or an enemy, to stand still until they have satisfied themselves about the strength of the wind. Wind may be very important to the competition shot, but it is not so vital to the sniper who is intent on a killing shot at comparatively short, hunting ranges. And the idea of the sniper draping an adjacent bush with a

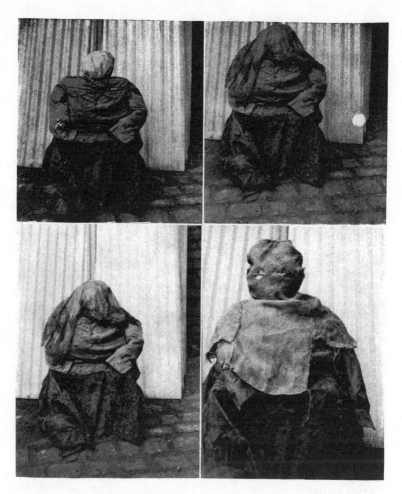

SNIPER TRAINING TARGETS

Upper left: Shows one of the trunk dummies which were used for sniping
shooting and observation exercises. Points to note are the Sniper Badge on
the right sleeve—officer's pip on shoulder—ribbons.

Below the dummy is seen a German camouflage groundsheet and cape.
Upper right: Shows same dummy with camouflage veil draped around head
and shoulders, covering sniper badge and most effectively breaking outline.
There is one mistake and that is it is still possible to see one of the medal
ribbons, and this could easily be picked up with a telescope.

Lower left: Similar to No. 2 but with all ribbons covered.

Lower right: Shows dummy covered by a sniper cowl which was made (from
a couple of sandbags—the head section lined with a handkerchief for comfort!—painted and stitched, very amateurishly)—AND USED!

A "One Man" Sniping School

The first R.A.F. Sniping School was organized at Sylt, Holland, in January, 1946. Here is one of its "graduating classes" and two of their dummy targets. Instructor is in center of back row.

Such "schools" have unlimited possibilities for regimental and battalion units, when placed in charge of the right type of qualified rifleman-instructors.

piece of cloth overnight is reminiscent of the Crimea. There is nothing positively reliable about wind. A second's study of a wind vane will confirm that to anyone. *Natural* experience is the only way in which wind determination, and its affect on shooting, will be truthfully compiled.

Winchester Carbine. Throughout the course the second man in the sniper team carried my Winchester carbine, and its use confirmed the formerly held opinion that this is *the* weapon for the job—light, completely mobile and with sufficient accuracy up to 200 yards to make it a killer in the hands of a man who knows how to use it.

Sniper Equipment. It is sincerely felt that it is a bad thing to lay down hard and fast rules and fashions for the equipment of a sniper. A sniper turning out, on some jobs, in all the regalia laid down would be festooned like a Christmas tree. He would need only a "dummy head" to be a veritable Santa Claus.

Close Combat Fighting. Since it was felt that close quarter combat might easily fall to the lot of a sniper at night, or on patrol, the students were trained in the use of self-loading pistols and revolvers both by night and day. One short period was given to dagger training. It was not my wish to turn these fellows into Commandos, but snipers *must* be versatile.

"Reading the Signs." Exercises in "reading the signs" were staged. One of the dummies was placed lying on its back, in the path of a sniper team returning to "headquarters." The dummy had been shot in the back from very close range with a 7.65mm pistol. The empty cartridge case was left in the sand at the spot where it had flown from the pistol on ejection. Two sets of tracks, footprints in the sand, lead to the spot but only one set of prints came away. (Instructor being carried on the back of fatigueman.) The insignia of a lieutenant, two pips, was on the epaulettes of the dummy and all other flashes and badges had been removed. In one pocket there was an

empty cigarette packet on the inside of which were pen-
cilled notes as though they had been hastily scribbled at
some conference. The sniper team found the "body" and
were asked "what are you going to do about it?" This is
what happened:— a cautious approach by one of the team,
the other covering him. Very cautious examination made
for booby traps; body was searched, not very thoroughly,
for papers, etc., and the cigarette packet was found. It was
opened, the writing noted, and retained. In their log for
the Intelligence Officer the finding of the body was reported
at "X"; mention of the fact that the body was that of a
lieutenant was made, and the cigarette packet attached to
the report. Nothing more.

Correct method of procedure was then explained and
demonstrated. Body observed; tracks noted—two sets of
prints to body, only one away; cautious approach; search,
just as careful, for booby traps; condition of body noted;
search of body and pockets; finding of cigarette packet,
only material avaliable; body turned over; examination
of wound at point of entry—in heart region, back—
Suspicious; noticed that size of wound consistent with
shooting by small calibre weapon at very short range
since there was evidence of scorching of the cloth of the
battle-dress blouse, extensive blackening and some unburnt
powder grains, latter suggestive of use of short-barreled
handgun; looked around, noticed empty cartridge case in
sand; examined it—Geco 7.65mm; pips and base cut off
epaulette, coloured base may denote something to IO;
made rough drawing of areas upon which flashes and
badges had been sewn and torn off—may be of use to
IO . . . and so on. *Full* report made in Log Book for
Intelligence Officer, for transmission along with evidence.
Combination of all these things, writing on cig., packet,
evidence of shooting in back without sign of struggle,
(bad feeling in enemy troops?) and visual evidence may
result in matters of supreme importance being deduced.

It was pointed out that the hunter reads the signs on a kill, and so should the sniper. It is not desired that snipers should be the products of a police college, but they must, or should, be able to use common-sense, powers of observation and *read* the evidence available. They are not Sherlock Holmeses, but they are hunters!

During the course as one of the general interest lectures the students were given a talk on the identification of firearms and forensic ballistics, which included mention of scorching, blackening and unburnt powder ranges; fatal shot ranges of handguns, rifles, etc. Discussion of a "case" which occurred a few weeks earlier added piquancy and interest to this lecture. In November 1945 the body of a Polish fighter pilot with a bullet pierced heart was found on Westminister Bridge, London. The problem was— Murder or Suicide? Did the deceased press the gun, of small calibre, to his heart and then fling it over the bridge? His raincoat showed powder marks consistent with the shot being fired at close range; no one heard the shot; there was no sign of the weapon; and there were no traces of blood on the spot. The police supposition was that the Pole had leaned against the narrow parapet put the pistol to his heart and pressed the trigger, the recoil had hurled the pistol from his hand over the parapet into the river, the shock of the bullet threw his body into the position in which it was found on the pavement, and the fact that the bullet extinguished life instantaneously stopped circulation and so accounted for the entire absence of blood.

Hunting Points Given to the Students. To become a finished stalker you must, in addition to knowing the secrets of silent movement, inconspicuous dress, and using cover to the great advantage, know the weak points of each animal species, in your case the enemy, and how to take advantage of those weaknesses. Just as all animals have habits peculiar to themselves so has your enemy. But the wise hunter knows that there are exceptions to all rules so it is not advisable to be dogmatic as to what the enemy will, or will not, do. Good stalking makes a good hunter; a good hunter makes a good sniper. Learn it, and enjoy· to the full that unsurpassed thrill that arises from matching your skill against that of the enemy—and winning!

If a hunter is wise he "sights in" his rifle on as near natural a target as possible. You have seen the "deer targets" used for this purpose by hunters. If it is possible snipers should do the same; "sighting in" marks can be the vital areas on dummy targets.

In assessing the shooting qualification of the students *every* practice fired was taken into consideration including AFV "slit" shooting using AP ammunition; sniper team schemes; "vital area"; "forfeit" practices where a miss paid forfeiture of points; actual hunting shots on deer and all practices fired during really vile weather.

I was very sorry when the long course came to an end with two days stalking and shooting in the River Eide and Keil Canal area. I had enjoyed every minute of it, despite the cold and rain and mist and eye-irritating sand of Sylt, and the snow and ice of Schleswig. Our training area at Sylt was a sniper training paradise; there was no question of normal, orthodox ranges—despite the hazard of maybe-forgotten mines we roamed and shot at will over the extensive sandhills which changed in feature overnight by the caprice of the wind; it was the finest training ground imaginable.

When the students first arrived to take the course they were united in the opinion that sniping was a waste of time now that the war was over; but their viewpoint changed in a matter of hours, and when I said "Cheerio" to them in late January 1946 it was pleasant and heart warming to know that one was God-speeding a number of fervent disciples each eager to spread the gospel of sniping into the dull, dark consciousness of they who know nothing of the faith!

INDEX

S & W .38, 55, 57, 119, 201, 251
 adapted (?) to .22, 56
Sylt, 58, 63, 105, 134, 195, 251, 272,
 334, 346

Target shot vs. Game shot, 128
Target shot not necessarily a Sniping
 shot, 129
Targets
 "Rommel's Runners," 20
 two dimensional, 134
 three dimensional, 137, 336
Telescope, 104, 108, 110, 166, 333
Telescope sights, 125, 128, 136
 German, 180
 unreliability of in Middle East
  theatre, 111
"Ten Little Nigger Boys 1944," 34
Tokarev (pistol), 203
Towers—shooting, 264
Trees
 German snipers in, 19, 87
 training in tree shooting, 231
 another comment on tree shooting,
  266, 332

Underhill, O., OBE, Major, 47, 143,
 277, 284, 297, 313

Vickers Machine guns, 12, 210

Volksturm, 50
Volume of fire—emphasis on in World
 War II, 322

Walther, 27, 54, 178, 187, 197, 202, 209,
 216
Weapon training (German), 226
Webley .455, 201, 325
Welcome
 in Normandy, 13
 in Brussels, 26
 in Eindhoven, 27
Whelen's "Telescopic Rifle Sights," 181
Winchester carbine, 29, 32, 191, 194,
 263, 343
Wild-life—use of knowledge of, 85, 333
Wills, F. A. H., the Hon. Major, 104,
 143, 284, 317
Women sniper stories, 12, 315
"Wooden" bullets
 6.5 caliber, 8, 219
 7.9 caliber, 8, 219
 8.0 caliber, 8, 219
 20.0 caliber, 8, 219
World War I, 141, 276
Wounded (most hideously wounded
 man seen), 13
Wounds, 324

Zeroing—dry, 332

Samworth Books on Firearms

Above are listed the Samworth Books on Firearms now offered for sale or in
process of publication by

THOMAS G. SAMWORTH

Small-Arms Technical Publishing Company

Georgetown, South Carolina

U. S. A.

September, 1948

Twenty-two Caliber Varmint Rifles

By Charles S. Landis

This is a book of 521 pages devoted exclusively to the increasingly popular .22 caliber "wildcat" rifles and their ammunition. Everything from the rebuilt single shot action to the most elaborate custom built center fire bolt action, good for 200 to 400 yard work on turkeys, woodchucks, crows, hawks, coyotes and wolves, is treated in this extensive work. The best selection for any type of shooting, every sort of neighborhood, every distance and every size pocketbook. All the good loads are listed, with their possibilities, their average accuracy at each relative distance, their killing power on different kinds of game and varmints, plus a wide assortment of loads for these various purposes. With this book, you don't have to guess at the right rifle, cartridge, loads or sights . . . or the type of hunting in which to use them.

Here, for the first time, is presented full and correct technical information on the assembly, adjustment and finishing of most of the leading popular wildcat .22s of the day—boring, straightening and rifling of barrels; chambering problems, with special attention to the making of chambering reamers and their attendant and correct use; headspace adjustments; throating principles and processes; breeching and firing pin alterations and adjustments.

An extensive and important section of the book is that devoted to the suitability and application of all the various types and makes of commercial and military rifle actions for conversion into thoroughly safe and highly accurate varmint rifles. Most of the leading custom riflemakers of the United States and Canada have contributed their eminently qualified views upon this vitally important subject, and have discussed it from every conceivable angle.

The vital matter of high pressure .22 center fire ammunition has been equally well handled; here are given dimensional specifications and essential loading data for all of the popular .22 wildcats. The acquisition, conversion and preparation of their special cartridge cases and bullets has been adequately covered:—here is the real dope on fire-forming; necking down; shortening necks; truing bases; reaming out case necks; primer pocket check-up . . . cartridge assembly such as never before presented to the handloaders.

Regardless of how much money you want to put into your varmint outfit "*Twenty-two Caliber Varmint Rifles*" tells all about that outfit. It tells about every well known wildcat cartridge which, to date, has been used sufficiently to prove itself. Every woodsman, every small game hunter, every farmer, rancher, stockman, professional varmint hunter or rifleman will find this to be the book he has long been looking for. Profuse with group reproductions, illustrations and cartridge drawings.

Professional Gunsmithing

By Walter Howe

Gunsmithing methods and textbooks, like everything else, are matters of evolution and change for the better. This is particularly true of the many technical books on gunsmithing now in existence—each in part records or augments the gradual but positive progress of the craft.

Here is a new work written entirely from the professional outlook and devoted mainly to the repair and modification of existing stock weapons. *"Professional Gunsmithing"* approaches the subject from an entirely new angle, supplementing and enhancing all other previous Samworth Books on Firearms treating of this vital matter of gun repair and upkeep. It combines both business and technical phases of gunsmithing, in that matters such as time, ethics, price estimation, how to deal with shooters as customers, and the idea of doing the job exactly as someone else demands and not as the gunsmith himself might want to do it, are given paramount consideration throughout the text.

How to best set up a gunshop and what is more important, how to keep it going on a profitable basis is included in this volume. Subjects such as business set-up and customer relationship are presented in a clear, understandable manner. Several speciality lines which will provide a satisfactory source of revenue are included and the listing of sources of supplies for all gunsmithing materials is the most extensive yet published.

Anyone entering the gunsmithing field, either as a means of livelihood or merely to work on their personal firearms, will find a mass of applicable material herein. The subject of commercial gunsmithing is taken up by Howe in a broad and comprehensive manner, approached from the angle of basic principles and logical reasoning. He tells how to diagnose gun troubles when the weapon is brought in for repair and explains the general reasons and causes for necessity of such repairs. By applying Howe's "approach" to the problem in hand any gunsmith will be enabled to correctly and profitably remedy the fault or repair the defective part.

Walter Howe's instruction is concise and practical because he knows whereof he writes. Specific jobs and types of repair work which have proved to be most frequently brought into the gunshop during his experience as a practicing gunsmith, are treated in detail. The amateur will appreciate this instruction as the advice of a master craftsman; the professional will be impressed with its clarity and practical application to the problems which daily confront him.

"Professional Gunsmithing" is today's outstanding textbook for the gunsmithing profession, and is now being used as such in colleges and training schools which include gunsmithing in their curriculum. 520 pages, 120 special drawings, 21 plates.

A Rifleman Went To War

By Capt. Herbert W. McBride

This pioneer work on sniping and battle marksmanship was written by one of the outstanding American riflemen of all times, the late Captain Herbert W. McBride, whose name appeared high up on the lists of prizewinners at Sea Girt and Camp Perry for many years before the First World War. At the outbreak of that war, he enlisted in the Canadian Army and spent some 18 months in Belgium and France with the 21st Battalion, Canadian Expeditionary Force. The greater portion of this period found Mac (as he was known to thousands of us), actually in the front line trenches, with German infantrymen only a matter of yards away.

His book, first published in 1936, is still an applicable and authoritative work on the use of the modern military rifle and telescope on the battlefield. In World War II it was of incalculable benefit to American and British forces in the training of their men in rifle marksmanship and the principles which McBride taught therein were very favorably commented upon by high ranking officers who observed and fought both in Europe and the Pacific.

McBride served with the Canadians as a machine gunner, his work as a rifleman being confined largely to sniping, though he used the rifle in repelling enemy attacks on more than one occasion and writes all about it. He carried a pistol, used it, and tells you what he thinks of it. He made something of a reputation on patrols and raids—having been decorated for work of this sort. There are chapters on each of these several subjects, dealing not only with his experiences but with his observations and conclusions. But the outstanding features are the chapters devoted to sniping and the rifle in battle. Captain McBride was one of the best qualified snipers in the Allied Army and he made a reputation in the Canadian Corps on his shooting ability. In his narrative, he goes into full details regarding the many tricks of the sniper—sniping equipment and its care and use—observation with the big telescope—concealment—range finding—counter sniping—and battle firing. No sob stuff and no dramatics—just a complete and truthful statement of facts, telling you how to "get your man" and get him "fustest."

The instructions given, and the tricks Mac tells of, can be applied on any battlefield of today and in any static position where modern rifles and ammunition are used. His teachings are in no way obsolete; they still stand. Material and extracts from this book have been widely copied and quoted in many more recent domestic and foreign works and it is acclaimed as an outstanding contribution to our shooting literature. 412 text pages and frontispiece.

Shots Fired in Anger

By Lt. Col. John B. George

Johnny George is remembered by Illinois riflemen as a State Team member at Camp Perry; as the youngest .30 Caliber champion the State ever had; and as a many-times-winner in various local and regional rifle competitions. He knew plenty about the peace-time use of rifles. He got into World War 2 early, as a lieutenant in the 132nd Infantry, Americal Division, on Guadalcanal. This was the first Infantry Division to be used aggressively against the Axis Powers in any theatre. After the Guadalcanal Campaign, he volunteered and went through Burma with "Merrill's Marauders." Subsequent wartime assignments took him more than twice around the globe. He saw *plenty* of shooting.

"Shots Fired in Anger" is a book covering George's rifle shooting experiences up to and including his platoon-leader and sniping ventures on Guadalcanal. He wrote it particularly for other riflemen.

Half of the text of this work is in narrative form, giving a shot-by-shot account of Lt. George's part in the Battle of Guadalcanal and the events leading up to it. He discusses rifleman training and tactics first, then tells the actual stories of how he and his fellow Infantrymen killed the enemy with rifles and other Infantry weapons. Throughout the book George disclaims being a warrior, but he seems to remain somewhat this side of those who condemn War as a monotonous bore, devoid of thrills. His account sometimes takes the slant of a good big game hunting story as told by one alive to the dangers, as well as the thrills, of the chase. One thing he makes clear is the fierce pride he takes in having been a doughboy and a rifleman. He believes ardently in the traditions of the foot soldier—and more than ever before he believes in accurate rifle fire.

The second half of this book, entitled "The Tools Used," gives a gun-nut's description of the weapons used and encountered in the field, relating their manners of performance. This presentation almost brings the Japanese and American weapons to life; George shows here that he certainly regards guns as much more than inanimate bits of metal and wood.

Every American rifleman and member of the National Rifle Association should read this book. Aside from its entertainment value, it contains a world of practical information which will prove of worth to the younger members of our shooting clan, who may well be called upon to use our American military rifles in another war. It tells you just what to expect of the modern military rifle when shooting "for keeps"—and also what to look out for from the rifle of the other fellow. The sketches illustrating this work were done by one of the best artists in Japan. 421 pages well illustrated.

Ordnance Went Up Front

By Roy F. Dunlap

In reality, this book is the elaborated technical diary of an American gun nut who served as an enlisted man in the 27th Ordnance Company of the United States Army and whose duties consisted mainly of going over practically all types of the rifles, pistols and machine guns of World War II, both enemy and allied.

The author's services in both Eastern and Western theatres of war puts him right up into the "been everywhere and seen everything" classification. He really did get around a bit; Aberdeen Proving Ground; Egypt; Mississippi; New Guinea; Leyte; Luzon and Tokyo.

Working on all types of small arms, usually right in the combat area, was Roy Dunlap's job during most of the war, and he consequently describes and treats these various arms within the light and knowledge of his own first hand experience—plus that of the men up on the firing line. When a particular weapon is described, it is actual performance you are reading about—those details of suitability, report, recoil, feel and actual results, known only to practical shooters—and the type of knowledge so desired by other shooting men. These are the facts *you* want to know.

To the owners of these foreign military weapons—the veterans who brought them back as trophies or the individuals who have since purchased them—*Ordnance Went Up Front* is the book to tell you *everything* about that weapon; its specifications; the cartridge it shoots; its limitations; and in particular, what can be done with it to make it up into a top-grade sporting rifle or target arm.

Herein are the most detailed and informative descriptions of German, Italian, British, American and Japanese small arms that have so far been published, with much additional data given on the ordnance of many of the smaller nations. Weapons and cartridges are treated extensively, and in their proper relation to each other. This is the book many shooters thought they were getting when they purchased earlier works on these subjects. It is the first such work really written from the practical-user and not the catalog-reader standpoint, with Dunlap's previous training as an experienced gunsmith and Camp Perry marksman standing him in good stead. He *knows* what *you* want to know—and *writes* it. Here is a trained rifleman's qualified opinions, formed after having examined, dissected, repaired and fired all types of modern military weapons used in the past war. 414 pages, with 44 plates.

African Rifles and Cartridges

By John Taylor

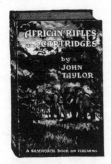

John Taylor is a professional ivory hunter who has spent some 30 years in the African Bush engaging in his chosen vocation of elephant hunting. His total bag runs better than 1,500 elephant, almost as many buffalo, innumerable rhino, hippo, lion and leopard, besides the larger antelope and countless "small buck" that have fallen to his rifles during these years and which were, of necessity, shot to feed his camp retinue and followers.

During this 30 years of continuous hunting he has owned, experimented with, tried out, and otherwise used all of the various suitable British, German and American big-game cartridges, from the 6.5mm to the .600 Nitro. Some of these calibers he acquired two or three times for use on extensive safaris. Single-shots, doubles and magazines; he has tried them all; black powder to smokeless; soft lead bullets to "solids."

The practical aspect of his work is foremost on every page in this book. Here, for the first time, is an actual analysis of the suitability and killing power of *all* modern big-game rifles when used on game ranging from the mighty African elephant on down to the tiny dik-dik antelope. Every question on hunting ballistics that the rifleman can think of has been answered in this book; with much of it never before having been put in type.

This volume sets a new high for actual gun and cartridge suitability, performance and killing effect. There has never been a book before which contains the amount of real, down-to-earth gun and hunting data such as John Taylor herein gives. He takes up every caliber cartridge by cartridge, and discusses each individually. With his opinion of each cartridge, he tells the value and effect of each bullet available for that cartridge—solids, soft-point, split jacket, hollow-point, or plain lead—and this in all the various weights. Interspiced throughout the text are authentic hunting incidents, quoted from his voluminous notes and given solely to prove some ballistic point in question.

Our staff artist, Ned Smith, has turned out a new style of technical cartridge illustration, fully in keeping with the style and originality of the text of this book. Here are the cartridges reproduced full-size, with case and bullets laid open and analyzed visually for your inspection and knowledge; with jacket construction, turn-in, thickness and coverage shown; all supplemented by elaborate explanations as to the suitability and action of each cartridge and type of bullet.

Whether you intend to hunt in Africa or in Arizona—for lion or for white-tail deer—you will find this book of extreme value in the selection, handling and shooting of your modern big-game rifle. 426 text pages, profuse with accurate and original technical drawings and plates.

Samworth Prints on Firearms

Concurrently with the preparation and editing of the *Samworth Books on Firearms* over the past several years, it became necessary to devote much time and study to the composition and arrangement of the special illustrations and paintings to be used along with our books. This, in most instances, turned out to be no small job.

Fortunately, we made contact with Gayle Hoskins, the famous artist of Wilmington, Delaware. Mr. Hoskins has an especial aptitude for historical scenes and outdoor subjects involving firearms, and to our critical demands for accurate weapons-and-period correctness he has given a most satisfying degree of interest and study. As a result of several of his paintings which we have so far used, there has been created a steady and insistent demand from our book buyers to furnish them, in proper form for framing, certain of the rifle shooting scenes he has so accurately and interestingly depicted.

Consequently, we are now offering *Samworth Prints on Firearms*— a series of attractive and authentic pictures, reproduced in the very best and most modern process of this day—six and seven colors done in color-gravure—which will prove highly suitable for the walls of the rifleman or sportsman's home.

Here is "Trade From the Monongahela," depicting a party of backwoodsmen in from the headwaters of the Ohio, who have a pack-load of deer hides to barter for new rifles and a supply of powder and lead. The smithy shown is also the riflemaking establishment of Phil Lefevre, of Lancaster County, Pennsylvania, time is around 1750. Print surface is 17 x 25 inches in size, plus wide margins.